Victims, Crime and Society

Victims, Crime and Society

Edited by
Pamela Davies, Peter Francis, Chris Greer

SAGE Publications
Los Angeles ▪ London ▪ New Delhi ▪ Singapore

SAGE Publications Ltd
1 Oliver's Yard
55 City Road
London EC1Y 1SP

SAGE Publications Inc.
2455 Teller Road
Thousand Oaks, California 91320

SAGE Publications India Pvt Ltd
B 1/I 1 Mohan Cooperative Industrial Area
Mathura Road,
New Delhi 110 044

SAGE Publications Asia-Pacific Pte Ltd
33 Pekin Street #02-01
Far East Square
Singapore 048763

British Library Cataloguing in Publication data

A catalogue record for this book is available from the
British Library

ISBN 978-1-4129-0759-0
ISBN 978-1-4129-0760-6

Library of Congress Control Number Available

Typeset by C&M Digitals (P) Ltd, Chennai, India
Printed in Great Britain by The Cromwell Press, Trowbridge, Wiltshire
Printed on paper from sustainable resources

Contents

List of Contributors

Hazel Croall, School of Law and Social Sciences, Glasgow Caledonian University.

Pamela Davies, School of Arts and Social Sciences, Northumbria University.

Peter Francis, School of Arts and Social Sciences, Northumbria University.

Chris Greer, Department of Sociology, City University London.

Jason L. Powell, School of Sociology and Social Policy, University of Liverpool.

Azrini Wahidin, School of Sociology, Social Policy and Social Work, Queen's University Belfast

Sandra Walklate, School of Sociology and Social Policy, University of Liverpool.

Acknowledgements

We owe a debt of gratitude to a number of people, without whose contributions, encouragement and support this book would never have reached the point of publication. First, our thanks goes to Caroline Porter at Sage for her tireless efforts, enduring patience and remarkable capacity to mix (and down) a heady cocktail of good humour, attention to detail, and consummate professionalism. To our contributors, Hazel Croall, Jason Powell, Azrini Wahidin, and Sandra Walklate – whom we have known for years and worked with before – the experience, as usual, has been a pleasure. If you haven't had enough of us by now, we look forward to working with you again soon. To the various people who read various drafts of various chapters, thank you for your helpful comments. Finally, to our friends, families and loved ones, thank you for being around.

Pamela Davies, Peter Francis and Chris Greer,
October 2006

Victims, Crime and Society

Pamela Davies, Peter Francis, Chris Greer

Introduction

Our central organizing theme in this book is the nature of victimization in relation to the intersecting and overlapping social divisions of class, race, age and gender. Under this rubric, the book explores the unequal distribution of victimization, the patterning and nature of risk, the experiences of crime victims, and the social, political and criminal justice responses to criminal victimization. It foregrounds how the major social divisions in England and Wales – class, race, age and gender – provide a useful starting point for understanding the complex and dynamic nature of victimization in society. The book also explores the frequent tensions between social divisions, victimization, social harm and state policy and practice. Specifically, chapters within this book do the following:

- establish the importance of social division – class, race, age, gender – in understanding crime victims and victimization;
- examine the media representation of social divisions, inequality and victimization;
- map the unequal distribution of victimization in relation to social divisions and inequalities, and explore how victimization impacts upon and is experienced differently by a range of groups and individuals;
- evaluate the various political and policy responses to crime victims and victimization and assess the role of the voluntary and community sectors in supporting victims of crime;
- explore the political, cultural and social context of criminal victimization and review key theoretical, methodological and empirical approaches which are important in understanding victimization in contemporary society.

Our aim in the rest of this Introduction is to map out the core themes of the book, identify various 'golden threads' that run throughout its pages and, in so doing, introduce, contextualize and interconnect the chapters that follow. First, we introduce the concept of social divisions as social categories and identify their constructed nature. Second, we examine the connectedness between social divisions, inequality and victimization. Third, we introduce the importance of media analysis to an understanding of victims, crime and society. Fourth, we outline the various social research methods that have been used to help understand the nature, extent and impact of victimization. Fifth, we discuss political and policy responses to victimization. Sixth, we situate an understanding of victims, crime and society within a broader theoretical framework. And, finally, we introduce the various pedagogic features used within the book, and present an outline of each chapter's structure.

Social divisions as social categories

Everyday social existence involves the definition and continual reassessment of 'who we are'. An important part of defining 'who we are' is determining who we are *not*. Our sense of 'self', therefore, our construction of 'who we are', is defined to a significant extent in contradistinction to conceptions of the 'other'. Notions of 'self' and 'other' can be isolated and highly individualized or shared and deeply embedded in culture. Sometimes they are institutionalized and become custom or law. Sometimes they remain marginal, and are considered quirky or eccentric. Sometimes their expression provokes censure and approbation. What is crucial is that constructions of 'self' and 'other' are intimately connected to the power relations that permeate the social and cultural world. We all live in a set of patterned and structured relations of unequal status and power – political, cultural or economic, for example. These relations can both free up and constrain our everyday lives. Having more money opens up certain opportunities which remain closed to those who have less. Having power and influence may open doors that would otherwise remain shut. These relations of power, which help to shape our everyday experiences, are bounded by social divisions.

Social divisions are social categories. Such categories can include race, gender, age, class, sexuality, mental health and physical disability. Social categories are not static, but dynamic and change over time, space and place. As Best (2005: 324) states, 'Social categories are not simply given, they have to be established and maintained and the process through which they appear is known as *social division*.' They are situated historically, culturally, economically, and politically. Cultural and economic transformations in the past two decades, such as deindustrialization and globlization, have impacted upon the nature of social division. Best (2005: 2), for example, discusses how in recent years the concept of globlization has 'racialised our notions of citizenship, and led us to question the validity of the nation state as a political entity'. Social divisions can be arbitrary, yet they are also enduring. For Best, the most enduring social divisions are those we believe are rooted in nature. In this sense, then, the most enduring social divisions portray continuity. Being young and working class, for example, continues to represent disadvantage, marginalization and exclusion.

We are conscious of the problems relating to structuring the book according to what may appear, superficially at least, to be distinct and separate structural variables. From the outset we want to acknowledge that we recognize that the intersectionalties of class–race–age–gender or multiple inequalities (Daly, 1993) variously combine 'as intersecting, interlocking and contingent' (Daly, 1997: 33). Indeed, we could have stretched the content of the book to include chapters on sexuality, mental health and disability, and we would have done so were it not for the fact that, in relation to victims of crime and victimization, these three areas remain under-researched.

The four social categories upon which this book primarily focuses – class, race, age, and gender – happen also to be the major social inequalities in our society. To be poor, to be black, to be young and to be female, simultaneously represents different distinct social categories with combined significance and relationship to relative disadvantage, exclusion, marginalization and powerlessness. We do not all start life equally. We come into it as unequal individuals. Advantage and disadvantage, therefore, are with us from the start, and the nature and impact of inequalities persist and change over time, place and space. Moreover, inequality is situated across and within generations. Our experiences in childhood may well affect our experiences later in life; and these will often affect our children's experiences as well. Crucially for this book, our experiences, fears and perceptions of crime and victimization are experienced through social divisions of inequality.

In the chapters that follow, Hazel Croall explores class (Chapters 3 and 4), Sandra Walklate and Pamela Davies explore gender (Chapters 6 and 7), Peter Francis explores race and age (Chapters 5 and 8), Azrini Wahidin and Jason Powell explore age (Chapter 9), and Chris Greer and Pamela Davies explore the connections between social divisions in the context of media representation (Chapter 2) and criminal injustice (Chapter 10) respectively.

For more on social divisions as social categories and on the relationship between social inequality and victimization, read:

Best, S. (2005) *Understanding Social Divisions*, London: Sage.

Carrabine, E., Iganski, P., Lee, M., Plummer, K., and South, N. (2004) *Criminology: A Sociological Introduction*. London: Routledge.

Croall, H. (1998) *Crime and Society in Britain*. London: Longman.

Inequality, risk and victimization

Whereas social division is the central organizing theme of the book, individual chapters are connected by four 'golden threads'. These are: social inequality, risk and victimization; media representation and victims of crime; researching crime and victimization; and political and policy responses to victims of crime.

The British Crime Survey (BCS) for 2005/06 reports that crime and victimization is stabilizing after long periods of reduction. In 2005/06, there were 10.9 million crimes committed against adults living in households in England and Wales (Walker et al., 2006). Since peaking in 1995, the BCS estimates that crime has reduced by 44 per cent, representing 8.4 million fewer crimes, with burglary (59 per cent) and vehicle crime (60 per cent) falling by more than half, and violent crime by 43 per cent. Indeed, 'The risk of becoming a victim of crime has fallen from 40% at its peak in 1995 to 23% according to BCS interviews in 2005/06, representing just over 6 million fewer victims. This is the lowest level recorded since the BCS began in 1981' (Walker et al., 2006: 13). Police data indicate that recorded rates for burglary and theft of and from vehicles have continued to fall over the same period. Furthermore, although police figures reveal an increase in recorded crime over the same period up until 2004 (largely as a result of the NCRS),[1] the figures for 2005/06 indicate a reduction from the previous year. There were 5.6 million crimes recorded by the police for 2005/06. In general terms, and without disaggregating the crime and victimization figures, England and Wales are probably safer places in 2005/06 than they were in the mid-1990s.

However, it must be noted that such figures can also be misleading:

- Walker et al. (2006), for example, confirm findings from previous surveys that suggest there are fairly high rates of under-reporting and under-recording of crime and victimization, and that rates of both are contingent on a range of interrelated factors. These include, for example, offence type, victim characteristics (young, old, black, white, male, female, straight, gay), previous experiences, and perception of the likely police response.
- The BCS has, since its inception, provided evidence that crime and victimization are unevenly distributed across and between groups of individuals based upon their ethnicity, gender, age, class, lifestyle, relationships, and so on. The BCS 2005/06 indicates that geographic patterns and concentrations of offences varied by crime type. Variations differed across regions; in urban and rural areas; by Crime and Disorder Reduction Partnership (CDRP)[2] area; and between most employment-deprived and least unemployment-deprived areas.

- The impact that victimization has upon an individual is dependent upon a range of factors, many of which are, to use Daly's phrase, intersecting, interlocking and contingent (1997: 33).

In examining the relationship between inequality, risk and victimization, Mike Dixon and colleagues (2006) offer a useful introduction and overview of recent crime and social inequality data. Examining data drawn from the BCS alongside socio-economic data, they attempt to unmask the unequal impact of crime.

They point out that both crime and public perceptions of it differ by income and area. Those with incomes less that £10,000 and those residing in deprived neighbourhoods are more likely to experience acquisitive crime, and more likely to pronounce themselves very worried about being physically attacked (see Figure 1.1). Dixon et al. (2006: 13) highlight three specific findings in relation to income, victimization and concern. These are:

- Richer households are more likely to be victims of some crimes, such as vehicle crime and criminal damage.
- Poorer households are more likely to be victims of serious intrusive crime such as burglary, mugging and domestic violence.
- Poorer households are much more likely to report being very worried about specific types of crime and feeling unsafe when walking alone after dark. Importantly, the difference in concern is greater than the difference in victimization.

Obviously, there are broader issues at play here which relate to an individual's ability to undertake avoidance behaviour and protect themselves and their household from crime and victimization; their willingness to report their victimization to an interviewer or the police; and their ability to deal with the cumulative physical and psychological effects of experiencing and worrying about victimization. Nevertheless, the broad finding remains the same – that those people most likely to be victimized by crime and to experience social harm in England and Wales are often the most marginalized social groups living in the poorest areas (Zedner, 2002). Vulnerability to crime, risk and fear of crime are exacerbated by social, economic, cultural and political exclusion.

Dixon et al. (2006) provide similar findings for ethnicity, age and gender. The differential risk rates associated with specific categories of social division are considered in detail in the different chapters in this book. What we want to stress here is that these categories should not be viewed as static and separate but as interconnecting and closely related. Thus,

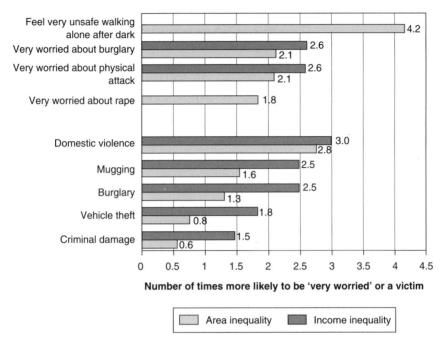

Figure 1.1 Inequality in concern and risk of victimization, by income and area

Source: Dixon et al. (2006), based on British Crime Survey data, various years.

Note: Income inequality compares households with incomes of less than £10,000 per year to households with incomes of more than £30,000 per year. Area inequality compares households in 'hard-pressed' or 'striving' areas to households in 'wealthy achiever' or 'thriving areas (ACORN definitions). Income data from 2004/05, area data from 2003/04. Concern about crime data by area is from 2002/03.

recent BCS reports suggest that black and minority ethnic groups are more likely to be victims of crime, but this is because, on average, they are more likely to be younger (Dixon et al., 2006: 14). Once age is accounted for, risk and rates of vulnerability are minimal (Salisbury and Upson, 2004). There are also interesting points to be noted in relation to age and gender. Young people, for example, are often the most likely to be criminally victimized, and risk of victimization declines with age. But gender also affects the risk and vulnerability of younger and older people. Dixon et al. (2006: 16) point out that while women are less likely to be to be victims until they reach the age of 65, 'they are more likely to be victims of domestic violence at any age'.

Each chapter in this book focuses upon social inequality, risk and victimization, and their connections with the social categories of class, race, age and gender.

> For more on inequality, risk and victimization, read:
>
> **Cook, D. (1997)** *Poverty, Crime and Punishment.* **London: Child Poverty Action Group.**
> **Dixon, M., Reed, H., Rogers, B. and Stone, L. (2006)** *Crime Share: The Unequal Impact of Crime.* **London: Institute for Public Policy Research.**
> **Walker, A., Kershaw, C. and Nichols, S. (2006)** *Crime in England and Wales 2005/06.* **Home Office Statistical Bulletin. London: Home Office.**

Media representation and victims of crime

The front cover of this book presents an image of legs and feet of people walking along a pavement. We don't know who they are, what they look like, whether they are male or female, black, mixed race, Asian, young or old. The cover is reflective of the second golden thread that runs the length of the book. The role of news media in constructing and (mis)representing victims of crime and victimization. While the media do not necessarily tell us what to think, they can tell us what to think about. They are of fundamental importance to those who would promote a particular view of crime victims and victimization, or seek to challenge or change existing views. They are a key site where policy-makers seek to secure popular acceptance and legitimacy of new measures affecting victims of crime, and groups espousing competing values, interests and beliefs struggle to secure 'ownership' – and, with it, political power – of various victim-related issues and debates.

In the information age (Webster, 2005), where communications technologies occupy a central and increasingly important role in most people's lives, understanding complex social issues such as crime and victimization, control and social order requires engaging with the media. As one of us has argued elsewhere (Greer, 2005: 157):

> The rapid and relentless development of information technologies over the past 100 years has shaped the modern era, transforming the relations between space, time and identity. Where once 'news' used to travel by ship, it

now hurtles across the globe at light speed and is available 24 hours-a-day at the push of a button. Where once cultures used to be more or less distinguishable in national or geographical terms, they now mix, intermingle and converge in a constant global exchange of information. Where once a sense of community and belonging was derived primarily from established identities and local traditions, it may now also be found, and lost, in a virtual world of shared values, meanings and interpretations. In short, media are not only inseparable from contemporary social life; they are, for many, its defining characteristic.

The 'problem of crime', as many have pointed out, is a socially constructed problem. What we mean by this is that, since most people have little first-hand experience of crime and victimization, we are reliant on other sources of information for much of our knowledge about it. Few of these are more important than the media. Media representations influence what the issues of crime and victimization 'mean' to people. They help to socially construct these issues by presenting particular 'views of reality'. There is no necessary connection, however, between what is presented in the media and what is happening 'in the real world'. The issues of crime and victimization, then, are highly mediatized issues. On this basis, it is our contention that any comprehensive sociological exploration of crime victims and victimization must engage with the media and media representation. For a failure to engage with the media in analyses of this nature is a failure to acknowledge one of the key sources through which the concepts of crime, victim and victimization are given meaning in contemporary society.

One need only skim the chapter headings and index pages of the vast majority of victimology books to realize that media representations scarcely feature. This, for us, represents an important gap in the literature, and in this book we seek to contribute to filling that gap. It is not our intention to suggest that victimization has no external reality, or that this reality is 'unknowable' in any meaningful, empirical way. Nor indeed would we suggest that the reality of crime, inasmuch as it can be known empirically or experientially, is of secondary significance to what people *believe to be* the reality of crime. On the contrary, aligned with a critical criminological approach, we are keen to point out that victimization tends to be disproportionately concentrated among some of the most vulnerable, marginalized and powerless sections of society. For these groups the pains of victimization are experienced not only most often, but also most acutely. What we would insist, however, is that popular understanding of this unequal distribution of pain and suffering, of the nature and extent of victimization, of the experiences of victimization and fears of being a victim, of the measures that might be taken to reduce victimization, of victims' needs and victims' rights – all these issues are, to a greater or lesser extent, shaped in the media.

In addition to Chapter 2 by Chris Greer, which is dedicated to exploring media representations through an in-depth analysis of general issues and specific cases studies, each successive chapter acknowledges in some sense the key role that the media can play in defining, problematizing and reshaping dominant conceptions and popular understandings of crime victims and criminal victimization.

For more on media representation and victims of crime, read:

Chermak, S. (1995) *Victims in the News: Crime and the American News Media.* **Boulder, CO: Westview Press.**
Greer, C. (2003) *Sex Crime and the Media: Sex Offending and the Press in a Divided Society.* **Cullumpton: Willan.**
Jewkes, Y. (2004) *Crime and the Media.* **London: Sage.**

Researching crime and victimization

The third golden thread connecting the chapters in this collection concerns the methodologies and the tools and techniques used to find out about crime victimization and victims of crime. Since the 1970s, the direct questioning of the victim has been central to the criminological enterprise, some of the features of which are generic to social surveys, whereas others are specific responses to the problems of studying victimization (Davies et al., 2003).

The belief that official criminal statistics indicate more about the organizational processes of collation and collection than about levels of crime and criminal activity has had an enormous impact upon engaging criminologists in alternative and competing strategies of collecting data about crime, such as the utilization of data other than that from the police (Maguire, 2002). A further impetus to the development of victim surveys came from direct concerns for the victim within criminology and also within criminal justice policy. It was only with the growth in interest in victims of crime and criminal activity in the late 1970s in the United States and in the 1980s in Britain, coupled with the enormous impact of feminist research and methodologies, that information about victims of crime and victimization slowly started to appear in the form of the crime survey (Goodey, 2005). Since then, surveying victims has for many criminologists become one of the most flexible and rewarding research approaches, facilitating the generation of details about the circumstances of the offence, relationships between victims and their experiences of the various criminal justice agencies. In the early 2000s the Home Office moved from only presenting the BCS and police-recorded crime in separate reports to combining key findings of each (see, for example, Walker et al., 2006).

Davies et al. (2003) demonstrate how victimization surveys have played an important role in criminology and in policy-making by providing better estimates of the extent of crime and victimization than those provided by the police and by giving insight into victims' experiences, perceptions and worries of crime and of the criminal justice system. Indeed, victimization surveys provide information about rates and trends, reasons for under-reporting; the correlates of victimization; the risk of victimization; the fear of crime and its relationship to the probability of victimization; the experience of crime from the viewpoint of victims; and the treatment of victims in the criminal justice system. In particular, five broad patterns in victim surveys are discernible. These are local cross-sectional sample surveys, 'appreciative' surveys, national trend sample surveys, cross-national surveys and police 'consumer' surveys (Davies et al., 2003; Spalek, 2006).

Victimization surveys, however, are not without their critics. Criticisms of victim surveys range from the simple, e.g. they can often assume a level of literacy or understanding among the sample population that may not be available, to the more complex. In particular, they have been criticized for not being able to get behind the mere appearance of things. What goes on behind our backs constitutes the things we are not aware of (but which may still result in our victimization) such as mass pollution and corporate victimization fraud.

Moreover, victimization surveys are unable to situate and contextualize victimization in the everyday lives and routine activities that we all engage in. They are unable to locate our experiences of crime and victimization within socio-economic, cultural and political contexts. In addition, surveys can often reflect the agenda and priorities of those carrying out the research or consultation rather than the participants involved as subjects. Victim surveys are closely tied to the confines of the criminological and victimological enterprises. Therefore, such surveys are often viewed as inappropriate to questions raised by forms of thinking which view such enterprises as constraining and instead seek to add a critical edge by locating victimization in wider structural issues.

As a consequence, some victimologists have looked beyond the victimization survey to more qualititative and ethnographic methods of research and inquiry. Indeed, many have heeded the clarion call for triangulation to pick and mix and match different methods for different types of research. Sandra Walklate (2003: 41), for example, has suggested that an exploration of the complexity of human interaction through time and space demands a research agenda which goes beyond the victimization survey. The kind of framework supported by Walklate is one that locates victimization within a socio-economic, cultural and political context and which examines the processes that go on behind people's backs which contribute to the victims (and the crimes) we see. For Walklate (2003), research may involve comparison, triangulation of method and longitudinal studies.

Class, race, age and gender all play their part in locating victimization in wider structural issues as do personal histories, habits and behaviours. Throughout the book, each chapter explores the ways in which victims of crime are rendered visible through documenting and cataloguing their experiences. The chapters examine how criminal victimization is measured and how unreported victimization remains an issue, and they trace the development of the ways in which the socially divided nature of victimization is increasingly appreciated and understood.

For more on researching victims and victimization, read:

Davies, P., Francis, P. and Jupp, V. (2003) *Victimisation: Theory, Research and Policy.* Basingstoke: Palgrave

Goodey, J. (2005) *Victims and Victimology: Research, Policy and Practice.* London: Longman

Spalek, B. (2006) *Crime Victims: Theory, Policy and Practice.* London: Palgrave.

Political and policy responses to victims of crime

The final golden thread connecting each of the chapters in this book concerns the political and policy response to victims of crime. Victims of crime who appear in the public arena usually do so because they have made contact with the police. These individuals are already a selective category of crime victim. They have become separated from other victims because they have become part of the political and policy process, and thus, in relative terms, are what we might call 'visible victims'. These are the people whose victimization has come to official notice. Their experiences are officially known and they may qualify for assistance and support.

However, even at this stage, they may experience secondary victimization. Secondary victimization results from the insensitive treatment of victims of crime – often inadvertently – by the criminal justice system. For example, a child or adult may have their accounts questioned by a police officer or social worker, casting doubt upon their truthfulness and integrity (Davies and Francis, forthcoming).

A range of supportive provisions and victim assistance schemes can be identified in most social systems across the world, all of which will have differing relationships to their respective criminal justice systems. Some victimagogic services are at arm's length or fully independent of the government and the criminal justice system, some are provided under statute, others by voluntary groups and charities. In England and Wales, particularly since the 1990s, there has been a proliferation of different victimagogic activities blurring the boundaries of whether help and assistance is public, private or voluntary and whether it is offered as of right. For a discussion of the development of victims support and victim services, consult Williams (1999) and Davies et al. (2003). Landmark dates in the development of victim support and services are detailed in Table 1.1.

A number of the contributions to this volume consider the nature and impact of the political and policy response to victims of crime. Each addresses a number of questions in relation to the connections between political and policy responses and victims of crime. These are:

- How appropriate are the various state responses to victimization?
- What has been the political and policy response to specific victims of crime?
- How do victims experience criminal justice systems and processes?

Table 1.1 illustrates the numerous developments relating to victims policy and practice over the past four decades. Many have had a positive impact, especially in terms of changing the status of the victim. Some measures have significantly improved victim's experiences in connection with helping achieve social justice. Other developments have been

Table 1.1 Some landmark dates in the development of victim support policy

Date	Procedure
1964	Establishment of statutory criminal injuries compensation arrangements
1972	First UK women's refuge set up
1975	Victim Support set up
1976	First UK rape crisis centre set up
1981	Creation of British Crime Survey
1982	Roger Graef's TV documentary on the treatment of women reporting rape
1985	UN declaration of the basic principles of justice for victims of crime and abuse of power
1986	Childline set up
1987	First national government funding for Victim Support
1990	Victims Charter
1991	Criminal Justice Act
1996	Victims Charter revised
1998	Crime and Disorder Act – reparation for victims of young offenders
1999	Youth Justice and Criminal Evidence Act – vulnerable witness provision
2004	Domestic Violence, Crime and Victims Act
2004	Victims Fund – to develop services for victims of sexual offending
2004	Establishment of the Victims Advisory Panel – giving victims a greater voice in policy-making
2005	*Rebuilding Lives: Supporting Victims* Green Paper – victim support to prioritize practical and emotional help, as well as financial compensation
2006	Code of Practice for Victims of Crime – creation of statutory obligations on the Criminal Justice System to provide minimum standard of service to victims
2006	Recruitment of a Commissioner for Victims and Witnesses

Source: Dixon et al. (2006: 7)

helpful in meeting victims needs in the short, medium and longer term. Certain time periods correspond with specific social groups achieving victimological recognition. The emergence of the second wave of feminism in the 1970s, for example, was enormously influential in the development of services for victims of rape, sexual assault and domestic violence. Developments in the 1990s were also highly significant. This decade produced the Stephen Lawrence Inquiry which acknowledged police institutional racism. The same decade also witnessed the rediscovery of popular punitiveness towards young offenders which youth victimology has since heavily criticized.

Despite an array of victim-oriented activities and measures, there continues to be a lack of any coherent victims policy, and victims continue to occupy a position defined by their need rather than by a notion of rights.

Victims' 'lived experiences' of criminal justice and its agencies – namely, the police, the courts and the prosecution process – continue to be problematic. For example, much literature details the fragile nature of police–victim relations, especially when the victim comes from a marginalized or oppressed group, such as ethnic minorities, women, young people and those from low socio-economic backgrounds. Furthermore some victims continue to be traumatized by inappropriate treatment from public sector services, including the criminal justice system.

For more on political and policy responses to victims of crime, read:

Davies, P. and Francis, P. (forthcoming) *Victims in the Criminal Justice System.* **Cambridge: Polity Press.**

Dignan, J. (2005) *Understanding Victims and Restorative Justice.* **Maidenhead: Open University Press.**

Spalek, B. (2006) *Crime Victims: Theory, Policy and Practice.* **London: Palgrave.**

Political economy of criminal victimization

This penultimate section situates the book within a broader theoretical and methodological framework – one that we hope is broadly critical in aim and approach. It is informed by the importance of delivering social justice (see also Walklate, 2007).

As noted at various stages already, the contributors to this volume are concerned not only to explore and explain the nature and extent of victimization in contemporary society, but also to understand the unequal distribution and experience of that victimization through reference to social division and inequality. Inequality is understood as being a necessary by-product of the current political-economic and social-cultural arrangements of late modern society. Crime, victimization, social division and inequality all simultaneously derive from and feed into wider structures of inclusion and exclusion, power and subordination, containment and control. As such, they are defining features of the contemporary social and criminal justice landscape.

A central contention of this book is that victimization is felt most often and most acutely by the most marginalized and powerless sections of society. At the same time, prevailing definitions of crime victim and victimization – in terms of who can or cannot legitimately claim victim status, who is or is not deserving of social support or media attention – do much to reify dominant white, male, middle-class, heterosexual discourses on crime and control. They reinforce rather than challenge existing structures of power. In so doing, they help to maintain the social, political and economic conditions under which much victimization takes place. It is within this critical criminological framework, sensitized in particular to the issues of inequality, social justice, and inclusion and exclusion, that all the contributions in this book are located.

Critical criminology has a long and varied history within the academy. Partly in response to the a–theoretical, a–historical, situationally-oriented approaches of the administrative criminologies resulting from the Home Office 'what works' mantra since the 1980s, critical criminology has undergone something of a recent resurgence. One of its central aims is to reinforce and tighten the links between criminology and its theoretical and political moorings at a time when mainstream criminology risks casting it adrift from both. While administrative criminologists pay at best secondary attention to the causes of crime, critical criminologists consider an appreciation of aetiology to be fundamental, not least because many of the sources of criminal behaviour and social harm can be found in the political and economic structures of late capitalist societies. Whilst administrative criminologists retain a narrow definition of crime – in many ways, reflecting tabloid representations of street violence, burglary, car theft and vandalism – critical criminologists are keen to convey that much suffering through criminal victimization results from the activities of the powerful. Corporate and white-collar offending, state crimes, deaths in custody, everyday experiences of racial and sexual violence and prejudice, and social exclusion can all be understood in terms of political and economic power and the unequal distribution of social justice in society.

Whether discussing race, age, gender, class or media constructions of these social categories and their connection to images of crime and victimization, analysis is informed by an appreciation of the political economy of crime and victimization, and a desire to highlight victimization caused by the powerful as a pressing and ongoing concern.

For more on the political economy of criminal victimization, read:

Cook, D. (2005) *Criminal and Social Justice*, London: Sage.
Hillyard, P., Pantazis, C., Tombs, S. and Gordon, D. (eds) (2004) *Beyond Criminology: Taking Harm Seriously*. London: Pluto Press.
Mawby, R. and Walklate, S. (1994) *Critical Victimology*. London: Sage.

The structure of the book

To ensure consistency across all chapters, and to secure a thorough review of the academic and policy literature, we were keen to identify from the outset a common format for each chapter. Each chapter includes the following:

- a critical review of the theoretical and research literature on the area of study;
- an assessment of the development of policy and legislative responses;
- a discussion of key developments/issues in the area of study;
- a discussion of any future research directions;
- a concise summary.

In addition, each chapter provides:

- a glossary of key terms used within the body of the chapter; highlighted by ▶▶
- questions for reflection and discussion; presented in shaded boxes
- an annotated bibliography; at the end of each chapter in a shaded box.

In outlining this format for each chapter, we were particularly keen to balance the authors' wish to explore and discuss what they wanted to, in relation to the particular substantive area that they were writing on, and the needs of the reader, new to the discipline of victimology and the study of victimization. In doing so, we think that the format strengthens the student-centred nature of the book and allows cross-referencing to be made within and between chapters.

Notes

1 The National Crime Recording Standard (NCRS) was introduced in April 2002 to ensure better consistency of crime recording across police force areas and offence categories. Visit http://homeoffice.gsi.gov.uk/rdscountrules.html for a more detailed discussion of the nature and detail of the NCRS.
2 The Crime and Disorder Act 1998, as amended by the Police Reform Act 2002, introduced a statutory responsibility on the police and local authorities to work together in partnership with other relevant agencies and organizations to prevent and reduce crime and disorder. As a result, there are, at the time of writing, 354 CDRPs in England and 22 CDRPs in Wales.

References

Best, S. (2005) *Understanding Social Divisions.* London: Sage.

Carrabine, E., Iganski, P., Lee, M., Plummer, K. and South, N. (2004) *Criminology: A Sociological Introduction.* London: Routledge.

Chermak, S. (1995) *Victims in the News: Crime and the American News Media.* Boulder, CO: Westview Press.

Cook, D. (2005) *Criminal and Social Justice.* London: Sage.

Cook, D. (1997) *Poverty, Crime and Punishment.* London: Child Poverty Action Group.

Daly, K. (1993) 'Class-race-gender: sloganeering in search of meaning', *Social Justice*, 20(1–2): 56–71.

Daly, K. (1997) 'Different ways of conceptualising sex/gender in feminist theory and their implications for criminology', *Theoretical Criminology*, 1(1): 25–51.

Davies, P. and Francis, P. (eds) (forthcoming) *Victims in the Criminal Justice System.* Cambridge: Polity Press.

Davies, P., Francis, P. and Jupp, V. (eds) (2003) *Victimisation Theory, Research and Policy.* Basingstoke: Palgrave.

Dignan, J. (2005) *Understanding Victims and Restorative Justice.* Maidenhead: Open University Press.

Dixon, M., Reed, H., Rogers, B. and Stone, L. (2006) *Crime Share: The Unequal Impact of Crime.* London: Institute for Public Policy Research.

Goodey, J. (2005) *Victims and Victimology: Research, Policy and Practice.* London: Longman.

Greer, C. (2003) *Sex Crime and the Media: Sex Offending and the Press in a Divided Society.* Cullumpton: Willan.

Greer, C. (2005) 'Crime and media: understanding the connections', in C. Hale, K. Hayward, A. Wahidin and E. Wincup (eds), *Criminology.* Oxford: Oxford University Press.

Hillyard, P., Pantazis, C., Tombs, S. and Gordon, D. (eds) (2004) *Beyond Criminology: Taking Harm Seriously.* London: Pluto Press.

Jewkes, Y. (2004) *Crime and the Media.* London: Sage.

Maguire, M. (2002) 'Crime statistics: the data explosion and its implications', in M. Maguire, R. Morgan and R. Reiner (eds), *The Oxford Handbook of Criminology*, 3rd edn. Oxford: Clarendon Press.

Mawby, R. and Walklate, S. (1994) *Critical Victimology.* London: Sage.

Salisbury, H. and Upson, A. (2004) *Ethnicity, Victimisation and Worry about Crime: Findings from the 2001/02 and 2002/03 British Crime Survey Findings 237.* London: Home Office.

Spalek, B. (2006) *Crime Victims: Theory, Policy and Practice.* London: Palgrave.

Walker, A., Kershaw, C. and Nichols, S. (2006) *Crime in England and Wales 2005/06.* Home Office Statistical Bulletin. London: Home Office.

Walklate, S. (2003) 'Can there be a feminist victimology?' in P. Davies, P. Francis and V. Jupp (eds), *Victimisation: Theory, Research and Policy.* Basingstoke: Palgrave.

Walkate, S (2007) *Imagining the Victim of Crime*, Buckinghamshire: Open University Press.

Webster, F. (2005) 'Making sense of the Information Age: sociology and cultural studies', *Information, Communications and Society*, 8(4): 439–58.

Williams, B. (1999) *Working with Victims of Crime*. London: Jessica Kingsley.

Zedner, L. (2002) 'Victims', in M. Maguire, R. Morgan and R. Reiner (eds), *The Oxford Handbook of Criminology*, 3rd edn. Oxford: Clarendon Press.

News Media, Victims and Crime

Chris Greer

Chapter aims

- To problematize media representations of crime and criminal victimization.
- To discuss methods of researching criminal victimization and media coverage.
- To assess media representations of different forms of criminal victimization.

Introduction

The definition of who may legitimately claim victim status is profoundly influenced by social divisions including class, race, ethnicity, gender, age and sexuality, and, as such, remains a point of contention and debate. Such debates are framed and inflected, to a significant extent, in the news media. This chapter, then, is concerned critically to explore how the status of victim, and different acts and processes of criminal victimization, are defined and represented in the news media.

It is now widely acknowledged that, across news and entertainment formats, media focus overwhelmingly on the most serious examples of crime and victimization, foregrounding images of violent and frequently sexual interpersonal offending (Marsh, 1991; Reiner et al., 2000a). By contrast, lower-level property offences that make up the significant majority of recorded crime (Maguire, 2002), and white-collar and corporate offences that place a major social and financial burden on society (Hillyard et al., 2004; Tombs and Whyte, 2001, 2003; Croall, this volume), are given sparse attention, if not ignored altogether. However, the mass media focus on violent crime is also highly selective. Ferrell (2005: 150) points out that news media representations highlight 'the criminal victimization of strangers rather than the dangerous intimacies of domestic or family conflict'. Stanko and Lee (2003: 10) note that violence in the media is constructed 'as 'random', wanton and the intentional acts of evil folk'. News reporting of crime and, further, of the particular types of crime on which journalists disproportionately focus, is selective and unrepresentative. News reporting of crime victims is equally so.

Critically exploring media representations of crime victims is important because, over the past few decades, victims have taken on an unprecedented significance in media and criminal justice discourses, in the development of crime policy, and in the popular imagination. Indeed, as Reiner and colleagues have noted, the foregrounding of crime victims in the media is one of the most significant qualitative changes in media representations of crime and control since the Second World War (Reiner et al., 2000a, b, 2003).

The chapter is structured into three main parts. First, it takes a critical look at some theoretical and methodological issues which are important when researching news media representations of crime victims and criminal victimization. Why and how these particular issues are important is illustrated by examining the portrayal of murder victims, where the influence of factors such as social divisions and inequalities and the determinants of news production is starkly illustrated. Second, it explores news representations of a range of different types of crime victim, focusing in particular on those groups and individuals who are variously over-represented, under-represented and misrepresented in media reports. Finally, the chapter identifies significant gaps in the existing research literature, raises a number of questions for further reflection, and suggests some potentially fruitful areas for future research and investigation.

News media and the 'ideal victim'

Not all crime victims receive equal attention in the news media. Occasionally, intense media coverage may be devoted to victims who can be discredited on the basis of, for example, a criminal, promiscuous or otherwise questionable past. More often, however, media resourses are allocated to the representation of those victims who can be portrayed as 'ideal'. Christie (1986: 18) describes the '**ideal victim**' as 'a person or category of individuals who – when hit by crime – most readily are given the complete and legitimate status of being a victim'. This group includes those who are perceived as vulnerable, defenceless, innocent and worthy of sympathy and compassion. Elderly women and young children, it is suggested, are typical 'ideal victims', whereas young men, the homeless, those with drug problems, and others existing on the margins of society may find it much more difficult to achieve legitimate victim status, still less secure a conviction in court (Carrabine et al., 2004). In this sense, there exists a **hierarchy of victimization**, both reflected and reinforced in media and official discourses. At one extreme, those who acquire the status of 'ideal victim' may attract massive levels of media attention, generate collective mourning on a near global scale, and drive significant change to social and criminal justice policy and practice (Greer, 2004; Valier, 2004). At the other extreme, those crime victims who never acquire legitimate victim status or, still worse, are perceived as 'undeserving victims' may receive little, if any, media attention, and pass virtually unnoticed in the wider social world.

▶▶ **Ideal victims** *a person or category of individuals who – when hit by crime – most readily are given the complete and legitimate status of being a victim, including those who are perceived as vulnerable, defenceless, innocent and worthy of sympathy and compassion.*

▶▶ **Hierarchy of victimisation** *describes a pecking order of sorts, representing the differential status of particular types and categories of crime victim in media and official discourses, including ideal victims (for example, some child murder victims) at the top of the hierarchy, and non-deserving victims (for example, habitually violent youths injured in a drunken fight) near the bottom.*

In the summer of 2002, two 10-year-old girls, Holly Wells and Jessica Chapman, went missing from their home in Soham. Their disappearance attracted international media attention and precipitated the biggest ever manhunt in Britain. In 1996, two boys of similar age, Patrick Warren and David Spencer, went missing from their homes. Their disappearance failed to register much outside the local press. Shortly after 13-year-old Milly Dowler went missing in 2002, the body of a teenage girl was recovered from a disused cement works near Tilbury docks (Jewkes, 2004). Amidst press speculation that it was another missing teenager, Danielle Jones, who had disappeared almost a year earlier, the body was identified as that of 14-year-old Hannah Williams. Yet it was Milly's story that continued to dominate the headlines. Hannah received only a few sentences on the inside pages.

How might this media selectivity be understood? The answer lies, at least partly, in dominant conceptions of legitimate and ideal victims. Holly and Jessica were archetypal 'ideal victims'. They were young, bright, photogenic girls from stable and loving, middle-class family backgrounds, and each had an exemplary school record. David and Patrick were working class, they were boys, and they had been brought up on a rough West Midlands council estate. They had been in trouble at school and one of them, David, had been caught shoplifting. While Holly and Jessica captured the hearts and minds of a nation, Patrick and David did not attract the same media or public interest, and few ever knew about their disappearance. Like Holly and Jessica, Milly Dowler epitomized the notion of an 'ideal victim'. By contrast, Hannah Williams was working class, raised by a single mother on a low income, and had run away before. Her background denied her 'deserving' victim status and, eclipsed by Milly's ongoing story, Hannah was forgotten almost immediately. Hannah Williams' murder generated just over 60 articles in the British national press, mostly after she was found. In its first two weeks alone, the hunt for Holly and Jessica produced nearly 900 (Fracassini, 2002).

The attribution or otherwise of ideal or legitimate victim status and related levels of media interest are clearly influenced by demographic characteristics.

The cases of missing and murdered children discussed above indicate that both 'class' – or perhaps better, a middle-class notion of 'respectability' – and gender can be defining factors. Race, too, can be central. In 1993, black teenager Stephen Lawrence was fatally stabbed in a racist attack. At first, the police assumed that because the victim was a young, black male, the murder must have been gang-related (McLaughlin and Murji, 1999; Cottle, 2004; Heaven and Hudson, 2005). For a week after the stabbing in 2000 of 10-year-old Damilola Taylor in South London, news reports focused almost exclusively on the issue of community policing (Jewkes, 2004). It was not until later that both these individuals were recognized and reported as legitimate victims worthy of national media attention. Partly because of their race, and partly because of their gender, legitimate victim status was not automatic as it was for Holly, Jessica and Milly, but needed to be won. The murder of white London solicitor Tom ap Rhys Price in 2006 received 5,525 words in the national press, while the murder on the same day, of Asian London cement merchant Balbir Matharu, received only 1,385 (*Guardian*, 27th January 2006). For some, including the Chief Commissioner of the London Metropolitan Police, Sir Ian Blair, the explanation was sad but simple. The British news media are institutionally racist in how they report murder.[1]

There was some limited media debate regarding the merits of this allegation. Overwhelmingly, though, the media response was hostile. Outraged newspaper editors reproduced high profile coverage of black and Asian murder victims – including Stephen Lawrence and Damilola Taylor – as 'proof' that they were not racist. The conservative *Daily Mail*, known for its 'traditionally reactionary stance on race issues in Britain' (McLaughlin and Murji, 1999: 377), reprinted its infamous front page which risked legal action by sensationally naming and picturing the alleged killers of Stephen Lawrence beneath the headline – 'Murderers: The Mail accuses these men of killing. If we are wrong, let them sue us!' (see Figure 2.1).

In the end, little was resolved, but the brief bout of mediatized claim and counter-claim usefully illustrated the complexity of the problem. Demographic characteristics such as class, race, gender, age, and sexuality can at times determine news media interest in a fairly straightforward manner. But they can also cut across each other and interact with other variables in nuanced and unpredictable ways that do much to invalidate blanket claims that 'the press' or, still worse, 'the media' are institutionally prejudiced. The influence of victim demographics needs to be considered within the wider context of the news production process, the other elements of the case, and the prevailing cultural and political environment at that time. In order to unravel this complexity a little further, it is helpful to explore the concept of newsworthiness.

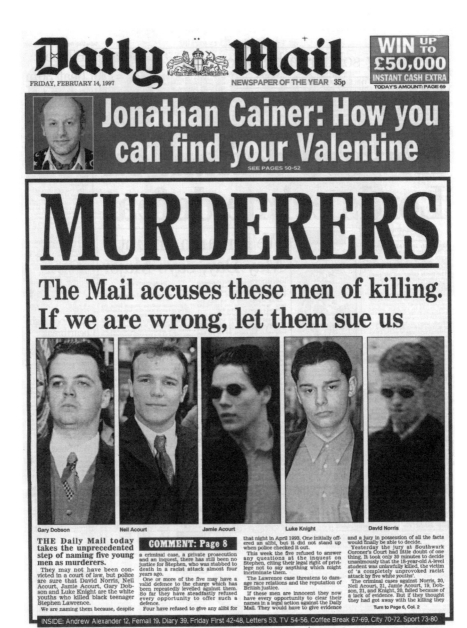

Figure 2.1 *Daily Mail* front page, 14 February 1997

QUESTIONS

Stop now and try to think of some well-known victims of crime. How would you describe these victims?

What are their demographic characteristics? Other than their victimization, do they share anything in common?

What do your recollections tell you about media representations of crime and criminal victimization?

What do your recollections tell you about yourself?

Newsworthiness, crime and criminal victimization

There exists an extensive literature on the various criteria that make events attractive – or 'newsworthy' – to journalists (Chibnall, 1977; Hall et al., 1978; Katz, 1987; Ericson et al., 1989; Schlesinger and Tumber, 1994; Greer, 2003; Jewkes, 2004). Newsworthiness is shaped by **news values** – those criteria that determine which events come within the horizon of media visibility, and to what extent, and which do not. Since the first sociological statement of news values by Galtung and Ruge in 1965, numerous commentators have offered their own interpretation of the key determinants of newsworthiness. Three important contributions are summarized in Table 2.1.

▶▶ **News values** those criteria that influence, often implicitly, the selection, production and prioritization of events as news. Key news values include drama and action, immediacy, violence, celebrities, and sex.

Most accounts agree on certain criteria, which can be thought of as core or fundamental news values. With specific reference to crime news, most accounts highlight the importance of violence. The observation made by Hall et al. (1978: 68) three decades ago about the production of crime news still holds today:

> One special point about crime as news is the special status of violence as a news value. Any crime can be lifted into news visibility if violence becomes associated with it ... Violence represents a basic violation of the person; the greatest personal crime is 'murder'... Violence is also the ultimate crime against property, and against the State. It thus represents a fundamental rupture in the social order.

Table 2.1   Three sociological accounts of 'news values'

Galtung and Ruge (1965)	Chibnall (1977)	Jewkes (2004)
Threshold (importance)		Threshold (importance)
Unexpectedness (novelty)	Novelty (unexpectedness)	
Negativity (violent, harmful, deviant, sad)		Violence
Unambiguity (clear and definite)	Simplification (removing shades of grey)	Simplification (removing shades of grey)
	Dramatization (action)	
Frequency (timescale, fit within news cycle)	Immediacy (the present, fit within news cycle)	
Elite-centricity (powerful or famous nations or people)	Personalization (notable individuals, celebrities)	Celebrity or high-status (notable individuals)
	Structured access (experts, officials, authority)	
Composition (balance, fit with other news)		
Personification (individual focus or causality)	Individual pathology (individual causality)	Individualism (individual focus or causality)
		Children (young people)
Continuity (sustainability)		
	Graphic presentation	Spectacle or graphic imagery
	Visible/spectacular acts	
Meaningfulness (spatial and cultural relevance)		Proximity (spatial and cultural relevance)
Consonance (fit with existing knowledge and expectations)	Conventionalism (hegemonic ideology)	Predictability (expectedness)
	Titillation (exposé, scandal)	
		Risk (lasting danger)
	Sexual/political connotations	Sex
	Deterrence and repression	Conservative ideology or political diversion (deterrence, distraction from wides problems)

Despite enduring similarities between accounts, it is important to recognize that news values are also culturally specific in that they reflect the historical and social moment in which they are situated (Naylor, 2001). As media and society change, so too can the criteria that influence the selection and production of events as news. The recent 'celebrification' of society (Rojek, 2001) would appear to have rendered anything and everything related to 'celebrity culture' newsworthy. Celebrity crime is especially so. The sexualization of society has also affected the news (Greer and Jewkes, 2005). With the breaking down of many sexual taboos in recent decades, sex and violence are presented more frequently and graphically across all media forms (Presdee, 2000), including crime news (Reiner et al, 2000a).

At the same time, specific criminal incidents – what Martin Innes (2003, 2004) calls '**signal crimes**' – can have a lasting influence on crime reporting. 'Signal crimes' are those crimes which impact not only on the immediate participants (victims, offenders, witnesses), but also on wider society, resulting in some reconfiguration of behaviours or beliefs (Innes, 2003). For example, the murder of toddler James Bulger by two 10-year-old boys in 1993 (re)generated sustained debate on the concept of 'childhood' and its intersections with 'evil and purity', 'guilt and innocence', 'care and control' (James and Jenks, 1996; Goldson, 1997; Morrison, 1997; Scraton, 1997). The racist murder of Stephen Lawrence in the same year, and evidence of institutional racism in the police (mis)handling of the case (Macpherson, 1999; see also Chapters 5 and 10 in this volume), intensified interest in race and racism and their connection with 'crime and victimization', 'law and order', 'policing and criminal justice' (McLaughlin and Murji, 2001; Cottle, 2005). The sexually-motivated abduction and murder of 8-year-old Sarah Payne in the summer of 2000 by a convicted paedophile crystallized fears around the image of the predatory child sex offender and fuelled debate on 'risk and dangerousness', 'surveillance and control', and the suitability of new legislation, to be called Sarah's Law, allowing limited public notification regarding the whereabouts of convicted sex offenders in the community (Silverman and Wilson, 2002; Evans, 2003). In the wake of these cases, further incidents of child violence, racist violence, predatory sexual violence were rendered more newsworthy still because they could be considered and constructed in relation to the defining incident at that time – the signal crime – which in turn could be revisited, reactivated and recreated in the media for a mass audience (Peelo, 2006). Thus, while violence endures as a core news value, its newsworthiness can be intensified considerably when focused through the lenses of celebrity, childhood, sex and race, among others – categories which are not in themselves new, but which have gained increased and lasting media currency due to wider social change and/or specific, high profile, signal crimes.

Figure 2.2   Cops Losing Fight on Violent Crime, *Sun*, page 33, 27 January 2006

▶▶ **Signal crimes**   *A term coined by Martin Innes which refers to those particularly serious or high profile crimes which impact not only on the immediate participants (victims, offenders, witnesses), but also on wider society, resulting in some reconfiguration of behaviours or beliefs (Innes, 2003).*

Newsworthiness, crime victims and the importance of the visual

What is missing from traditional accounts of crime newsworthiness is sufficient acknowledgement of the 'visual'. The rapid development of information technologies in recent decades has changed the terrain on which crime is reported. Today, crime stories are increasingly selected and 'produced' as *media events* on the basis of their visual (how they can be portrayed in images) as well as their lexical-verbal (how they can be portrayed in words) potential.

Of course, television stations are primarily concerned with producing an 'appealing visual product' (Chermak, 1995: 110). But press representations too have become intensely visual phenomena, incorporating: photographs of victims, offenders, or loved ones; diagrams mapping out a route taken, a geographical area, a weapon, or a crime scene; graphic illustrations of offending rates, prison populations, and police numbers; satirical cartoons lampooning bungling criminal justice professionals; the list goes on (see Figure 2.2). These visual elements of the news product depict immediately, dramatically, and often in full colour what it may take several paragraphs to say in words. If the visual has always played an important part in the manufacture of crime news (Hall, 1973), today it has become a universally defining characteristic.

Where victims of crime are concerned, the potential to visualize a case can have a direct impact on its perceived newsworthiness. Steve Chermak begins his book *Victims in the News* (1995) as follows:

> As the surviving family members begin to struggle with the realities of murder, they are asked by the news media to make a public obituary to the deceased victim. Journalists hope the family members can articulate their pain, suffering, and confusion in a newsworthy fashion so others can attach some meaning to the family's loss. The newsworthiness of this crime increases significantly if members of the family weep on camera, provide a descriptive photograph, or express their pain dramatically in words.

▶▶ **Visualisation of crime news**   *the increasing prevalence and importance of visual representations of crime news, crime victims and criminal victimisation in the information age, generally to enhance the immediate accessibility, human interest and overall communicative impact of the news product on media consumers.*

The press conference has become integral, both to the police investigation and to the media coverage of murder cases. Indeed, today it is almost expected that victims' loved ones will express their emotions and share their pain and suffering with media audiences, at once horrified and fascinated by the spectacle unfolding before them. As well as being assumed to increase the likelihood of public co-operation in a murder investigation, police are also aware that 'emotional displays of this kind make a good story for journalists and thus the case may receive more media attention than it might otherwise do' (Innes, 2003: 58). There is an important intersection here between the demographic characteristics of the victim and his/her relations, the availability or perceived suitability of loved ones to feature in press conferences, the overall newsworthiness of the case, and the amount of media attention it receives as a result.

The parents of Holly Wells and Jessica Chapman, Sarah Payne, and Milly Dowler all made emotional television appeals for the safe return of their children, and in some cases for information regarding the identity and whereabouts of their child's killer. Because of the ideal nature of the victims and the drama of the story, media interest in these cases was automatic. The task for the parents of Stephen Lawrence and Damilola Taylor was not as straightforward. It was not *until* Damilola's father travelled from Nigeria to make press and television appearances that this victim became newsworthy in his own right. And Doreen and Neville Lawrence campaigned tirelessly for justice, actively soliciting media attention and successfully raising the profile of the case when interest was sparse (Cathcart, 2000). Ultimately, in all of these cases, articulate and 'respectable' parents were not only able, but willing, and in some cases driven to engage with the media and withstand the potentially constant glare of its spotlight. Their suitability and capability in this regard made the stories more newsworthy and, crucially, kept the cases in the public eye. Those less able or less willing to engage with the media, or those whom the police consider less suitable for media exposure for whatever reason, may find that, deprived of new and newsworthy material, media attention quickly dries up. A police spokesperson said that Hannah Williams' background made it difficult to launch a national media campaign around her. Hannah's mother, it was claimed, a single parent on a low income, 'wasn't really press-conference material' (Bright, 2002).

Even more powerful than press conferences, victim photographs familiarize media audiences, instantly and enduringly, with victims of crime in a way that words cannot. 'Photographs', Susan Sontag (2004: 2) argues, 'have an insuperable power to determine what people recall of events.' Gerrard (2004: 14), writing about the Soham murders, suggests that 'We understand with words and stories, through the linked chain of events. But we recollect in pictures. Memory freeze-frames. Our lives are held in a series of vivid stills inside our head, and so it is with more public events.' And in the words of one journalist, 'If the public can see ... a victim, it adds something. There is nothing to a name. When you see a picture, you see the life, the potential' (cited in Chermak, 1995: 104). In missing persons and murder cases, victim photographs are rendered more poignant still by the understanding that those featured may be, or already are, dead. They present an idealized personification of innocence and loss. At the same time, they serve indirectly to highlight the monstrosity and evil of the offender, and to endorse the extent to which this monstrosity 'should inform justice' (D'Cruze et al., 2006: 22). In Western culture where 'seeing is believing' (Doyle, 2003: 138), photographs humanize crime victims, adding a sense of the 'real' to that which may otherwise remain abstract and difficult to latch on to or invest in emotionally.

Thus, it is not only what is known or imagined about victims, in terms of background, life history, future potential, but also how vividly that history and potential can be communicated to media audiences. In signal crimes featuring 'ideal victims', whose innocence is uncontested and whose potential is palpably felt, photographs may take on an iconic status, becoming an instant, powerful and lasting reference point. The photograph of Holly Wells and Jessica Chapman posing in their matching Manchester United shirts, or the school portraits of Damilola Taylor or Sarah Payne are good examples of victim photographs which were used relentlessly throughout each case and its aftermath, and became deeply embedded in the popular imagination. The power of these images, the newsworthiness of the crime type, the social characteristics of the victims and their families, and the suitability and willingness of those involved to engage with the media coalesced with other factors to produce a compelling narrative that connected deeply and on a profoundly personal level with media audiences, and stayed with them. Another crucial factor in sustaining their high profile presence in the news media was that these victims' cases featured evidence of serious failure by key institutions and agencies tasked with the role of 'public protection'.

Newsworthiness, crime victims and institutional failure

A key element in the construction of a compelling crime narrative is the attribution of responsibility or blame (Chibnall, 1977; Sparks, 1992). Blame for serious and violent crimes may be individual and directed at offenders, or, less often, social and directed at society. Importantly, however, it can also be institutional. When there is evidence that official agencies and state bodies assigned to protect the 'innocent' have somehow failed in this task, the potential to develop and sustain a compelling narrative is increased considerably. Media interest in the deaths of James Bulger, Stephen Lawrence, Sarah Payne, Holly Wells and Jessica Chapman, and Damilola Taylor was maintained in part by evidence of serious institutional failings – variously implicating the police, the courts, the education system, even the core social institution of the family – which were portrayed either as serving to maintain the conditions that allowed the offence to occur in the first place, or as impeding the case's investigation and prosecution afterwards. Now sensationally located at the heart of a scandal, the symbolic power of the victims extended beyond their individual cases and they became representative of wider issues and debates on public safety, social and criminal justice, or the nature of society itself.

When crime victims come symbolically to represent a problem that resonates with and potentially affects many in society – school safety, racist violence, knife crime – mediatized campaigns, particularly when launched in the victim's name, are likely to garner high levels of public support. Faced with collective moral outrage and a sustained barrage of critical media coverage, agencies publicly implicated as part of the problem, or the authorities to which those agencies are answerable, are required to respond. In each of the cases discussed above, the response was some form of official inquiry which, in turn, led to recommendations for change in structures of training and accountability, professional practice and criminal justice and social policy. The murder of James Bulger is inextricably linked to the 1998 Crime and Disorder Act's abolition of *doli incapax* – the centuries-old legal doctrine which maintained that children between the ages of 10 and 13 could not be held fully responsible for crimes committed because they are incapable of understanding the consequences and implications of their acts. The Macpherson Report (1999) investigating the mismanagement of the Stephen Lawrence murder case branded the London Metropolitan Police 'professionally incompetent and institutionally racist' and called for fundamental change to police training and accountability, and engagement with black communities across the UK. Sarah Payne's abduction and murder by a convicted paedophile generated media debate and public outrage which informed the legislative changes embodied in the Sex Offences Act 2003. The murders of Holly Wells and Jessica Chapman led directly to the Bichard Inquiry, which scrutinized the police's 'intelligence-based record keeping, vetting practices and information sharing with other agencies' (http://www.bichardinquiry.org.uk/report/) and made recommendations relevant for police, social services, education establishments, vetting services and government aimed at improving national child protection. Most recently, the conviction of two boys in 2006 for the murder of Damilola Taylor comes after three trials and claims that crucial forensic evidence was missed during the initial investigation. An inquiry into these institutional failures was, at the time of writing, under way. The extent to which the changes or recommendations for change following these cases have been appropriate or adequately implemented remains a matter for debate (Haydon and Scraton, 2000; Bowling and Phillips, 2002; Foster et al., 2005). For current purposes, however, what is important is the role news media played in generating, sustaining and shaping the preceding debate. It would be overstating things to suggest that media representations led directly to the policy and legislative developments that followed. But they were instrumental in publicly defining the cases, rooting the victims' images in the popular imagination, generating and focusing collective moral outrage and support for change, and, crucially, keeping the stories alive in both political and popular consciousness, in some cases, long after the initial investigation had closed.

QUESTIONS

Revisit your list of crime victims. Now, consider how you are thinking about those crimes? What is it that you recall about each case? Is it the details of the offence; the media coverage – television, radio, Internet, press; the images that were released during the investigation; evidence of institutional failure?

Do you recall different things about different cases?

Are you imagining the cases in words, pictures, or both?

The previous sections have discussed the significance of social divisions and inequalities, the contemporary nature of news production, and the wider criminal justice environment for the representation of crime victims in the news media. More specifically, it has sought to demonstrate the complexity of the interconnections between these factors and the impact they can have on the attribution of legitimate or ideal victim status, media interest, and the public construction of particular cases of murder. The second half of this chapter broadens out the analysis by considering news representations of a range of different types of crime victim under three broad headings: under-representing victims of crime, over-representing victims of crime, and misrepresenting victims of crime. It should be noted that these headings are not mutually exclusive: victims who are under-represented, for example, are by definition also misrepresented. The aim, however, is not to establish hermetically sealed categories of crime victim, but rather to stimulate critical thinking by demonstrating some of the ways in which crime victims and criminal victimization can be distorted in news media representations.

Under-representing victims of crime

Victims of street crime

Though it is true that some of the most serious examples of criminal offending grab the biggest headlines, images of street crime and anti-social behaviour maintain a constant and foreboding presence across news media. Given the newsworthiness of violence, it is not surprising that robbery and assault feature heavily. News reports and broadcasts are replete with images of anti-social and criminally violent behaviour. Elderly women are archetypal 'ideal victims' of street crime and may attract considerable

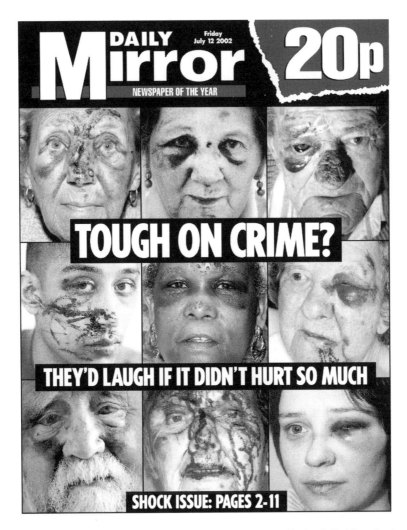

Figure 2.3 Tough on Crime? They'd Laugh if it Didn't Hurt so Much, *Daily Mirror* front page, 12 July 2002

media attention when they become victims (see Figure 2.3). However, despite the impression given on some newspaper front pages, elderly women constitute one of the least 'at risk' groups (see also Walklate, Chapter 6 in this volume). As Leishman and Mason (2003: 13) point out, contrary to media stereotypes, 'victims of street muggings are typically not the vulnerable old lady having her handbag snatched, but the teenager being relieved by a coeval of a mobile phone'. What is striking about news media representations of street crime is that they relentlessly promote the image of young people as offenders, while downplaying their everyday experiences as victims. News media portrayals of young people as victims tend to be reserved for particularly grievous incidents resulting in serious injury or death – when they can be presented as innocent, naïve or vulnerable. This distortion led the authors of one UK media analysis to conclude, 'according to our daily press, a typical adolescent is a sporting youngster, criminally inclined [and] likely to be murdered or injured in an accident' (Porteous and Colston, 1980: 202).

The under-representation of young people as victims of street crime is even more pronounced for those who are non-white. High profile examples of racist murder and child killing, as we have seen, can generate enormous levels of media attention. And particular forms of criminal victimization may be reported in racialized terms which cast black youth as victims as well as offenders. The BBC News (30 September 2006), for example, ran a feature on gun crime which reported that 35per cent of UK shootings involve black victims, and that black youths are 30 times more likely to be killed through gun crime than white youths. Reinforcing Porteous and Colston's (1980) findings, however, this coverage followed a series of incidents resulting in death and portrayed the problem as an issue of 'race' as much as an issue of 'criminal victimization'. The everyday experiences of black people as victims of crime and racial prejudice seldom make the headlines.

For decades, black youth have been demonized in media discourses as the 'criminal other'. Whether as pimps, rioters, muggers, Rastafarian drug dealers, gang members, or Yardies (Hall et al., 1978; Gilroy, 1987; Solomos, 1988; Alexander, 1996; Muncie, 2004), the association between race and crime has been forcefully established and remains resonant today. This association has more recently extended to Asian youth (Alexander, 2000). Once perceived as more likely to fall victim to street violence than perpetrate it (Muncie, 2004), participation in events such as the anti-Rushdie protests of 1989 and demonstrations against the first and second Gulf Wars have resulted in an intensified media interest in potential Asian criminality. An *Independent* article in 1995, warning of 'an Asian crime "timebomb"', cautioned that 'the country is on the verge of an outbreak of disorder caused by Asians ... which could shatter the belief that Asians are more law-abiding than white or black people'. In a post-September 11th world of heightened 'Islamophobia', fear and suspicion of Asian youth are exacerbated by news reports which crudely, but commonly, marry the terms 'Asian' and 'Muslim', on the one hand, and 'Islam' and 'Islamic fundamentalism', on the other. Racialized discourses on asylum and immigration inflame tensions still further (Greer and Jewkes, 2005; ICAR, 2007).

Meanwhile, Asian youth 'resistance' against perceived or actual victimization by the state and wider society becomes 'synonymous with criminality and upheaval, with the breakdown of perceived traditional values and the growth of a pathologised culture of alienation and confusion' (Alexander, 2000: 7). The apparent news media obsession with the criminality of non-white youth displaces interest in their experiences of all but the most serious forms of criminal victimization.

Victims of white-collar and corporate crime

The most notable thing about white-collar and corporate offending in the media is their general lack of prevalence and prominence relative to 'traditional' or 'conventional' crimes of interpersonal and sexual violence. This apparent lack of media interest can be related back to the previous discussion of newsworthiness and the allocation of blame. Unlike many street crimes, corporate and white-collar offences are often 'morally ambiguous in terms of crime, criminal and victim; they unfold slowly; and they do not culminate in a clear resolution' (Cavender and Mulcahy, 1998: 699). While traditional crimes at some point necessarily involve a degree of proximity between victim and offender, victims of corporate and white-collar crime may never actually encounter the offender and, moreover, may never realize they have been victimized, for example, in cases of large-scale financial fraud or embezzlement, where individual losses are small but the cumulative total may run into millions (Stephenson-Burton, 1995). When individuals are aware of their victimization, it may be impossible to evidence the precise source of harm, still less prove individual or corporate legal culpability, for example, in cases of long-term environmental pollution or corporate negligence resulting in deaths at work (Tombs and Whyte, 2001). Even when both crime and victim are clearly identifiable, the media's preferred image of the 'ideal victim' can be difficult to establish. In the case of health and safety violation, as Tombs and Whyte (2007) point out, attempts to portray employees as innocent victims may be directly challenged by corporate discourses that seek to abrogate liability by presenting individuals as 'accident-prone' and thus partly to blame for their own injury. Investors who are defrauded may be perceived as partly responsible for making 'risky' or 'ill-informed' financial choices and, as a result, receive little attention outside the specialist business and financial press. Older people who are 'taken advantage of', or ordinary folk who are victimized by corporate 'fat cats', may be seen as more deserving of 'legitimate' victim status (Levi, 1999), and receive more favaurable mainstream media attention unchallenged by competing interests.

Due to the difficult to prove and frequently diffuse nature of the harm caused by white-collar and corporate victimization, these offences feature much less in our immediate experience. They do not arouse the same levels of fear and moral indignation as offences of interpersonal violence. The language of news coverage contributes further to muting moral outcry and inhibiting emotional identification with victims of these offences. Reports describe health and safety 'accidents' rather than 'criminal negligence'. Financial assets are 'plundered' or 'lost', rather than 'stolen'. Individuals are 'defrauded' rather than 'robbed'. Furthermore, as Stephenson-Burton (1995: 147) notes, there is often a 'grudging respect, or at the very least a lessening of antipathy, within media representations of the white collar criminal'. So despite the fact that the economic, social and physical harm done can be enormous (Croall, 2001b; Tombs, 2005), white-collar and corporate offending continue to suffer from relative media invisibility, with the victims remaining less visible still.

Over-representing victims of crime

Police and prison officers as crime victims

Discussions of ideal and legitimate victims have so far focused on members of the public. Another important manifestation of the 'ideal victim', at times no less potent in terms of generating sustained media attention and public outcry, is the police or prison officer killed in the line of duty. While many victims of crime are under-represented in the news media, it can cogently be argued that the criminal victimization of police and prison officers is, if anything, over-represented. Greer (2005: 165) has noted the news media priority given to police officers killed on duty: 'On 26th December 2003 Iran was struck by an earthquake which killed upwards of 25 thousand Iranian citizens. This was a natural disaster on a massive scale, and the second story reported on the UK evening News at Ten. The headlining item disclosed that an English police officer had been shot.'

The suggestion is not that those state servants killed in the line of duty are undeserving of media attention or, in some cases, national recognition and public mourning. Rather, the point is that news media representations tend to exaggerate both the prevalence and the seriousness of incidents involving prison and police officers, while the victimization of the marginalized and the powerless is frequently overlooked. Sim (2004) argues that this mediatized impression of vulnerability and danger is, in fact, at odds with the available statistical information. Most of the deaths of on-duty police and prison officers occur through natural causes, such as heart attacks, or accidents, such as car crashes. Very few deaths result from murder by inmates or offenders. Nevertheless, the murders of police and prison officers are highly newsworthy to journalists because they can be portrayed as ruptures to the social fabric of society, reinforcing the perennially popular media themes of decline, disorder and lack of respect for authority (Chibnall, 1977). At the same time, these statistically rare, isolated incidents allow representative bodies, like the Prison Officer Association and the Police Federation, to symbolically construct *all* their members as both 'heroes' and 'victims', carrying out dangerous work under constant threat of murderous violence from inmates and offenders. Prisons are portrayed as harmful and dangerous places for prison staff alone, while the dangers faced by prison inmates at the hands of staff and each other receive scant media attention. The number of police officers killed in the line of duty is eclipsed by the number of people who die in police custody each year, yet while the former may dislodge the deaths of 25,000 Iranian citizens as lead news item, the latter seldom causes much of a news tremor. As Sim notes (2004: 116), the cumulative effect of over-representing 'the victimised state', while at the same time under-representing the victimization of some of society's most powerless and marginalized groups, sometimes at the hands of the state, contributes to building a 'consensus around the essential benevolence of state institutions and their servants – particularly police and prison officers – while simultaneously socially constructing these same servants as living in perpetual danger from the degenerate and the desperate'. For critical criminologists, this ideologically loaded selectivity contributes to buttressing the legitimacy of the prevailing criminal justice system, maintaining the perceived sanctity of state servants as guardians of order, and supporting the development of authoritarian, law and order politics.

Misrepresenting victims of crime

Victims of the criminal justice system

When they are victims of serious criminal victimization, police and prison officers tend to attract high levels of ideologically loaded media coverage. When those who have been caught up in the criminal justice net, and are therefore already branded offenders, fall victim to the pressures of the criminal justice system, media coverage is often less copious, but no less ideologically loaded. Drakeford (2006) illustrates how the 2004 prison suicide of 14-year-old Adam Rickwood – the youngest child ever to take his own life while in the care and custody of the British penal system – was characterized in the conservative *Daily Mail* as bad from the start. His death was described as the closing scene in 'a bleak tale of family breakdown, and an absence of discipline, as well as a blasé acceptance of drug-taking, underage drinking and petty theft' (*Daily Mail*, 16th August, 2004, in Drakeford, 2006). As Drakeford (2006: 218) notes, a 'cultural hegemony, reinforced by media reporting, links "youth" and "crime" in the public mind in a way which dissolves these categories into one, regarding those caught up in the criminal justice system as simply reaping the rewards of their own culpability'. The death of Zahid Mubarek in Feltham Young Offenders Centre in 2000, bludgeoned to death with a table leg by his racist cellmate, led to an official inquiry. The release of the Inquiry Report (Keith, 2006) received considerable media attention, not least because it listed more than 180 'failings' in the penal system, branding the sequence of events 'institutional racism leading to institutional murder'. News stories in this case were less about the deprived or depraved background of the victim, and more about the gaping holes in criminal justice policy and practice which would allow a vulnerable inmate to be incarcerated in the same cell as a persistently violent offender with a history of racist assault and suspected severe personality disorder. Even here, then, while there was no 'spoiling' of the victim's identity, as there was with Adam Rickwood, it was the newsworthiness of exposing institutional failure and attributing blame to those in authority that dominated coverage.

Adult victims of sex crime

Several commentators have pointed to the highly gendered reporting of male sexual violence against women (Soothill and Walby, 1991; Benedict, 1992; Lees, 1995; Greer, 2003). Soothill and Walby (1991: 22) argue that during the tabloid wars of the late 1970s sex crime was presented by some newspapers as a form of 'soft pornography' to increase sales. Twenty years on, Lees (1995: 125) evidenced little change and found much rape reporting in a sample of four British newspapers to be 'biased, inaccurate and irresponsible', and frequently 'directed at discounting women's allegations of rape, and justifying the masquerading of rape as seduction'. Benedict (1992) has highlighted the tendency for news media to polarize women in sex crime cases into either 'virgins' or 'whores', or, in the language of this chapter, 'ideal' and 'undeserving' victims. These binary oppositions do not necessarily result from individual journalistic malice. Rather, they arise from the gender-biased nature of language and prevailing myths about women, sex and rape. These myths implicitly guide news-making in a way that can influence even the most well-meaning commentators, so 'a myth-saturated woman will be just as insensitive to rape cases as a myth-saturated man, especially given the conditions and habits of newsroom behaviour' (Benedict, 1992: 6). Meyers (1997: 119) has found a similarly biased coverage of female victims of sexual violence, noting that news coverage is influenced heavily by the 'virgin–whore' dichotomy, and by notions of race, class and age which result from the convergence of 'male and white supremacist ideologies'. The findings across these studies and others are remarkably consistent. News media representations of adult victims of sex crime, if seldom presented as soft pornography today, are frequently structured and couched in masculinist terms. Such narratives do much to maintain traditional patriarchal stereotypes of femininity, masculinity and 'appropriate' female sexuality, while doing little to challenge prevailing myths about rape and tackle the problem of male sexual violence against women.

Child victims of sex crime

Perhaps the most significant shift in media reporting of sex crime in recent decades has been the emergence of child victims as a news staple, and the decline in attention to adult rapes unless there is some additional, novel aspect to the case, for example, the involvement of celebrities, or multiple victims or offenders (Greer, 2003). Even though child sex abuse reporting has proliferated, it is only certain types of offence that receive regular and sustained coverage. News stories tend to feature very young victims – well below the age of consent and thus easily presented as completely 'innocent' – who have been abused by a stranger, someone in a position of authority – say, a teacher, youth leader or member of the clergy – or, more recently, groomed online (Martellozzo, 2007). Sexual victimization often takes place within the home, and it is more likely a child will be abused by someone to whom they are related than by a stranger or someone just met (Grubin, 1998). Yet images of familial abuse are virtually absent from mainstream media representations. Kitzinger (1999) points out that while people may on some level be aware that the greatest dangers to children frequently come from within the home, their fears focus on external threats – scrubland rather than living rooms, strangers rather than family members – because this is both practically and emotionally more manageable on a day-to-day basis. While such fears may be understandable and are no doubt shared by many of the journalists who produce the news, they nonetheless contribute to sustaining a highly selective and misleading representation of child sexual abuse in the media. In particular, the emphasis on the most serious examples of child sexual victimization by strangers reinforces fears of the unknown predatory 'other', and at the same time inhibits full and informed discussion about the nature and extent of sexual violence in society and the measures that might best be taken to protect those most at risk.

QUESTIONS

Why is it that some crime victims and forms of criminal victimization feature so prominently in the media, while others are scarcely mentioned or discussed?

What additional forms of criminal victimization, not discussed in this chapter, are reported in the media?

What characterizes those media representations?

Summary

This chapter has identified and explored some of the key influences that shape the representation of crime victims and criminal victimization in the news media. It has explored the relationship between social divisions, inequality and 'ideal' or 'legitimate' victim status, examined how changes in the media environment and the news production process have impacted on the representation of crime victims, and considered reporting of a range of different victim types who are variously over-represented, under-represented or misrepresented in news media discourses. These closing paragraphs offer a few points by way of summary, raise some questions which seem pertinent at the present time, and suggest a number of potentially fruitful areas for further research and investigation.

In the past 30 years or so, shifts in 'official' and 'academic' thinking, accompanied by wider political and cultural change, have contributed to generating a climate in which 'system discourses' are often pitched in vain against 'victim discourses' (Garland, 2000). At a time of widespread intolerance, anxiety and fear of the unknown 'other' (Young, 2007), those who are seen to represent the interests of offenders occupy an uncomfortable and, at times, deeply unpopular place within public hearts and minds (Greer, 2003). In stark contrast, those who speak for victims are seen to speak for us all. Yet the victim voices that find resonance in the media represent only a small fraction of those who experience criminal victimization. What this chapter demonstrates, along with the other contributions in this volume, is that those who feel the pains of victimization most acutely are often those whose voices are stifled rather than amplified in news media discourses.

It is not simply the case that race, gender or any other social division retains an overarching and static defining influence over media interest in crime victims and their subsequent representation in the news. Reporting criminal victimization is more fluid and dynamic than this, and can change from case to case and over time. Implicitly promoting the view that news media, like any other institution, are capable of reflexive learning, many journalists would contend that since Stephen Lawrence, the news media have learned how to 'do race', if perhaps not yet 'class'. That there is evidence both for and against this claim – some of which has been discussed in this chapter – serves to further highlight the variability of news representations and the dangers of settling for blanket generalizations about the prejudices of the 'the press' or 'the media'. Nevertheless, it remains the case that much news coverage of criminal victimization both reflects and reinforces social divisions and inequalities, and in so doing feeds into the wider structures of power, dominance and subjugation from which they derive. It is perhaps less in the sensational reporting of high profile murder cases, and more in the representation of victims of everyday crime, prejudice and abuse that these inequalities, though less dramatically conveyed, continue to have the greatest impact. This impact can be seen in the selective portrayal of those victims who come within the horizon of newsworthiness. Equally, however, it can be evidenced through consideration of those who do not.

The selective representation of crime victims in the news media is similarly reflected in much criminological research. With the important exception of feminist studies on sexual and domestic violence, and the work of some critical criminologists discussed above, what little research there is exploring crime victims in the media has tended to focus on those types of crime and victim that maintain a strong media presence. It is also crucial to consider those victims and processes of criminal victimization which remain absent from the news. More attention, for example, could be directed at researching the media representation (or lack of representation) of victims of the powerful: corporate crimes, deaths in custody, war crimes and genocide. A number of key and as yet largely unanswered questions stem from these observations:

- How do different groups, interests and individuals go about soliciting and sustaining media interest in particular crime victims, or types of victim?
- What precisely are the conditions that need to be in place before victimized members of marginalized and powerless groups are deemed worthy of media attention and public sympathy?
- What are the hierarchies of credibility and power in a multi-mediated society where images increasingly interweave with the worldwide practice of crime, violence, war and justice?
- What precisely is the everyday impact of the selective representation of crime victims and criminal victimization on popular crime consciousness?

The answers to these questions are complex and difficult to research, and anything short of an **ethnographic approach** is unlikely to make much headway (Chermak, 1995; Greer et al., 2007). But this does nothing to diminish their importance. In the information age (Webster, 2005), news images and media debates are a central influence in shaping popular notions of who can rightly claim legitimate victim status, informing victim policy formation and, ultimately, helping to shape the structures of training, accountability and professional practice directed at protecting the public and responding to victims of crime. Deconstructing the power dynamics, information flows, social relations and political struggles between all those involved in the news production process is a pressing sociological project. Just as so many crime victims remain marginalized or ignored in official discourses, understanding the role of media in constructing and representing crime victims and criminal victimization cannot remain on the periphery of academic enquiry. Rather, it should be a central concern for all those wishing seriously to engage with the political economy of crime, control and social order in contemporary society.

▶▶ **Ethnographic approach**   a qualitative research methodology concerned with studying subjects within their own natural environment, frequently involving detailed observation and in-depth interviews, geared towards developing an appreciation and understanding of the social world as seen through the eyes of the researched population (see also qualitative methodologies in Chapter 8 in this volume).

ANNOTATED BIBLIOGRAPHY

Chermak, S. (1995) *Victims in the News: Crime and the American News Media.* **Boulder, CO: Westview Press.** One of the only book-length studies to be conducted specifically on media representations of crime victims, this study is an in-depth qualitative analysis of the American news media with a strong ethnographic edge.

Cottle, S. (2004) *The Racist Murder of Stephen Lawrence: Media Performance and Public Transformation.* **Westport, CT: Praeger.** A sophisticated book-length analysis of the Stephen Lawrence case and its construction and 'performance' in the media, exploring the rhetoric of journalism, the dynamics and contingencies within both politics and storytelling, and the strategic interventions of various groups, interests and identities.

Crime, Media Culture: An International Journal **(edited by Yvonne Jewkes, Chris Greer and Jeff Ferrell).** This journal offers a forum for exchange between scholars who are working at the intersections of criminological and cultural inquiry. It promotes a broad cross-disciplinary understanding of the relationship between crime, criminal justice, media and culture, and regularly features articles on media methodology, news production, and criminal victimization.

Greer, C. (2003) *Sex Crime and the Media: Sex Offending and the Press in a Divided Society*. **Cullumpton: Willan.** This book presents an in-depth quantitative and qualitative analysis of the press reporting of sex crime, including interviews with all the key players in the news production process and, like Chermak's study, has a strong ethnographic edge.

Schlesinger, P. and Tumber, H. (1994) *Reporting Crime: The Media Politics of Criminal Justice*. **Oxford: Clarendon Press.** Still one of the best qualitative studies of crime reporting in the press and on television, this book includes general discussions of newsworthiness, crime reporting and the wider crime and justice environment, and in-depth case studies exploring how particular acts of criminal victimization are portrayed in the British news media.

Note

1 The author is currently exploring, with Eugene McLaughlin, the troubled relationship between Sir Ian Blair and the media, and the reporting of murder in the British press. A number of issues raised in this chapter emerged during discussions related to this ongoing research.

References

Alexander, C. (1996) *The Art of Being Black*. Oxford: Oxford University Press.
Alexander, C. (2000) *The Asian Gang: Ethnicity, Identity, Masculinity*. Oxford: Berg.
Benedict, H. (1992) *Virgin or Vamp*. Oxford: Oxford University Press.
Bichard, Sir M. (2004) *The Bichard Inquiry: Report*, HC653. London: The Stationery Office.
Bowling, B. and Phillips, C. (2002) *Race, Crime and Justice*. London: Home Office.
Bright, Sir M. (2004) 'The vanishing', *Observer Magazine*, 15 December.
Carrabine, E., Iganski, P., Lee, M., Plummer, K. and South, N. (2004) *Criminology: A Sociological Introduction*. London: Routledge.
Cathcart, B. (2000) *The Case of Stephen Lawrence*. London: Penguin.
Cavender, G. and Mulcahy, A. (1998) 'Trial by fire: media constructions of corporate deviance', *Justice Quarterly*, 15(4): 697–719.
Chesney-Lind, M. and Eliason, M. (2006) 'From invisible to incorrigible: the demonisation of marginalised women and girls', *Crime, Media, Culture: An International Journal*, 2(1): 29-47.
Chermak, S. (1995) *Victims in the News: Crime and the American News Media*. Boulder, CO: Westview Press.

Chibnall, S. (1977) *Law and Order News: An Analysis of Crime Reporting in the British Press*. London: Tavistock.

Christie, N. (1986) 'The ideal victim', in E. Fattah (ed.), *From Crime Policy to Victim Policy*. Basingstoke: Macmillan.

Corner, J. (2004) 'Afterword: framing the new', in S. Holmes and D. Jermyn (eds), *Understanding Reality Television*. London: Routledge.

Cottle, S. (2004) *The Racist Murder of Stephen Lawrence: Media Performance and Public Transformation*. Westport, CT: Praeger.

Cottle, S. (2005) 'Mediatized public crisis and civil society renewal: The racist murder of Stephen Lawrence', *Crime, Media, Culture: An International Journal*, 1(1): 49–71.

Croall, H. (2001a) *Understanding White Collar Crime*. Buckingham: Open University Press.

Croall, H. (2001b) 'The victims of white collar crime', in L. Sven-Ake (ed.) *White-Collar Crime Research: Old Views and Future Potentials: Lectures and Papers from a Scandinavian Seminar*. National Council for Crime Prevention, Sweden Bra-Report, 2001: 1.

D'Cruze, S., Walklate, S. and Pegg, S. (2006) *Murder*. Cullumpton: Willan.

Doyle, A. (2003) *Arresting Images: Crime and Policing in front of the Television Camera*. Toronto: University of Toronto Press.

Drakeford, M. (2006) 'How to explain a prison suicide', *Crime, Media, Culture: An International Journal*, 2(2): 217–23.

Ericson, R., Baranek, P. and Chan, J. (1989) *Negotiating Control: A Study of News Sources*. Milton Keynes: Open University Press.

Evans, J. (2003) 'Vigilance and vigilantes: thinking psychoanalytically about anti-paedophile action', *Theoretical Criminology*, 7(2): 163–89.

Ferrell, J. (2005) 'Crime and culture', in C. Hale, K. Hayward, A. Wahidin and E. Wincup (eds), *Criminology*. Oxford: Oxford University Press.

Foster J., Newburn, T. and Souhami, A. (2005) *Assessing the Impact of the Stephen Lawrence Inquiry*, Home Office Research Study 294. London: Home Office.

Fracassini, C. (2002) 'Missing', *Scotland on Sunday*, 18 August.

Galtung, J. and Ruge, M. (1965) 'Structuring and selecting news', in S. Cohen and J. Young (eds) (1981) *The Manufacture of News: Deviance, Social Problems and the Mass Media*, revised edition. London: Constable.

Garland, D. (2000) 'The culture of high crime societies: some preconditions of recent "law and order" politics', *British Journal of Criminology*, 40: 347–75.

Gerrard, N. (2004) *Soham: A Story of Our Times*. London: Short Books.

Gilroy, P. (1987) *There Ain't No Black in the Union Jack*. London: Hutchinson.

Goldson, B. (1997) 'Children in trouble: state responses to juvenile crime', in P. Scraton (ed.), *'Childhood' in 'Crisis'?* London: UCL Press.

Greer, C. (2003) *Sex Crime and the Media: Sex Offending and the Press in a Divided Society*. Cullumpton: Willan.

Greer, C. (2004) 'Crime, media and community: grief and virtual engagement in late modernity', in J. Ferrell, K. Hayward, W. Morrison and M. Presdee (eds), *Cultural Criminology Unleashed*. London: Cavendish.

Greer, C. (2005) 'Crime and media: understanding the connections', in C. Hale, K. Hayward, A. Wahidin and E. Wincup (eds), *Criminology*. Oxford: Oxford University Press.

Greer, C., Ferrell, J. and Jewkes, Y. (2007) 'It's the image that matters: style, substance and critical scholarship', *Crime, Media, Culture: An International Journal*, 3(1): 5–10.

Greer, C. and Jewkes, Y. (2005) 'Extremes of otherness: media images of social exclusion', *Social Justice*, 32(1): 20–31.

Grubin, D. (1998) *Sex Offending Against Children: Understanding the Risk*, Police Research Series, Paper 99, Policing and Reducing Crime Unit. London: Home Office.

Hall, S. (1973) 'The determination of news photographs', in S. Cohen and J. Young (eds) (1981) *The Manufacture of News: Deviance, Social Problems and the Mass Media*, revised edition. London: Constable.

Hall, S., Critcher, C., Jefferson, T., Clarke, J. and Roberts, B. (1978) *Policing the Crisis: Mugging, the State and Law and Order*. London: Macmillan.

Haydon, D. and Scraton, P. (2000) 'Condemn a little more, understand a little less': the political context and rights implications of the domestic and European Rulings in the Venables-Thompson case', *Journal of Law and Society*, 27(3): 416–48.

Hayward, K. and Yar, M. (2006) 'The "chav" phenomenon: consumption, media and the construction of a new underclass', in *Crime, Media, Culture: An International Journal*, 2(1): 9–28.

Heaven, O. and Hudson, B. (2005) 'Race, "ethnicity" and crime', in C. Hale, K. Hayward, A. Wahidin and E. Wincup (eds), *Criminology*. Oxford: Oxford University Press.

Hillyard, P., Pantazis, C., Tombs, S. and Gordon, D. (eds) (2004) *Beyond Criminology: Taking Harm Seriously*. London: Pluto Press.

ICAR (2007) *Reporting Asylum: The UK Press and the Effectiveness of PCC Guidelines*. London: City University.

Innes, M. (2003) 'Signal crimes: detective work, mass media and constructing collective memory', in P. Mason (ed.), *Criminal Visions: Representations of Crime and Justice*. Cullompton: Willan.

Innes, M. (2004) 'Signal crimes and signal disorders: notes on deviance as communicative action', *British Journal of Sociology*, 55(3): 335–55.

James, A. and Jenks, C. (1996) 'Public perceptions of childhood criminality', *British Journal of Sociology*, 47: 315–33.

Jewkes, Y. (2004) *Media and Crime*, London: Sage.

Katz, J. (1987) 'What makes crime "News"?', *Media, Culture and Society*, 9: 47–75.

Keith, B. (2006) *Report of the Zahid Mubarek Inquiry*, HC 1082–1. London: The Stationery Office.

Kitzinger, J. (1999) 'A sociology of media power: key issues in audience reception research', in G. Philo (ed.), *Message Received*. London: Longman.

Lees, S. (1995) 'The media reporting of rape: the 1993 British "date rape" controversy', in D. Kidd-Hewitt and R. Osborne (eds), *Crime and the Media: The Post-Modern Spectacle*. London: Pluto Press.

Leishman, F. and Mason, P. (2003) *Policing and the Media: Facts, Fictions and Factions*. Cullompton: Willan.

Levi, M. (1999) 'The impact of fraud', *Crininal Justice Matters*, 36: 5–8.

Macpherson, Sir W. (1999) *The Stephen Lawrence Inquiry: Report of an Inquiry by Sir William Macpherson of Cluny*, CM4262–1. London: HMSO.

Maguire, M. (2002) 'Crime statistics: the "data explosion" and its implications', in M. Maguire, R. Morgan and R. Reiner (eds), *The Oxford Handbook of Criminology*, 2nd edition. Oxford: Oxford University Press.

Marsh, H.L. (1991) 'A comparative analysis of crime coverage in newspapers in the United States and other countries from 1960–1989: a review of the literature', *Journal of Criminal Justice*, 19(1): 67–80.

Martellozzo, E. (2007) Policing Child Sexual Abuse Online: Understanding Grooming in the 21st Century, Paper presented at the European Society of Criminology Conference, Bologna, Italy.

McLaughlin, E. and Murji, K. (1999) 'After the Stephen Lawrence Report', *Critical Social Policy*, 19(3): 371–85.

McLaughlin, E. and Murji, K. (2001) 'Ways of seeing: the news media and racist violence', in M. May, E. Brunsden and R. Page (eds), *Understanding Social Problems: Issues in Social Policy*. Oxford: Blackwell.

Measham, F. and Brain, K. (2005) '"Binge" drinking: British alcohol policy and the new culture of intoxication', *Crime, Media, Culture: An International Journal*, 1(3): 262–83.

Meyers, M. (1997) *News Coverage of Violence Against Women: Engendering Blame*. London: Sage.

Morrison, B. (1997) *As If*. London: Granta Books.

Muncie, J. (2004) *Youth and Crime*. London: Sage.

Naylor, B. (2001) 'Reporting violence in the British print media: gendered stories', *Howard Journal*, 40(2): 180–94.

Peelo, M. (2006) 'Framing homicide narratives in newspapers: mediated witness and the construction of virtual victimhood', *Crime, Media, Culture: An International Journal*, 2(2): 159–75.

Porteous, M. and Colston, N. (1980) 'How adolescents are reported in the British press', *Journal of Adolescence*, 3: 197–207.

Presdee, M. (2000) *Cultural Criminology and the Carnival of Crime*. London: Routledge.

Reiner, R. (2002) 'Media made criminality: the representation of crime in the mass media', in M. Maguire, R. Morgan and R. Reiner (eds), *The Oxford Handbook of Criminology*, 3rd edition. Oxford: Oxford University Press.

Reiner, R., Livingstone, S. and Allen, J. (2000a) 'Casino culture: media and crime in a winner-loser society', in K. Stenson and D. Cowell (eds), *Crime, Risk and Justice*. Cullompton: Willan.

Reiner, R., Livingstone, S. and Allen, J. (2000b) 'No more happy endings? The media and popular concern about crime since the Second World War', in T. Hope and R. Sparks (eds), *Crime, Risk and Insecurity*. London: Routledge.

Reiner, R., Livingstone, S. and Allen, J. (2003) 'From law and order to lynch mobs: crime new since the Second World War', in P. Manson (ed.), *Criminal Visions: Media Representations of Criminal and Justice*. Cullompton: Willan.

Rojek, C. (2001) *Celebrity (FOCI)*. London: Reaktion Books.

Schlesinger, P. and Tumber, H. (1994) *Reporting Crime: The Media Politics of Criminal Justice*. Oxford: Clarendon Press.

Scraton, P. (1997) 'Whose "childhood"? What "crisis?", in P. Scraton (ed.), *'Childhood' in 'Crisis'?*, London: UCL Press.

Silverman, J. and Wilson, D. (2002) *Innocence Betrayed: Paedophilia, the Media and Society*. Cambridge: Polity Press.

Sim, J. (2004) 'The victimised state and the mystification of social harm', in P. Hillyard, C. Pantazis, S. Tombs and D. Gordon (eds), *Beyond Criminology: Taking Harm Seriously*, London: Pluto Press.

Solomos, J. (1988) *Black Youth, Racism and the State*. Cambridge: Cambridge University Press.

Solomos J. (1999) 'Social research and the Stephen Lawrence Inquiry', *Sociological Review Online*, 4(1). Available at: www.socresonline.org.uk/soresonline/4/lawrence/solomos.html; accessed 23 September 2006.

Sontag, S. (2004). 'What have we done?', *The Guardian* (UK), 24 May, section G2, pp. 2–5.

Soothill, K. and Walby, S. (1991) *Sex Crime in the News*. London: Routledge.

Sparks, R. (1992) *Television and the Drama of Crime: Moral Tales and the Place of Crime in Public Life*. Buckingham: Open University Press.

Stanko, E. and Lee, R. (2003) 'Introduction: methodology reflections', in R. Lee and E. Stanko (eds), *Researching violence: Essays on Methodology and Measurement*. London: Routledge.

Stephenson-Burton, A.E. (1995) 'Through the looking glass: public images of white collar crime', in D. Kidd-Hewitt and R. Osborne (eds), *Crime and the Media: The Post-Modern Spectacle*. London: Pluto Press.

Strange, C. (2006) 'Hybrid history and the retrial of the painful past', *Crime, Media, Culture: An International Journal*, 2(2): 197–215.

Tombs, S. (2005) 'Corporate crime', in C. Hale, K. Hayward, A. Wahidin and E. Wincup (eds), *Criminology*. Oxford: Oxford University Press.

Tombs, S. and Whyte, D. (2001) 'Reporting corporate crime out of existence', *Criminal Justice Matters*, 43: 22–4.

Tombs, S. and Whyte, D (eds) (2003) *Unmasking the Crimes of the Powerful: Scrutinising States and Corporations*. New York: Peter Lang.

Tombs, S. and Whyte, D. (2007) *Safety Crimes*. Cullompton: Willan.

Valier, C. (2004) *Crime and Punishment in Contemporary Culture*. London: Routledge.

Webster, F. (2005) 'Making sense of the Information Age: Sociology and Cultural Studies', *Information, Communications and Society*, 8(4): 439–58.

Young, J. (2007) *The Vertigo of Late Modernity*, London: Sage.

Social Class, Social Exclusion, Victims and Crime

Hazel Croall

Chapter aims

- To contextualize the relationship between socio-economic status and criminal victimization.
- To explore victimization from 'conventional' violent and property crime.
- To examine the extent to which crime, victimization, criminal justice and crime reduction policies are related to broader processes of social inclusion and exclusion.
- To illustrate that the impact of crime falls most heavily on the poorest and most excluded sections of society.
- To demonstrate that crime and victimization play a major role in exclusionary processes and policies.

Introduction

While criminologists have long associated crime with lower-class *offenders*, the relationship between criminal *victimization* and socio-economic status has proved more complex although crime has been described by one noted criminologist as a 'regressive tax on the poor' (Downes, 1983). This chapter will focus on victimization from 'conventional' violent and property crime and Chapter 4 will address victimization in relation to the so-called 'crimes of the powerful'.

One of the major issues facing any exploration of the relationship between social inequality and victimization is separating the effects of indicators of social class from those of lifestyle, gender or age, and identifying the different ways in which the risk of crime can be related to social status. In the first place, the amount and impact of victimization experienced by different socio-economic groups have to be established along with differences in levels of fear and worry about crime and experiences of the criminal justice process. These questions have been addressed by surveys such as the British Crime Survey (BCS) which, while providing much relevant information, also have major limitations. In relation to socio-economic status, they may, by focusing on individual experiences, neglect structural dimensions. They also omit the experiences of some of the most socially excluded and cannot explore the more complex processes which link social exclusion to crime and victimization. It will be seen later, for example, that in seeking to avoid the risks of crime, citizens also avoid people and areas that they perceive to be 'dangerous'.

Research on the differential distribution of risks of victimization must therefore be treated with caution. While analyses of BCS data, as will be seen below, do reveal heavy concentrations of crime victimization, these are largely quantitative studies and there are few qualitative studies which might better capture the nature of people's experiences of and responses to crime and victimization (Foster, 2002). Many victimization surveys have been dominated by a crime reduction agenda, and questions asked about 'high crime' areas more often relate to 'technical' factors such as the presence or absence of security devices, CCTV, or street lighting than to the economic and social deprivation which characterizes these areas.

This chapter aims to explore many of these issues, paying particular attention to the relationship between social class, as measured by indices such as income, employment and area of residence, and the following:

- amounts of victimization and repeat victimization;
- the impact of crime;
- the 'fear of crime';
- experiences of the criminal justice process and victim support services.

The chapter will also explore the extent to which crime, victimization and criminal justice and crime reduction policies are related to broader processes of social inclusion and exclusion by looking at:

- the situation of some of the most excluded groups in society;
- the exclusionary impact of individual crime prevention strategies;
- the exclusionary potential of recent developments in criminal justice policy.

Conceptualizing social class, crime and victimization

While the relationship between social class and offending has dominated many criminological perspectives, its relationship to victimization has been less rigorously questioned, with some perspectives such as labelling or critical criminology seeing lower-class offenders as 'victims' of over-policing and criminalization. Early victimological approaches tended to focus on individual victims rather than on socio-economic or structural factors although the greater impact of crime on the poor has long been recognized. More contemporary analyses, which make fewer distinctions between 'criminals' and 'victims', have also had to take account of the massive social and economic changes of the latter part of the twentieth century which have been linked to the development of an '**exclusive society**' (Young, 1999, 2002).

▶▶ **Exclusive society**   *refers to a social order which manifests various features of social exclusion as opposed to social embeddedness.*

While positivist victimology, with its focus on individual risk factors and its reliance on quantitative research, has severe limitations, it has, through victim surveys, produced vast amounts of data which do indicate some of the many ways in which crime affects different socio-economic groups and is concentrated in particular areas. Its analyses have, however, tended to focus on the type and design of housing or the lifestyles of inhabitants, rather than the socio-economic deprivation which also typifies these areas. Attributing victimization, for example, to housing design, an absence of security precautions or travelling through what administrative victimologies would describe as 'risky areas' fails to take account of socio-economic factors such as the inability of residents to afford security devices or avoid those 'risky' areas.

Both radical and critical victimologies criticized this lack of a structural analysis. The radical victimology associated with the left realist approach in criminology (Lea and Young, 1993) challenged the impression given by 'conservative' victimology that there was a low average risk for burglary which to them concealed higher risks of victimization in poorer areas. They also called for studies which were more appreciative of the '**lived reality**' of crime, particularly among the poor. Yet they were in turn criticized for a focus on street rather than suite crime, for a reliance on the individualized, quantitative victim survey, and for focusing on class at the expense of gender, race or age. Nonetheless, they did raise important questions about the wider socio-economic framework of victimization (Davies et al., 2003; Walklate 2003).

▶▶ **Lived reality**   *refers to properly and accurately conceptualizing criminal victimization as people experience it.*

Critical victimology also asks many relevant questions in relation to class (Walklate, 2003; Mawby and Walklate, 1994). It asks us, for example, to look 'behind our backs' and to reflect on the victimization which we 'do not see' and argues that the processes of victimization are socially, economically and culturally situated. This is relevant as the role of social class is often overlooked and the victimization of the most socially excluded is often not 'counted'. Walklate also identifies a need to transgress the dualism between victims and offenders by recognizing that they are more often drawn from the same social groups. A more nuanced approach would therefore look at experiences of both offending and victimization which can be seen as part of a process rather than as single events involving individual offenders and victims.

The tendency to neglect structural factors on the part of 'conservative' criminologies and victimologies reflects the ideology underlying much criminal justice policy and theories of crime. To the conservative governments of the 1980s and early 1990s, linking crime to social and economic inequality was tantamount to 'excusing' crime which was seen as a matter of individual and familial responsibility. The poor were 'blamed' – for their poverty, their offending and in effect for their victimization. In the popular notion of the criminal **'underclass'**, writers such as Charles Murray (1996) identified a 'culture of dependency' on welfare benefits in which people chose not to work, and single parent families without fathers lacked clear role models, leading to greater participation in crime.

▶▶ **Underclass**   *this refers to a class consisting of the most disadvantaged and poor who are seen as a class below the rest of society.*

This was heavily criticized and other theorists pointed to the impact of the massive social changes of the latter part of the twentieth century in which many communities, hitherto economically reliant on manufacturing, were blighted by high rates of unemployment, casual employment and environmental decline (Bagguley and Mann, 1992; Taylor, 1997; Young, 1999). This was accompanied by the growth of a global economy and an individualistic culture in which consumption featured strongly. This arguably produced a society of 'winners' and 'losers', of conspicuous affluence accompanied by relative deprivation, as income differentials continued to widen. The 'losers' became more economically and spatially segregated from the 'winners' with the most excluded suffering deprivation across areas of income, employment, housing and health. Whereas the notion of the underclass had tended to 'blame the poor' by stressing the role of human agency, the concept of social exclusion can involve a greater recognition of structural factors, although there are 'weak' and 'strong' versions with the former stressing the role of individuals and families (Young, 2002). To Young, crime, deviance and state responses to them are a crucial feature of the 'exclusive society' whose features are summarized in Box 3.1.

Box 3.1   The exclusive society

Young (1999) argues that the change from 'modernity' to late modernity has involved a shift from an *inclusive* to an *exclusive society*.

An inclusive society is associated with:

- material and ontological security, for example, security of employment and feelings of safety;
- incorporating members;
- attempts to assimilate deviance and disorder as 'deviants' are dealt with in communities and families.

An exclusive society is associated with:

- material and ontological precariousness, for example, loss of secure employment and feelings of unsafety;
- response to deviance involves more exclusion, for example, higher rates of imprisonment.

Relative deprivation accompanied by a culture of individualism leads to increasing crime which in turn leads to exclusion.

Exclusion is associated with:

- fear of crime which leads to public avoidance of 'risky' situations;
- rising prison rates involving penal exclusion;
- exclusion from public spaces of groups suspected of 'crime'.

The exculsion of these groups from public spaces leads to:

- 'barriers' between areas in cities;
- a cordon sanitaire separating 'winners' from 'losers';
- the 'outgroup' become scapegoated or defined as 'underclass';
- processes of demonization.

Criminology and 'administrative' actuarial criminal justice policies based on 'risk management' are part of this exclusion.

An important element of Young's analysis is the relationship between crime, social exclusion and criminal justice policy, the latter of which underwent a series of transformations towards the end of the twentieth century, as crime continued to rise and it became evident that criminal justice and penal policies had a limited role in reducing the volume of crime. While some dispute the universality of these shifts, most commentators agree that they have involved a search for more cost-effective means of reducing crime and have included the development of **responsibilization strategies, actuarial justice, crime prevention, reduction and 'community safety' policies, bifurcatory strategies** and **'popular punitivism'.**

▶▶ **Responsibilisation strategies**   *whereby individuals and communities are expected to take more responsibility for protecting themselves from crime by, for example, installing security devices, taking out insurance policies, or involving themselves in strategies such as Neighbourhood Watch (Garland, 1996).*

▶▶ **Actuarial justice**   *this involves concerns with costs and efficiency, risk management and crime reduction targets (Feeley and Simon, 1994).*

▶▶ **Crime prevention, reduction and 'community safety' policies**   *these may involve 'situational crime prevention' which involves installing security and the use of CCTV, or may be more community-oriented through, for example, the work of Crime and Disorder Partnerships responsible for conducting 'audits' and meeting targets for the reduction of specific forms of crime.*

▶▶ **Bifurcatory strategies**   *strategies under which harsh punishment is reserved for the most 'serious' offenders with less serious offenders being dealt with more cheaply in the 'community'.*

▶▶ **Popular punitivism**   *where all political parties seek to be 'tough on crime' (Bottoms, 1994).*

These have been accompanied by the so-called 'rediscovery of the victim' and the introduction of more 'victim-centred' policies, which can be related to these overall shifts in policy. Victim surveys have been motivated by the perceived need to accurately assess the 'risks' of crime and to assist crime prevention policies. The criminal justice process needs victims to report crimes and provide evidence and appeasing them may be part of **managerialist policies** (Davies, 2003). Their involvement in restorative justice schemes could be seen as an expedient and low cost way of dealing with offenders (Goodey, 2004) and, as Ashworth (2000) has argued, victims' interests can be 'hi-jacked' in the interests of severity by being invoked to justify **punitive policies**.

▶▶ **Managerialist policies**   *in the context of criminal justice, generally refers to a management creed which includes bureaucratization, performance measurement and administrative control (Newburn, 2003).*

▶▶ **Punitive policies**   *in the context of penal policy, refers to being tough on crime.*

Criminal justice and penal policies have a further exclusionary potential. Imprisonment exacerbates the social exclusion of offenders and policies such as curfews, electronic tagging and anti-social behaviour orders all aim to exclude those perceived to pose a threat to 'order' in the community. While the notion of 'community' involvement in crime reduction is often viewed as 'inclusionary', important questions can be asked about whose notion of community takes precedence in crime and disorder partnerships (Gilling, 2001).

QUESTIONS

Can you find any empirical support for an 'underclass' or is this notion ideological?

Can the poor be blamed for their victimization?

Researching crime, class and victimization

The BCS has now amassed a considerable amount of data associating patterns of victimization with a range of factors related to socio-economic status such as income, type of housing or employment status and one of the most widely used indicators is the ACORN classification which groups postcodes according to demographic, employment and housing characteristics. Most relevant to this chapter are 'rising' and 'striving' areas, the former characterized by young professional couples and singles, and the latter by higher numbers of the elderly, single parents and unemployed residents. They are also multi-ethnic, low-income areas (Aitchison and Hodgkinson, 2003). Such surveys reveal a clear association between the risk of victimization and living in a deprived area. According to the most recent British Crime Survey, 'generally people living in more deprived areas are more likely to be a victim of crime than those living in less deprived areas' (Walker et al., 2006: 116). In Scotland, (not covered by the British Crime Survey), the 2004 Scottish Crime and Victimization Survey (SCVS) also found that:

> the experience of crime is strongly related to the type of area people live in. Households in the areas classified as most deprived using the Scottish Index of Multiple Deprivation experience more crime and anti-social behaviour than the least deprived areas (Hope, 2006).

Nonetheless, these characterizations are generalized and it cannot be assumed that areas are homogenous or that all victims living in a 'striving' area are poor (Pantazis and Gordon, 1998). Indeed, the 'rich' living in 'poor' areas report higher rates of victimization (Hope, 2000).

Because both the 'rich' and 'poor' are at risk of victimization, the effect of socio-economic factors on overall rates is far from clear-cut. Analyses of 1992 BCS data suggested that 'rich' households (measured by income) experienced the highest rates of victimization with the 'poor' experiencing least (Pantazis and Gordon, 1998). Recurrent surveys have found high risks of victimization in both 'rising' *and* 'striving' areas (Aitchison and Hodgkinson, 2003; Dodd et al., 2004). These seeming contradictions indicate the different ways in which socio-economic status is related to crime risk. Box 3.2, taken from the 2003–4 BCS, indicates, for example, that having no home security is strongly related to burglary, but, as will be seen below, the poor are far less likely to have home security. In general, the cars, houses and possessions of the 'rich' make them more attractive targets, but they are better able to afford security precautions. Taking simple incidence rates therefore reveals a mixed pattern.

Box 3.2 Factors associated with the risk of victimization

Burglary is associated with:
- no home security;
- areas with high perceived levels of anti-social behaviour;
- living at an address for less than one year;
- geographical area (but with no distinct pattern);
- single adult households.

Vehicle related theft is associated with:
- young heads of household;
- areas with high perceived levels of anti-social behaviour;
- geographical area;
- multiple vehicle ownership;
- living in flats or terraced houses.

Theft from the person is associated with:
- being female, single, widowed, separated or divorced;
- living in particular geographical areas (again with no distinct pattern);
- areas with high perceived levels of anti-social behaviour.

Criminal damage (vandalism) to the home is associated with:
- living in urban and low income areas;
- geographical area (no distinct pattern);
- age;
- living in a terraced house or maisonette.

Criminal damage (vandalism) to a car is associated with:
- owning one or more vehicle;
- living in a maisonette or converted flat;
- age (households aged between 25 and 44);
- living in urban and low income areas.

Violent crime is associated with:
- being young, particularly aged 16–24;
- being divorced, separated or single;
- being male.

Where there is 'no clear variation' in relation to area, risks were highest in 'striving', low income *and* 'affluent urban areas' (Ringham and Wood, 2004; Upson et al., 2004).

Source: Dodd et al. (2004)

Repeat victimization

A different picture emerges when looking at repeat and multiple victimization, and closer analyses of BCS data have revealed so-called 'hot spots' and concentrations of crime in areas such as 'mixed inner metropolitan' or multi-racial areas with a mixture of poor, private rented housing and owner occupation, non-family areas with a mix of affluent housing and private rented housing in multi-occupation, and the poorest local authority estates, located either in inner city or overspill areas (Evans and Fraser, 2003).

Hope (2001), summarizing analyses of BCS data, points out that:

- Around one-fifth of victims of household property crime live in the 10 per cent of residential areas with highest crime rates and experience more than one-third of household property crime.
- Over half of all property crime, and over one-third of all property crime victims, are likely to live in only one-fifth of communities of England and Wales. Conversely, the 50 per cent of communities with the lowest crime rates suffer merely 15 per cent of household property crime, spread between a quarter of victims.
- Victims who are multiply or repeatedly victimized are more likely to live in high crime rate areas than those less frequently victimized.
- Concentrations of crime risks coincide with concentrations of the 'poor'. Twenty per cent of communities with the highest crime rates have higher numbers of the 'poor' than the 'rich'.

Analyses of multiple victimization suggest correlations with other misfortunes, with one study reporting higher rates among young adults and those who live with children, rent from the local authority, live in poorer urban areas and have had a household fire (Hope et al., 2001). Taken together, these variables indicate an association between multiple victimization and the more economically deprived sectors of society and, the authors argue, it seems plausible that the relationship between victimization and other misfortunes is related to the concentration of social disadvantage in people's lives and in their communities.

For the inhabitants of some areas, therefore, crime of many kinds can be an almost daily occurrence although the 'lived reality' is not well represented in surveys that only look at individual incidents. Victims may not, for example, report all incidents, and reports may exceed the numbers which the survey can record (Genn, 1988). Some may seem like trivial incidents whereas repeated experiences of burglary, theft from the person along with harassment, name calling, intimidation and vandalism can have a cumulative and more serious impact which can itself lead to exclusion as victims may stay in to avoid victimization or in extreme cases leave home.

Fear of crime

Hardly surprisingly, residents in such areas report higher rates of fear and worry about crime, and research linking fear of crime with poverty (Pantazis, 2000) suggests that:

- Older people living in areas of multiple deprivation were seven times more likely to feel unsafe compared with those less deprived.
- Those in 'multiply deprived' households were nearly three times more likely to feel unsafe in their local neighbourhood compared to those in 'comfortable' households.
- People living in poor households are more than twice as likely as rich people to feel unsafe when alone either at home or in the street after dark, regardless of where they live.
- The effects of poverty may exceed gender differences.

Fear of crime must, however, argues Pantazis, be placed in the context of the other insecurities experienced more acutely by the poor – it is not the only reason people do not go out at night and people living in poverty worry more about illness for themselves or their families than they do about crime.

Impact of crime

The poor may worry more about crime because it has a more severe impact on them. Maguire and Kynch (2000) found, for example, that victims earning under £10,000, black or Asian victims and those in 'striving' areas were more likely to report that crimes had affected them very much. Those earning under £5,000 per annum, the uninsured, the 'very poor' with restricted mobility and single parents were considered as 'most vulnerable'. Poorer victims of property crime can less easily replace valuables or install home security and Box 3.3 illustrates how the 'commodification' of security can lead to a vicious circle, making the poor less able to avoid repeat victimization.

Box 3.3   Insurance and security

- Almost one-in-ten uninsured households experienced burglary in 1997 compared to 5 per cent insured households (Budd, 1999).
- The uninsured are generally poorer and live in council or housing association property; the 1998 BCS found that low income households are least likely to be insured and around half living in council or housing association accommodation were uninsured because of cost considerations (Victim Support, 2002).
- Many insurance companies will not insure those who have been previously victimized, they may charge higher premiums in certain areas or they may insist on the installation of expensive security measures (Victim Support, 2002; Goodey, 2004).
- Those who suffer a more severe impact from higher rates of property crime are least able to protect themselves from increasing risks of further victimization and feelings of insecurity.
- Lack of insurance also renders people more vulnerable to non-criminal harms such as fire or flood.

Overall, therefore, despite the limitations of standard victim surveys, there are strong indications that, while the rich and poor alike are victimized, the impact of crime falls far more heavily on the least affluent, living in multiply deprived areas. This victimization may also be compounded by indirect victimization from less visible crimes which are not counted in surveys. They may, for example, suffer from illegal trades in drugs, and from environmental and commercial crimes which will be outlined in Chapter 4. Moreover, surveys do not cover the most socially excluded such as the homeless, those with no permanent address and some immigrants, whose experiences will be explored below.

The impact of victim-oriented policies

A further set of issues relates to the uneven impact on different socio-economic groups of the range of policies introduced to limit the 'secondary victimization' experienced by victims in the criminal justice process (Davies, 2003).

Compensation

Crime victims are compensated in two main ways – by being granted awards under the Criminal Injuries Compensation Scheme (CICS) and by court-ordered compensation orders. A number of commentators have argued that these disadvantage least affluent victims in a variety of ways:

- The CICS in England and Wales distinguishes between 'deserving' and 'non-deserving' victims and does not make awards to anyone considered to have contributed to the offence or with a criminal record (Zedner, 2002). This reflects the tendency to segregate 'victims' from 'offenders' which does not apply well to areas with high concentrations of crime where victims may well come from the same group as offenders, already have criminal records or have families who do. The 'subjective' value judgements which are utilized also make these victims more likely to be perceived as having contributed to violence, which may result from a long history of intimidation (Victim Support, 2002).
- CICS only makes awards of over £1000, which excludes the majority of victims of minor assaults and robberies (Dignan, 2005) and a much smaller award could be of considerable benefit to those on a low income.
- Any award made to a victim in receipt of Social Security benefits is counted as capital for the purposes of assessing entitlement to income-related benefits. This

creates a significant difference between poorer and more affluent victims whose income is not affected by receiving an award (Victim Support, 2002).

- Court-ordered compensation may also disadvantage the least affluent as poorer victims are most often victimized by offenders who are also on low incomes or dependent on state benefits. Thus victims may only receive small amounts over a long period of time (Davies, 2003; Reeves and Mulley, 2000).

QUESTION

In what ways does criminal injuries compensation in England and Wales discriminate against the rich and the poor?

Access to support services

Victim Support organize schemes for supporting and advising victims and, overall, research carried out by Maguire and Kynch (2000) reported that a wide range of victims are contacted, with few differences between poorer areas and others. Indeed some poorer victims, particularly female victims of violence, were more likely to be contacted, although wealthier victims of burglary were more likely to be contacted than those from poorer areas. **Serial victims** of threats and intimidation and ethnic minority victims were, however, less likely to be contacted and there have also been suggestions that the police, responsible for referring cases, may 'filter' out young men from 'rough' areas in the belief that they are the aggressor.

▶▶ **Serial victims** *this concept is similar to that of repeat victimization where a person or location is a target for the same type of criminal victimization several times over.*

Victims and the criminal justice process

Little research has focused specifically on socio-economic factors and experiences of the criminal justice process, however a number of points suggest that the least affluent may experience greater difficulties:

- Victims have complained about cases and requests for protection not being taken seriously by the police, particularly in situations in which victims are likely to be seen as having contributed to an offence – which reflects positivist victimology's concern with deserving and non-deserving victims. As seen above, this may be the case with many poorer and vulnerable victims.

- Victims have also experienced difficulties giving evidence in court where they are pitched into an arena whose rules and language they may not fully understand and where, for example, cross-examination aims to discredit their evidence and they are prevented from telling 'their' story. While more often researched in relation to victims of sexual violence, it could reasonably be hypothesized that those from the most deprived backgrounds are also likely to be disadvantaged by a lack of understanding and skill in presenting themselves in a manner credible to the court.
- Social class, which is related to cultural and educational differences, also affects the ability to obtain and assimilate information, and to negotiate with those perceived to be in authority. Thus the more affluent are more likely to know about their rights as victims (Zedner, 2002) and seek advice about giving evidence. As Goodey (2004: 138) points out, 'the most marginalized and, arguably, the most vulnerable victims have no access to private services they can ill afford, and are often unaware of public services to which they may be entitled'.

Exploring the dynamics of crime, victimization and social exclusion

Thus far the evidence presented has been based largely on BCS data which, as argued, is limited to surveys of individual victims' experiences and misses out some important groups. It is therefore less able to capture the processes through which both individual and governmental responses to crime and victimization may exacerbate social exclusion. Some of these processes can be identified by looking at the situation of the most socially excluded and by further exploring the exclusionary dimensions of individual and state responses to crime.

Crime and victimization among the most excluded

The most excluded include those who lack a stable home, are denied state benefits and who have no legal status as citizens. The young homeless (Box 3.4) have widely been associated with higher rates of victimization associated with their situation (Pain et al., 2002; Gaetz, 2004). As Gaetz (2004: 445) comments in relation to Canada, street youth are excluded as 'they are not able to avail themselves of the safety practices, strategies and resources that many other Canadians have access to (e.g. a door to hide behind)'. Furthermore, they are

[made] vulnerable by their limited social capital, their exclusion from adequate housing and employment, their compromised physical and mental health, and

their inability to provide protected spaces for themselves. They are therefore at increased risk for criminal assault or robbery (Gaetz, 2004: 446–7).

Box 3.4 Homelessness, crime and victimization

- One major reason for young people running away from home, particularly for young women, is violence or sexual abuse within the home. Exclusion from school, which may result from persistent bullying, is also an important factor.
- The young homeless report very high rates of multiple and repeat victimization. On the streets, in hostels or in temporary accommodation, young people were at greater risk from robbery, assault and sexual violence. Young homeless men were more likely to be physically assaulted and young women to be sexually assaulted.
- This victimization is less likely to be reported due to mistrust of the police and young homeless people report harassment and violence from the police as they are more commonly labelled as offenders. They also fear being seen as undeserving victims because of their situation.
- In a wider sense of victimization, the homeless, and particularly the young homeless, can be seen as victims of other forms of social policy such as housing, education and welfare policies (Carlen, 1996) which contribute to the creation of homelessness.

Source: Pain et al. (2002).

Immigrants without appropriate papers are another group who are particularly excluded, as illustrated in Box 3.5, and also experience considerable amounts of victimization which contributes to a spiral of crime, victimization and exclusion:

- Victimization is often a direct cause of exclusion. Young people may leave home to escape violence, 'chronic' victims may make themselves 'intentionally homeless' (Victim Support, 2002), and political and state violence may force people to leave their home countries and seek refuge in other countries (Box 3.5).
- This exclusion increases risks of victimization. The homeless, for example, lack shelter to provide minimal security and 'illegal' immigrants are vulnerable to exploitation by gangmasters, employers or landlords.
- These victims are less likely to report crime as they fear the police and other 'authorities'.
- They are less likely to be offered support or to know about support services.
- The most excluded are also victims of 'criminalisation'. Groups such as 'beggars', 'street people', 'bogus asylum seekers' or 'illegal immigrants' are often assumed to pose a 'threat'.

Box 3.5 Immigrants, crime and victimization

- Illegal immigrants must enter Western Europe either by being smuggled or trafficked, the latter often involving victimization. Their status denies them the rights associated with citizenship and also leads to criminalization.
- According to Goodey (2003: 416):

  > Illegal migrants are ... at the mercy of individuals and groups who take advantage of their vulnerable situation ... from the human smugglers who profit from people's desire for economic betterment, through to employers who escape health and security payments for illegal workers.

- Women are typically recruited by traffickers with attractive offers of (legitimate) employment yet can suffer abuse including:

  - rape, assault and bullying by traffickers and pimps;
  - being held in brothels and forced to 'service' clients;
  - having their passports removed.

They are particularly vulnerable as they have little or no knowledge of the 'host' country's language and norms of behaviour.

- If assaulted or the victim of theft, illegal immigrants cannot go to the police for fear of being deported. Support services are not geared to their needs and victims are unlikely to approach them because they fear repeat victimization or intimidation from their attackers. Moreover they may lack information about the existence of agencies, have problems with language and mistrust public agencies.
- Such women are seen by the authorities in European states as 'witnesses' for the prosecution of organized crime, and are treated as criminals rather than victims. As non-EU citizens they are not entitled to benefits for victims.
- Governments should recognize, argues Goodey (2003: 428), that 'the victimization of illegal migrants, as some of the most economically, socially and politically marginalized people in the EU is central to any discussion of 'migration-crime-security''.

Source: Goodey (2003, 2004)

The largely **invisible victimization** of these groups is extremely important in discussions of victimization and exclusion. Not only does it provide a good example of the victimization that we 'do not see' which is excluded from surveys but it also enables us to question the extent to which these groups are excluded or included in supposedly victim- or community-centred policies – indeed, through their exclusion and crimi-nalisation they are more likely to be seen as the 'problem' than as part of the 'solution' (Gaetz, 2004).

▶▶ **Invisible victimization** *refers not only to victimization that we 'do not see' or 'know about' but also to an inability or omission in measuring different types, experiences and locations for victimization. It also signifies deficiencies in theoretical and policy development and political awareness.*

Purchasing security

One of the reasons that this victimization is 'unseen' is that many people avoid contact with these groups and live in 'exclusive' areas which are socially and geographically segregated. Some of the steps taken by top income earners to avoid the risk of victimization (Goodey, 2004: 138) include the following:

- choosing to buy homes in safer neighbourhoods;
- sending their children to safer schools;
- insuring their home, property and health;
- replacing stolen consumer goods regardless of insurance cover;
- employing private security;
- avoiding encounters with undesirable others in crime-ridden neighbourhoods, through use of private transportation;
- employing lawyers to ensure that justice is done on their behalf.

The combined effect of these individual choices contributes to social exclu-sion as, in a process reminiscent of the Chicago School's depiction of concen-tric zones, what Young (1999, 2003) describes as invisible barriers develop between areas. For Hope (2000, 2001), these responses reflect the use of economic and social capital. The housing market enables the more affluent to buy houses in 'exclusive' areas, a major feature of which is the absence of criminal threat and they purchase more private security devices. Thus they create what he describes as private security 'clubs' in which they exclude risk by spatially and culturally distancing themselves from **criminogenic** places and people. The ultimate example of this is the 'gated community' – protected by perimeter security and restricting entry to those who are per-mitted through the barriers. Cultural and social capital is also important in encouraging 'collective neighbourhood norms' of security which might include participation in Neighbourhood Watch, which has been found to work better in more affluent areas. There are therefore different 'pools' of security with the poor being trapped in poor neighbourhoods – as seen above, they are less likely to be able to afford security. Thus concludes Hope (2001: 216), 'in a risk society ... the threat of crime victimization is not just a consequence of social exclusion but also a contributory cause'.

▶▶ **Criminogenic**   *a term used mostly in connection with white-collar and corporate, organizational and occupational crimes. Criminogenic places allude to settings, environments and locations – usually workplaces, businesses or corporations – and criminogenic people refer to those in employment or working. The 'place' lends itself to criminal opportunities and inflicting victimization and the 'person' is offered similar opportunities to become corrupt.*

State responses to crime – inclusionary or exclusionary?

The exclusionary effect of the actions of individual, responsibilized, citizens is mirrored in many State responses to crime which have increasingly focused on cost-effective means of crime reduction and prevention through community partnerships. Government policy has also encouraged the development of restorative justice, which, while seeming to be more inclusionary and to involve victims, may fail to serve the interests of poorer victims.

CCTV – excluding the 'dangerous'?

The growth of surveillance through CCTV cameras has been a major feature of crime prevention strategies. While its effectiveness can be contested, CCTV has been justified as making citizens feel safer and more willing to engage in commercial transactions, thereby playing a role in economic regeneration. It may therefore operate to exclude those perceived to pose a threat. Research indicates that:

- operators of CCTV are guided by stereotypical assumptions of groups who 'do not belong' indicated by, for example, evidence of 'subcultural attire' (Norris and Armstrong, 1999).
- these groups were seen as threatening to disrupt the commercial image of malls – some of which practised formalized exclusion policies (McCahill and Norris, 2003).
- groups can therefore become 'victims of surveillance' and may be further victimized if convictions follow dubious CCTV evidence (McCahill and Norris, 2003).

- systems 'rather than contributing to social justice through the reduction of victim-ization ... may become a tool of injustice through amplification of differential and discriminatory policing' (Norris and Armstrong, 1999: 201).

Community safety: whose community? Whose safety?

Economic regeneration is also part of the agenda of policies falling under the general heading of 'community safety', a term which implies a broad and inclusive approach encompassing a range of harms (Hughes et al., 2002). The term was abandoned in the setting up of Crime and Disorder Partnerships in 1998, which must conduct safety audits and develop local plans. Critics point out that these have been dominated by a managerialist agenda with targets for the reduction of specific crimes being set by central government rather than reflecting consultation with local groups (Hughes, 2002; Tilley, 2002). Partnerships, which do include community groups, have been found to be dominated by the Police (Phillips, 2002) and the most mar-ginalized, the young, and particularly the young homeless are excluded. Although there are requirements to consult 'hard to reach' groups, young people are less likely to be represented as victims (Pain et al., 2001). In addi-tion, the introduction of a range of orders aimed at tackling disorder and anti-social behaviour have largely been seen as punitive and exclusionary – by imposing curfews and restrictions and targeting residents of social housing areas along with those, often the young or street people, who are perceived as a 'threat'. As has been seen, however, these groups are among the most victimized.

While community safety is often seen as 'communitarian' and inclusive, Gilling (2001: 392) points to the moral authoritarian overtones in notions of the 'ideal' community and, asking 'Whose voice is to be heard?', argues that it is the voice of the 'patriarchal, mono cultural dominant class, the moral standards of whom are imposed on the rest'. Its notion of inclusion, he argues, involves excluding those who do not fit or belong. Thus commu-nity safety is not addressing the insecurity of the victims of neo-liberalism (the socially dislocated underclass) but that of the 'respectable classes' whose enhanced freedom and affluence come at the expense of insecurity about the dangerous other (Gilling, 2001: 397). Thus, he continues, the 'communitarianism of community safety threatens to set the included against the excluded, whose behaviour is increasingly problematised as inci-vility, whose opinions are not convincingly canvassed, whose participation is not convincingly sought and whose mere presence is perceived as a threat to enterprise'.

Empowering the victim?

A more inclusionary and victim-centred approach is implied in the growing popularity of restorative justice which aims to involve offenders, victims and communities in mediation and reconciliation. Referral Orders, for example, introduced under the Youth Justice and Criminal Evidence Act of 1999, were presented as a move 'away from an exclusionary punitive justice and towards an inclusionary restorative justice capable of recognizing the social contexts in which crime occurs and should be dealt with' (Muncie, 2000: 14, cited in Crawford and Newburn, 2002: 476). These involve lay participation via Youth Offender Panels (YOPS), and victims may be represented along with a supporter. A 'contract' is agreed with an offender which should always include reparation for the victim or wider community.

In some respects, these orders reflect the wider limitations of restorative justice, particularly its application to the most marginalized. It is, for example, inevitably limited to reported crimes with a known offender (Goodey, 2004), whereas the most excluded groups often do not report crimes and are intimidated by offenders. It is also restricted to young offenders and less serious offences (Goodey, 2004). Many victims do not take up their options to participate, some feeling that they do not wish to face 'their' offender. In other cases, pressures for advancing cases prevent victims being contacted. While the social characteristics of non-participating victims have been a central feature of research, it could be argued that the most 'chronic' victims might fear intimidation rather than seek reconciliation and may feel less confident about participating in such projects. Like other 'community-based' initiatives such as Neighbourhood Watch, it may be less appropriate in areas without a clear sense of community (Crawford and Newburn, 2002; Goodey, 2004).

There are further issues about the representativeness of 'community representatives' reflecting, in respect of lay participation, a tension between a desire for broad involvement and a need to ensure that panel members have requisite skills, in effect, a tension between managerialism and communitarian appeals (Crawford and Newburn, 2002). In a study of pilot schemes of referral orders Crawford and Newburn (2002), found that:

- While, in theory, they seek to empower victims and offenders, in practice, there are serious questions about how representative panels are. While members are meant to be chosen according to personal rather than professional qualifications, they require training and tend to be drawn from more middle-class, professional sections of the community.

- The composition of the panels was 91 per cent white, 69 per cent female, 68 per cent over 40 years old and 50 per cent were employed in professional or managerial occupations. They were therefore predominantly 'female, middle class and middle aged: one panel member commented that they were "very, sort of *Gardener's World*"'.
- There is a 'risk of lack of correspondence between community representatives and communities they seek to represent'.

This may also provide an example of victims' interests being used to aid efficiency – as Goodey (2004: 211) comments, whatever the strengths of lay involvement, the reliance on largely middle-class volunteers could be seen as using non-professional labour who are unable to fully appreciate the lifestyles and circumstances of offenders. Thus, she argues, there is a danger that these kinds of schemes may be seen as second-class justice for marginalized social groups, for offenders, victims and their 'communities'.

QUESTION

To what extent do you agree with Hancock (2006) who argues that working-class communities are becoming increasingly marginalized by New Labour's emphasis on 'community safety' and being 'tough on crime' and its 'causes'?

Questions for further research

Despite the welter of information provided by crime surveys, there is still much to be explored about the relationships between social class, victimization and social exclusion. Particularly lacking is contemporary qualitative research involving the most marginalized groups which looks more closely at the lived realities of crime in so-called 'hot spots' or 'high crime' areas – at, as Foster (2002) argues, the 'people pieces'.

While we know, for example, that some areas characterized by social deprivation suffer from very high concentrations of crime, others do not and there is a tendency to assume a similarity between 'high crime areas' which may not exist. It is often said, for example, that such areas lack a sense of community which limits their ability to engage in steps to prevent crime – yet such research as there is suggests that people may have different ways of adjusting to crime and different senses of community (Foster, 2002).

There are a number of interconnected reasons for such a lack of research. It has already been seen that positivist victimology has been driven by a managerialist, actuarial agenda, which has tended to 'count' individual victimization and relate risks of victimization to factors, such as street lighting and architectural features, which can be manipulated in the interests of crime reduction. Left realist studies, as seen earlier in this chapter, were also criticized for adopting similar methodologies and focusing on individual victimization. The structural inequalities and ideological constructions through which those victims who, according to critical victimologies, we 'cannot see' are less visible and less amenable to crime reduction initiatives. Indeed, as has also been seen above, the most excluded groups are more likely to be regarded as offenders, rather than as victims. This reflects a more general demonization by the media of the excluded as 'deviant' and as 'other' (Greer and Jewkes, 2005).

This is related to the tendency, particularly in administrative criminology, to use what Young (2002) has criticized as binary oppositions –victim/offender, included/excluded. Yet as seen above, offenders and victims are often drawn from the same group and Young (2003) points out that the excluded are not rigidly separated from the included, either spatially or culturally. Indeed, it is their 'inclusion' by way of absorbing cultural goals and moving through the areas of the 'included' which is a source of that relative deprivation which leads to crime. The precariousness of the included also, he argues, gives rise to 'vindictiveness' and fuels a punitive culture. Social exclusion and inclusion are therefore complex processes irreducible to the quantitative methodologies of administrative criminology and a full understanding of the relationships between crime, victimization and social exclusion must recognize this context and attempt to capture the 'lived reality' of excluded areas.

Other issues concern the construction of crime and victimization and their relationship to other harms. Fears and worries about crime cannot be taken in isolation from other harms which affect the most marginalized including social and economic policies, transport, the environment, safety or illness yet few surveys have explored these relationships. Critics of the narrow way in which community safety has been conceptualized point to its potential to incorporate a more holistic or 'pan-hazard' approach to community safety and further criticize the 'criminalization' of social policy whereby many aspects of the social policy agenda have been dominated by the perceived need to reduce crime (Gilling, 2001; Hughes et al., 2002).

Summary

This chapter has outlined the many different ways in which crime and victimization are related to socio economic status, concluding that the impact of crime falls most heavily on the poorest and most excluded sections of society and furthermore that crime and victimization play a major role in exclusionary processes and policies. It has illustrated the greater impact of crime on the least affluent, particularly in terms of their experiences of repeat and multiple victimization, greater levels of fear of crime and the greater difficulties which poorer victims have in taking steps to protect themselves. This chapter has pointed to the many ways in which lower socio-economic status groups may be disadvantaged in relation to support and compensation following victimization. The chapter has also drawn attention to the way in which crime and victimization contribute to social exclusion, both through the experiences of the most socially excluded and by the combined effect of individual strategies to avoid risk. Finally, this chapter has explored the way in which crime prevention and reduction policies can further exacerbate the exclusion of those seen as a threat and, despite their inclusionary aims, fail to take account of the most deprived victims.

ANNOTATED BIBLIOGRAPHY

Hope, T. (2001) 'Crime victimization and inequality in risk society', in R. Matthews and J. Pitts (eds), *Crime, Disorder and Community Safety: A New Agenda?* London: Routledge, pp. 193–218. An extensive discussion of how steps taken to avoid the risk of crime are related to wider process of social exclusion.

Pantazis, C. (2000) 'Fear of crime, vulnerability and poverty: Evidence from the British Crime Survey', *British Journal of Criminology* 40(3): 414–36. This is a very good summary of the research and literature relating fear of crime to poverty.

Young, J. (1999) *The Exclusive Society.* London: Sage; Young, J. (2002) 'Crime and social exclusion', in M. Maguire, R. Morgan and R. Reiner, (eds), *The Oxford Handbook of Criminology*, 3rd edition. Oxford: Oxford University Press; Young, J. (2003) 'Merton with energy, Katz with structure: the sociology of vindictiveness and the criminology of transgression', *Theoretical Criminology* 7(3): 389–414. Jock Young has written extensively on the relationship between crime and the development of an exclusive society.

(Continued)

Walker, A., Kershaw, C. and Nicholas, S. (2006) *Crime in England and Wales 2005/6.* **London: Home Office RDS bulletin 12/06.** The British Crime Survey provides a useful starting point for exploring the impact of socio-economic inequalities and victimization. Subsequent versions can be accessed via the Home Office Website.

References

Aitchison, A. and Hodgkinson, J. (2003) 'Patterns of crime', in J. Simmons and T. Dodd (eds), *Crime in England and Wales 2002/3,* National Statistics. London: Home Office.

Ashworth, A. (2000) 'Victims' rights, defendants' rights and criminal procedure', in A. Crawford and J. Goodey (eds), *Integrating a Victim Perspective within Criminal Justice.* Aldershot: Ashgate Dartmouth.

Bagguley, P. and Mann, K. (1992) 'Idle thieving bastards? Scholarly representations of the 'underclass''', *Work, Employment and Society,* 6(1): 113–26.

Bottoms, A. (1994) 'The philosophy and politics of punishment and sentencing', in C. Clarkson and R. Morgan (eds), *The Politics of Sentencing Reform.* Oxford: Oxford University Press, pp. 17–49.

Budd, T. (1999) *Burglary of Domestic Dwellings: Findings from the British Crime Survey,* Home Office Research Development and Statistics Directorate, Statistical Bulletin 4/99. London: Home Office.

Carlen, P. (1996) *Jigsaw: A Political Criminology of Youth Homelessness.* Buckingham: Open University Press.

Crawford, A. and Newburn, T. (2002) 'Recent developments in restorative justice for young people in England and Wales: community participation and representation', *British Journal of Criminology,* 42(3): 476–95.

Davies, P. (2003) 'Crime victims and public policy', in P. Davies, P. Francis and V. Jupp (eds), *Victimisation: Theory, Research and Policy.* Basingstoke: Palgrave Macmillan.

Davies, P., Francis, P. and Jupp, V. (2003) 'Victimology, victimisation and public policy', in P. Davies, P. Francis and V. Jupp (eds), *Victimization: Theory, Research and Policy.* Basingstoke: Palgrave Macmillan.

Dignan, J. (2005) *Understanding Victims and Restorative Justice.* Buckingham: Open University Press.

Dodd, T., Nicholas, S., Povey, D. and Walker, A. (eds) (2004) *Crime in England and Wales 2003/4,* Statistical Bulletin 10/04 July 2004. London: Home Office.

Downes, D. (1983) *Law and Order: Theft of an Issue.* London: Blackrose Press.

Evans, K. and Fraser, P. (2003) 'Communities and victimization', in P. Davies, P. Francis and V. Jupp (eds), *Victimization: Theory, Research and Policy*. Basingstoke: Palgrave Macmillan.

Feeley, M. and Simon, J. (1994) 'Actuarial justice: the emerging new criminal law', in D. Nelken (ed.), *The Futures of Criminology*. London: Sage, pp. 173–201.

Foster, J. (2002) '"People pieces": the neglected but essential elements of community crime prevention', in G. Hughes and A. Edwards (eds), *Crime Control and Community: The New Politics of Public Safety*. Cullompton: Willan.

Gaetz, S. (2004) 'Safe streets for whom? Homeless youth, social exclusion and criminal victimization', *Canadian Journal of Criminology and Criminal Justice,* 46(4): 423–55.

Garland, D. (1996) 'The limits of the sovereign state: strategies of crime control in contemporary society', *British Journal of Criminology*, 36: 445–71.

Genn, H. (1988) 'Multiple victimization', in M. Maguire and J. Pointing (eds), *Victims of Crime: A New Deal?* Milton Keynes: Open University Press.

Gilling, D. (2001) 'Community safety and social policy', *European Journal on Criminal Policy and Research,* 9: 381–400.

Goodey, J. (2003) 'Migration crime and victimhood: responses to sex trafficking in the EU', *Punishment and Society*, 5(4): 415–31.

Goodey, J. (2004) *Victims and Victimology: Research, Policy and Practice*. London: Pearson, Longman.

Greer, C. and Jewkes, Y. (2005) 'Extremes of otherness: media images of social exclusion', *Social Justice* 32(1): 20–31.

Hancock, L. (2006) 'Community safety and social exclusion', in P. Squires (ed.), *Community Safety: Critical Perspectives on Policy and Practice*. Bristol: Policy Press.

Hope, S. (2006) *Scottish Crime and Victimization Survey 2004: Calibration Exercise*. Edinburgh: Scottish Executive Crime and Criminal Justice Research Programme Research Findings No. 86/2006.

Hope, T. (2000) 'Inequality and the clubbing of private security', in T. Hope and R. Sparks (eds), *Crime, Risk and Insecurity*. London: Routledge, pp. 83–106.

Hope, T. (2001) 'Crime victimization and inequality in risk society', in R. Matthews and J. Pitts (eds), *Crime, Disorder and Community Safety: A New Agenda?* London: Routledge, pp. 193–218.

Hope, T., Bryan, J., Trickett, A. and Osborn, D. (2001) 'The phenomenon of multiple victimization: the relationship between personal and property crime risk', *British Journal of Criminology*, 41(4): 595–617.

Hughes, G., McLaughlin, E. and Muncie, J. (eds) (2002) *Crime Prevention and Community Safety: New Directions*. London: Sage.

Maguire, M. and Kynch, J. (2000) *Public Perceptions and Victims' Experiences of Victim Support: Findings from the 1998 British Crime Survey*, Home Office Occasional Paper. London: Home Office Research, Development and Statistics Directorate.

Mawby, R. and Walklate, S. (1994) *Critical Victimology*. London: Sage.

McCahill, M. and Norris, C. (2003) 'Victims of surveillance', in P. Davies, P. Francis and V. Jupp (eds), *Victimization: Theory, Research and Policy*. Basingstoke: Palgrave Macmillan.

Murray, C. (1996) 'The underclass', in J. Muncie, E. McLaughlin and M. Langan (eds), *Criminological Perspectives*. London: Sage.

Newburn, T. (2003) *Crime and Criminal Justice Policy,* 2nd edition. London: Longman.

Norris, C. and Armstrong, G. (1999) *The Maximum Surveillance Society: The Rise of CCTV*. Oxford: Berg.

Lea, J. and Young, J. (1993) *What Is to Be Done about Law and Order?* 2nd edition. London: Pluto Press.

Pain, R., Francis, P., Fuller, I., Williams, S. and O'Brien, K. (2001). "'Hard-to-Reach" young people and community safety: a model for participatory, research and consultation', unpublished paper presented to the Home Office.

Pain, R., Francis, P., Fuller, I., O'Brien, K. and Williams, S. (2002) *Hard-to-Reach Young People and Community Safety: A Model for Participatory, Research and Consultation*. Police Research Series Paper 152, Home Office Research Development and Statistics Directorate. London: Home Office.

Pantazis, C. (2000) "'Fear of crime', vulnerability and poverty: evidence from the British Crime Survey', *British Journal of Criminology,* 40(3): 414–36.

Pantazis, C. and Gordon, D. (1998) 'Are crime and fear of crime more likely to be experienced by the 'poor'?' in D. Dorling and S. Simpson (eds), *Statistics in Society*. London: Arnold, pp. 198–212.

Phillips, C. (2002) 'From voluntary to statutory status: reflecting on the experience of three partnerships established under the Crime and Disorder Act 1998', in G. Hughes, E. McLaughlin and J. Muncie (eds), *Crime Prevention and Community Safety: New Directions*. London: Sage.

Reeves, H. and Mulley, K. (2000) 'The new status of victims in the UK: opportunities and threats', in A. Crawford and J. Goodey (eds), *Integrating a Victim Perspective within Criminal Justice*. Aldershot: Ashgate Dartmouth.

Ringham, L. and Wood, M. (2004) 'Property crime', in T. Dodd, S. Nicholas, D. Povey and A. Walker (eds), *Crime in England and Wales 2003/4*, Statistical Bulletin 10/04, July 2004. London: Home Office.

Taylor, I. (1997) 'The political economy of crime', in M. Maguire, R. Morgan and R. Reiner (eds), *The Oxford Handbook of Criminology*, 2nd edition. Oxford: Clarendon Press.

Tilley, N. (2002) 'Crime prevention in Britain, 1975–2010: breaking out, breaking in and breaking down', in G. Hughes, E. McLaughlin and J. Muncie (eds), *Crime Prevention and Community Safety: New Directions*. London: Sage.

Upson, A., Povey, D., and Gray, A. (2004) 'Violent crime', in T. Dodd, S. Nicholas, D. Povey and A. Walker (eds), *Crime in England and Wales* 2003/4, Statistical Bulletin 10/04, July 2004. London: Home Office.

Victim Support (2002) *Criminal Neglect: No Justice Beyond Criminal Justice*. London: Victim Support.

Walker, A., Kershaw, C. and Nicholas, S. (2006) *Crime in England and Wales 2005/6.* London: Home Office RDS bulletin 12/06.

Walklate, S. (2003) 'Can there be a feminist victimology?', in P. Davies, P. Francis and V. Jupp, (eds), *Victimization: Theory, Research and Policy*, Basingstoke: Palgrave Macmillan.

Young, J. (1999) *The Exclusive Society.* London: Sage.

Young, J. (2002) 'Crime and social exclusion', in M. Maguire, R. Morgan and R. Reiner (eds), *The Oxford Handbook of Criminology*, 3rd edition. Oxford: Oxford University Press.

Young, J. (2003) 'Merton with energy, Katz with structure: the sociology of vindictiveness and the criminology of transgression', *Theoretical Criminology,* 7(3): 389–414.

Zedner, L. (2002) 'Victims', in M. Maguire, R. Morgan and R. Reiner (eds), *The Oxford Handbook of Criminology*, 3rd edition. Oxford: Oxford University Press.

Victims of White-Collar and Corporate Crime

Hazel Croall

Chapter aims

- To consider how criminal victimization and harm have been conceptualized within criminology, victimology, and in the literature on white-collar and corporate crime.
- To explore research exposing the harms caused by major forms of white-collar and corporate crime.
- To consider issues of criminal justice policy in relation to these forms of victimization.
- To illustrate how victimization can be related to wider structural variables.
- To outline areas for further investigation and policy development.

Introduction

A major form of victimization excluded from the BCS and other crime surveys is that of white-collar and corporate crime. This is often seen to involve a very different set of relationships between offenders and victims, as there is less obvious direct harm or 'blood on the streets' (Clarke, 1990). It appears less personal as immediate victims are often 'employers', the 'government', the 'public health' or the 'environment' and in many cases, such as where safety laws are broken, causing the death or injury of employees, there is no direct intent to harm. There are also different images of the structural dimensions of victimization. To some, all citizens are victims of this kind of crime, irrespective of age, class or gender, whereas to others the crimes of the wealthy and powerful prey on the poor and powerless. Yet at the same time, victims of some financial frauds may fail to attract sympathy as they are assumed to be wealthy and to have willingly parted with their money (Shichor et al., 2000).

Scope and definition

Before exploring these issues, it is important to consider the scope of activities to be investigated. Box 4.1 outlines some of the problems of defining this contested area of crime (Croall, 2001a; Nelken, 2002), indicating that a major issue is which activities to include or exclude. This chapter will adopt an inclusive approach, covering activities which are subject to some form of legal regulation and penalty along with those perpetrated by both high and low status employees and large and small businesses. Whether offenders are at the top or bottom of the status hierarchy, it can be argued that their 'power' lies in the possession of occupationally-based trust or knowledge which victims do not have (Shapiro, 1990; Croall, 2001a) and from a victim's perspective, the harm, rather than the status of the offender, is the key feature.

Box 4.1   White-collar crime – definitional issues

- Sutherland (1949: 9) defined white-collar crime as 'crime committed by a person of respectability and high social status in the course of his occupation'.
- The role of class has been highly contested, as the status of an offender may matter less than the harm done by someone in a trusted occupational position.
- The term 'crime' is also contentious as many of the harmful activities of businesses or occupational groups are not subject to criminal law and punishment but to administrative or regulatory law and 'penalties' or 'sanctions'.
- An alternative definition is 'an abuse of a legitimate occupational role that is regulated by law' (Croall, 2001a: 163).

Forms of 'white-collar crime'

Many argue that the term 'white-collar crime' insufficiently describes the wide range of offences committed by the 'powerful', be they wealthy individuals or corporations. Most accept a distinction between:

- 'classic' white-collar crime, which involves *personal* gain, at the expense of employers, 'the government' or clients (which can also be described as *occupational crime*);
- offences which involve increased profits or the survival of the *organization* – often known as *organizational* or *corporate* crime (Slapper and Tombs, 1999).

Others prefer to use the broader term **economic crime** (used in many European, particularly Scandinavian countries, where the term 'white-collar crime' is rarely used).

▶▶ **Economic crime**   *defined as 'crimes of profit which take place within the framework of commercial activity' (Korsell, 2002: 201).*

A major feature of white-collar crime is its ambiguous criminal status (Nelken, 2002), and it is often not dealt with by criminal law. Should these activities be regarded as 'crime'? To critical criminologists, the role of class and power is crucial in understanding differences in criminalization.

Research knowledge

Compared to what are often described as 'conventional', non-white-collar crimes, there is less systematic research on victimization, the distribution of risk factors, repeat victimization and the impact of offences on victims. A major reason for this often criticized neglect is ideological. Offences are not generally seen as part of the 'crime problem', and the high status of offenders is generally assumed to lead to their being able to avoid the criminalization of their activities along with indirectly influencing the direction of criminological research through control over funding. In short, 'the powerful' are less likely to fund research critical of their own activities or to provide access to researchers (Tombs and Whyte, 2003; 2006a).

Technical and methodological problems deriving from the nature of offences also inhibit research. For example:

- Many victims are unaware of any harm and cannot detect it themselves as happens, for example, with some major frauds, pollution, food adulteration and descriptions of consumer goods.
- Victimization is often indirect and impersonal, affecting entities such as 'the government' although there are indirect effects on individuals – tax payers, for example, have to pay more and receive fewer benefits due to tax evasion.
- Individual victims may lose very little yet the 'illegal' profits may be large as in cases in which a bank employee takes one penny out of thousands of accounts or a firm sells goods which weigh less than indicated.

While this does not apply to all offences, many are difficult to capture in standard victim surveys. Some, such as frauds, are covered by the United States National Victim Survey, but information is limited to only frauds of which victims are aware. This means that different sources of information must be used, often lying outside criminological and victimological research. Although they may not be seen as 'crime', many of the activities involved are associated with harm, they are subject to regulation and linked to wider social issues such as workplace safety, the environment, consumerism or financial regulation. They are subject to investigation and research and useful sources of information include regulatory agencies, investigative journalism and relevant interest groups, along with a small amount of criminological research largely restricted to fraud.

Conceptualizing white-collar and corporate victimization

Analysing these kinds of victimization involves looking at how they have been viewed in different victimological traditions, and in the literature on corporate and white-collar crime. Positivist victimologies tended to neglect this whole area as they largely accepted conventional constructions of crime. Indeed, when 'business' or 'retail' crime surveys are carried out, they focus on offences, such as burglary or shoplifting, perpetrated against businesses by 'outsiders'. Analyses of 'lifestyles' or 'high crime' 'hot spots' do not consider the risks of working in an unsafe workplace, living in a heavily polluted environment or buying second-hand cars or counterfeit goods.

This focus has been challenged. Radical victimology did attempt to include the crimes of the powerful and the third Islington crime survey contained questions about workplace safety, unlawful trading practices and offences by landlords which were found to exceed experiences of conventional forms of crime (Pearce, 1992). This was an exception, however, and although it directed attention to the structural bases of victimization, other research largely focused on street and interpersonal crimes using, as outlined in Chapter 3, individualized victim surveys (Pearce and Tombs, 1998).

Critical victimology is also relevant to corporate and institutional victimization. This provides a major group of victims 'we cannot see' and, while later developments have focused more on gender (Walklate, 2003, and Chapters 6 and 7 in this volume), it provides a strong challenge to conventional constructions of crime and victimization. Moreover, while feminist victimology has tended to focus on the victimization of women and children, it also drew attention to sexual harassment and violence in the workplace and marketplace (Croall, 1995) and to the gendered dimensions of corporate victimization (Szockyj and Fox, 1996).

A major focus of 'white-collar criminology' (Slapper and Tombs, 1999), has been exposing the 'human misery' caused by the crimes of the powerful, often seen to exceed that caused by conventional crime. This has tended to use rather general categories to describe victims such as 'the general public', consumers and workers, and it has tended to explore the relationship between class, status and power and offending, criminalization, criminal justice and sentencing rather than victimization. In part, this is attributable to the difficulties, outlined above, of researching victimization which has been depicted as multi-layered – at the primary level affecting private individuals, at the secondary level, affecting organizations, or at the tertiary level, affecting 'society at large' (Lindgren, 2002). The 'rippling' effect of offences tends to downplay their impact on individuals and as Sutherland (1949) pointed out, it may also restrict the development of organized responses on the part of, for example, consumers. Other crimes, such as corruption, are seen as 'victimless', and yet others as having 'merely' an economic impact.

These constructions can be challenged and the existence of physical as well as economic harms stressed (Box, 1983). Crimes which largely affect 'the government' do, as seen above, affect all citizens and corruption damages the legitimacy of and trust in business and public service and, where it involves public service contracts, can lead to the construction of unsafe public buildings or inferior public services (Shover and Wright, 2001). Large bank failures not only harm individual wealthy investors who may be perceived as well able to afford the losses, but also smaller businesses and investors. Following the collapse of the BCCI, local services had to be cut in the Western Isles as the council there had invested in the bank (Croall, 2001a). Victimization is also 'hidden' by the construction of incidents resulting from systematic breaches of regulations as 'accidents' or 'disasters', a depiction which also suggests a more or less random effect, irrespective of class, age or gender. As will be seen, however, victimization can reflect these underlying social inequalities.

Notions of **deserving victims** and **undeserving victims** also affect this area of crime. Investors can be blamed for making 'risky' investments and seen as less deserving than older people victimized through pensions frauds (Levi, 1999). The principle of *caveat emptor*, let the buyer beware, has long dominated consumer law and consumers are blamed (and blame themselves) for being 'taken in' by counterfeit goods or other sales 'cons'. Workers may be blamed for ignoring safety regulations (Tombs, 1999) or women for choosing to have cosmetic surgery (Finlay, 1996). One of the most disturbing instances of **victim blaming** was involved in the Hillsborough disaster, in which 96 spectators died in a crush in a football stadium. Initially the police blamed the drunken state of many of the supporters which, by affecting subsequent investigations, led to a failure to fully explore the role of senior police officers whose decisions were subsequently alleged by inquiries and victim groups to have made a major contribution to the disaster (Scraton, 2004).

▶▶ **Deserving victims** *blameless, innocent and 'ideal' victims who did not provoke or invite their victimization.*

▶▶ **Undeserving victims** *victims who bear some responsibility and are in some part culpable or to blame for their victimization.*

▶▶ **Victim blaming** *similar to the concepts of victim precipitation, victim culpability and victim provocation. Each of these is also linked to the notion of 'lifestyle'. These concepts are used to try to explain the process of victimization and focus on the extent to which the victim can be held responsible for the events that occurred.*

What do we know about crime and victimization?

There is a considerable volume of information about the extent of different forms of white-collar and corporate crime which in turn provides some estimates of the extent of victimization, although it is less systematic than information on conventional crime. These kinds of crime have both physical and economic effects and the following sections illustrate victimization from a selection of major forms of crime grouped according to broad categories of victims.

Crimes against the government

The Government is a major victim of many forms of economic crime, which indirectly affects all citizens. Offences include:

- *Tax evasion*: The accountancy firm Deloitte and Touche estimated the cost of 'tax dodging' between 1976 and 1996 at around £2000bn, the equivalent of six years of government expenditure. Tax evasion takes place on a global scale through the use of offshore financial centres with the notorious company Enron having been revealed as avoiding US 409 million in taxes over five years (Johnson and Holub, 2003; Croall, 2005).
- *Fraud by public servants*: Fraudulent claims for expenses and allowances and frauds in relation to cash income, payroll and creditor payments were found by the Audit Commission (1993) to have led to Local Authorities losing £4.8 million.
- *Frauds on the NHS*: The Audit Commission (1993) also estimated losses for the NHS of around £5.9 million from frauds on the part of healthcare professionals including doctors, dentists and pharmacists.

Organizational victims

Organizations are victims of embezzlement, employee theft and many other frauds and are particularly vulnerable to offences involving the financial or technical expertise of employees. While organizations may be seen as 'legitimate' targets, losses are passed on to consumers and workers. For example:

- In one victim survey, Levi (1995) reported that: banks lost £3.2 million; clients or customers lost £1.8 million to 11 white-collar fraudsters; employers lost £1.7 million to 28 employees; suppliers of goods and services lost £1.1 million to 10 white-collar offenders and insurance companies lost £230,000 to 9 white-collar offenders.
- A European Economic Crime Survey by Price Waterhouse Coopers in 2001 found that up to 70 per cent of major companies reported economic crime in the previous two years – a high proportion attributable to employees (*Journal of Financial Crime*, 2002).

Investors and savers

Financial frauds and other offences such as 'misselling' where financial products are sold with misleading indications about their benefits have involved pensions, mortgage endowment policies (Fooks, 2003) and a host of other financial services. Two of the largest cases have involved:

- The Savings and Loan scandal in the United States, estimated to have involved total losses of up to one and a half trillion dollars amounting to a loss to every American of around $6,000 (Calavita and Pontell, 1995; Punch, 1996).
- The pensions misselling cases in the UK have been described as the 'worst financial scandal this century'. Following the 'privatization' of pension provision, 2 million or more pensions were sold on the basis of false or misleading information. By 1998, this had involved estimated costs of £11 billion and surveys found that only 9 per cent of pensions companies complied with legal requirements (Slapper and Tombs, 1999).

Crimes against consumers

Consumers are subject to a variety of outright frauds along with bogus bargain offers, misleading descriptions and substandard or counterfeit goods, as well as food poisoning and injuries from unsafe cars and other consumer goods. A variety of reports indicate the vast range of these offences, illustrated selectively in Box 4.2. To these could be added examples of what the Office of Fair Trading (OFT) describe as 'high pressure' and 'unscrupulous' sales techniques, some of which involve persuading customers to switch power suppliers and others involve doorstep selling. While consumers are often 'blamed' for not making 'informed' choices, they are increasingly unable to protect themselves as they cannot judge the contents or quality of mass-produced foods and goods.

Box 4.2   Consumer victimization

- **Cars**: The car industry has been described as 'criminogenic' with the sale of second-hand cars being subject to 'clocking' (the turning back of odometers) along with other problems. In Britain, a 'mystery shopping exercise' involving car servicing and repair was carried out in 2002. Trading Standards Officers rated over half the garages they visited as poor or very poor. Some 17 per cent carried out unnecessary work, 40 per cent missed or did not replace at least one item on the service schedule, 86 per cent missed at least one fault and 43 per cent provided no accurate quotes. Some 28 per cent of fast fit centres were rated poor or very poor, with around one-third unjustifiably recommending brake components and others unjustifiably recommending tyre replacements (Department of Trade and Industry, 2002). The British National Consumer Council (NCC) has calculated that the individual consumer typically loses £235 for each unsatisfactory repair or service and the DTI has estimated that consumers could lose up to £4 billion per annum (National Consumer Council, 2004).
- **'Cowboy' builders:** have been associated with shoddy work and charging for non-completed work. In North Wales, a local 'rapid response team' was set up to tackle cases of overpricing involving annual gains of around £200,000 (Powell, 2005). One insurance broker estimated that over a five-year period, nearly 5 million people in Britain were victimized by 'cowboy' traders. Victims reported sleepless nights along with feelings that their homes had been abused and some had to take time off work. Plumbers, builders, roofers and plasterers were the main offenders (Peake, 2004). A survey by British Gas in Wales estimated that more than 300,000 home owners were affected, with more than a third interviewed reporting having been 'ripped off' (Blake, 2004). In another investigation, Trading Standards officers were described as being 'appalled' by almost one quarter of 44 tradesmen invited to carry out simple jobs in a 'house of horrors' which they set up (Prynn, 2004).
- **Pricing offences:** These include falsely indicating a sale bargain when a higher price has not been charged and price fixing. On the introduction of legislation aimed at cartels, it was claimed that price fixing, market sharing and bid rigging cartels cost consumers and the economy hundreds of millions of pounds each year. The activities of major tour operators have been the subject of investigation by Trading Standards Officers including 'bait and trap' practices which attract customers by offering 'bargains' which

are subsequently revealed to involve travelling at unpopular times, and 'fluid pricing' where prices may be changed as often as every day.

- **Food frauds**: One of the oldest forms of food fraud is the adulteration of food with water or other ingredients. Mass production of food now enables basic meat to be processed with water and added additives. Samples of chicken tested by the Food Standards Authority in 2001 were found to contain only 54 per cent chicken along with water, salt, sugar, gum, flavourings and aromas. While not strictly illegal, these should be labelled to indicate their contents. Even more disturbing are suggestions that some mass-produced chicken is adulterated with pork and beef meat, raising issues about the spread of BSE (Lawrence, 2004). Other deceptive practices are involved in the marketing and labelling of foods such as the use of terms 'natural ingredients', 'diet' or 'organic' food, and the use, in most processed foods, of elements of genetically modified (GM) food whether or not declared on the label (Which?, 2004).
- **Food safety**: Consumers are also at risk of food poisoning, one of the most serious cases being the deaths of 21 pensioners from E.coli 0157 in Wishaw, Lanarkshire, in 1997 as a result of a butcher neglecting regulations. There has also been a rising volume of complaints to the Consumers Association about 'foreign bodies' in food such as nails or pieces of wood (Lawrence, 2002).

Crimes against workers

Workers are endangered by employers' neglect of health and safety regulations. As illustrated in Box 4.3, it has been estimated that occupationally caused deaths exceed those from homicide. Workers can also be exploited by employers failing to comply with wages legislation and other regulations about conditions of employment – which particularly affects those on low wages and migrant labour such as:

- Legal agencies' recruitment of foreign nurses from India, Africa and the Philippines to work in the NHS. In some reported cases they have been forced to work in private nursing homes, had their passports confiscated, and forced to sign illegal contracts and to work over 60 hours per week for £4 per hour (Browne, 2001).
- The Low Pay unit has reported the 'common experiences' of low paid workers working with no proper employment contract, enforced overtime and no rest breaks.

Box 4.3   Deaths at work

Tombs' (1999) analysis of figures for 1994-95 found the following:

- 376 fatal injuries reported under Reporting of Injuries, Diseases and Dangerous Occurrences Regulations (RIDDOR);
- 36 fatalities from the supply or use of flammable liquids;
- 27 fatalities in course of sea fishing, transport and communications work;
- 877 fatalities associated with driving in the course of employment

Total = 1316 fatal injuries.

This should be considered along with occupationally caused fatal illnesses such as asbestosis and occupationally caused lung disease which produce a further 1702 occupationally caused deaths.

Tombs (1999: 77) concludes that the scale of unlawful workplace deaths 'vastly outweighs the numbers of recorded homicides' – which stood in that year at 834 homicides in England, Wales and Scotland.

A series of investigations and official inquiries estimated that 70 per cent of fatalities at work could be attributed to managerial responsibility/violations of regulations (Slapper, 1993).

Crimes against 'the public'

Other offences such as 'environmental crime' affect the general public and local communities. This includes a vast range of activities including illegal emissions from industry, farming and transport, littering, waste dumping, the pollution of land, water and rivers and noise pollution. For example:

- The most serious case of industrial pollution involved the deaths of between 3,000 and 5,000 residents in Bhopal in India in 1984, following the release of methyl isocyanate, which while not resulting in a criminal prosecution was widely held to be the result of the company's neglect of safety rules (Pearce and Tombs, 1998).
- Wildlife and fish may also be endangered. In one incident in 1996, a British water company was prosecuted following a chemical leak which killed 33,000 salmon.

- Littering accounted for 14 per cent of prosecutions under Swedish Environmental legislation in 2000 (Korsell, 2002). In Britain, fly tipping, the illegal disposal of waste by businesses, has been described by the Environment Agency as a 'scourge of modern society' (Croall, 2004) and one major supermarket was prosecuted following the removal of 237 trolleys from a local river.

These, examples suggest a large volume of victimization which may well exceed that from the conventional crimes discussed elsewhere in this book, although few direct comparisons can be made. To these examples could be added many more – the more general area of 'safety crimes' involves public transport and the series of rail crashes including those at Hatfield and Southall which have accounted for many deaths (Slapper and Tombs, 1999; Tombs and Whyte, 2007).

Repeat victimization

These examples also suggest repeat and multiple victimization. A major characteristic of this area of crime is that prosecutions often follow a long history of offending. Financial frauds, for example, may have been continuing for years before discovery, tax evasion prosecutions are often for only selected offences for which evidence is available and safety or consumer prosecutions often follow a long history of warnings. Thus individual victims and groups of victims are likely to have experienced repeat victimization and, as is the case with conventional crimes, the risk of victimization may be higher following the success of previous offences. Moreover, some individuals and groups can be seen as 'serial' or 'multiple' victims as consumers, residents, workers and investors. And, as will be seen below, these will often be the least affluent.

The impact of offences

The above examples also suggest the considerable impact of these forms of crime. In extreme cases they cause injuries, ill health and death, in others, seemingly trivial effects, which, when 'added up' may, as South (1998: 44) suggests in relation to pollution, lead to 'modest to devastating changes in people's experience of the environment and conditions of life'. In addition, what may be seen as primarily economic harms also have emotional effects. Fraud victims report feelings such as bitterness and anger, depression, general health problems and loss of work (Titus, 2001). They may blame themselves and feel let down by a breach of trust. As Levi (1999: 7) comments:

> Not only does fraud lead to broken dreams, it also closes off opportunities which, once passed, are irrecoverable. For older people, vulnerable anyway to loss of confidence in themselves, frauds can destroy happiness permanently, just as readily as any other crime such as mugging or a more serious burglary. Indeed, more so, because victims know that they have supplied funds or goods voluntarily and because the loss of their financial cushion makes meaningless all their lifelong savings and sacrifices.

Policy and support in relation to victimization from white-collar and corporate crime

Despite this considerable impact, white-collar and corporate victims are generally excluded from 'victim-oriented' policies such as the state compensation scheme, or those offering assistance to victims and witnesses in court (Dignan, 2005). The regulatory process characteristic of these offences results in fewer prosecutions and lower sentences which often disappoint victims, and sentences are generally seen as deterrent rather than reparative.

Victims are represented not by the 'victim movement' but in a broad sense by campaign and interest groups such as the Consumers' Association, Friends of the Earth or Trade Unions. Support groups have also been set up following particular incidents such as the Hillsborough tragedy, the sinking of the *Herald of Free Enterprise* and the Clapham and Paddington rail crashes. These have highlighted the limitations of the criminal justice process, campaigned for changes in legislation and provided much-needed emotional and instrumental support for victims (Wells, 1995). Following 'disasters', victims need to share the experience of bereavement and attempt to explain 'what happened', which includes attributing responsibility. They also need help in coping with the legal process through inquests, investigations, and in relation to compensation, prosecution, and the eventual sentence, and there are now a number of lawyers and organizations with expertise in this area (Wells, 1995). The aims and work of one such group, the Centre for Corporate Accountability (CCA), is outlined in Box 4.4.

Box 4.4   The Centre for Corporate Accountability

The Centre's activities encompass advice, research and advocacy including:

Advice

- An advice service for families bereaved from work-related deaths.
- Free and independent advice on investigation and prosecution issues and Coroner's inquests to those who have been injured or bereaved due to workplace activities.
- Assisting people in drafting letters, meeting officials and informing them of their legal remedies.

Research

- Research on the adequacy of the law; the policies and practices of Government bodies and law reform.

Advocacy

- Discussions with Government bodies about changes in practices and procedures.

Source : www.corporateaccountability.org

These groups have highlighted many shortcomings in the criminal justice process from a victim's perspective, particularly concerning issues of corporations and their criminal liability, and the 'regulatory' process typical of many of these forms of crime (Slapper and Tombs, 1999; Croall, 2001a; Nelken, 2002; Tombs and Whyte, 2007).

Prosecution

Many forms of white-collar and corporate crime are not dealt with by the police but by regulatory agencies, such as the Health and Safety Executive, who have tended to adopt a 'compliance' approach in which prosecution is not seen as the best means of securing compliance with regulations and is considered a costly option. In addition, it is often difficult to establish sufficient evidence against any one individual within an organization and to establish the necessary *mens rea*, intent to harm, necessary for 'criminal' prosecution (Slapper and Tombs, 1999). This issue is now subject to legislative reform in both England and Wales and Scotland following the failure of high profile prosecutions involving Balfour Beatty and Railtrack in England and Wales who were involved in the Hatfield rail crash and TRANSCO, the gas company following the death, in a gas explosion, of a family of four in Scotland (Tombs and Whyte, 2007). Many prosecutions are therefore taken under 'regulatory' rather than criminal law, which does not carry the stigma of a 'criminal' conviction. Following injuries and deaths attributable to neglect of safety regulations, for example, companies are more often tried under Health and Safety legislation than the criminal law in relation to corporate manslaughter. A regular complaint of victim groups following major incidents is that those perceived to be responsible, particularly individuals, are not publicly brought to account for their offences. Some, victims such as those involved in the *Marchioness* and Hillsborough tragedies, have undertaken private prosecutions.

Sentencing

'Regulatory' prosecutions carry lower penalties and it is the breach of the regulation, rather than the outcome, be it death, injury or economic loss which is the primary consideration. While there is some evidence that judges do take victimization and the presence of 'innocent' victims into account, sentences are often seen as derisory from the victim's perspective (Croall and Ross, 2003; Croall, 2006a). In 1998, for example, the butcher responsible for the outbreak of E.coli which killed 21 pensioners was fined £2,500 following a 'regulatory' prosecution. The Sheriff indicated that he had taken account of the loss of business suffered by the company. Even very large fines can be seen as derisory. The fine following the Health and Safety prosecution in the Scottish TRANSCO case was a 'record' £15 million, with the judge commenting adversely on the company's lack of remorse (Adams and Bannerman, 2005). Yet it could be asked how victims' interests were served by such a fine which, although it was substantial, nonetheless amounted to less than 4 per cent of the company's profit, and will merely go to the Treasury (Croall, 2006b).

The fine is the main sentencing option for companies, although substantial compensation may be ordered. Reparative sentences are less often discussed for financial and corporate offences than deterrent ones, although many argue that offenders often have the resources and expertise to make substantial reparation (Croall, 2006a). Restorative justice can, argue some, work particularly well with companies (Dignan, 2005). Braithwaite (1995) reports 'shaming ceremonies' in which senior executives of an insurance company which had sold deceptive policies to Aboriginal communities were sent into the communities to negotiate settlements. Community orders also have reparative dimensions and the resources of corporate or white-collar offenders could be more imaginatively used. In the USA, for example, companies have been required to send executives to work in the community and those guilty of pollution to fund leisure amenities (Wells, 1993; Punch, 1996).

QUESTIONS

What are some of the main obstacles against preventing of victimization from corporate and white-collar crime?
Why don't corporations feature as victimizers on community safety and law and order agendas?

Individual and structural dimensions of victimization

One way of challenging the dominant perception that white-collar and corporate crimes are 'victimless' or have only trivial effects is to examine in more depth the many different ways in which individuals may experience these effects. Drawing largely on the examples of offences outlined above, Box 4.5 illustrates the way in which different offences affect individuals in key areas of everyday life. This includes not only financial and safety issues, but also takes account of how these offences, like conventional ones, adversely affect the 'quality of life' (Croall, 2001b, 2004). At home, for example, our safety is threatened by the supply and maintenance of power supplies and appliances, and doorstep selling continues to be a major issue of concern to the Office of Fair Trading. As the home has turned into a major area of sales through telemarketing and the Internet, there are many opportunities for fraudulent and misleading sales practices and arguably our quality of life is adversely affected by invasive and 'aggressive' sales practices. The quality of life in local neighbourhoods is also threatened by environmental crime and by the indirect effects, such as loss of resources for public services, of tax evasion or corruption. These examples are selective but they do illustrate that individual citizens face many risks from commercial activities across key areas of life whether at home or at work, at leisure, shopping, travelling, planning for the future or when ill. This underlines the likelihood of repeat, multiple and 'serial' victimization.

QUESTIONS

How many times have you been victimized by the activities discussed above in the last year?

How are the costs of corporate and white-collar crime calculated?

What are the problems associated with documenting and measuring victimization from white-collar and corporate crime?

Are the powerful the *Criminological Other*, – in other words, never the victimizers?

Are corporations the *Victimological Other*?

It could be argued that many of these activities are not generally regarded as 'crime'. Nonetheless the majority are subject to legal regulation or to calls for such regulation and are widely recognized risks which do occasion 'worry' and lead to avoidance strategies, albeit this is not perceived as 'fear of crime'. Looking at the impact of economic crime in this way also questions the focus of community safety on conventionally defined crime and the 'anti-social behaviour' associated with social housing tenants and disorderly young people. Companies may also be anti-social – the manager of a large record company recently received an Anti-Social Behaviour Order for fly posting (Whyte, 2004).

Box 4.5   Victimization from white-collar and corporate crime

In the home

Financial:

- Telemarketing frauds and scams; frauds via the Internet (e.g. sales of 'investment opportunities' and other goods);
- doorstep sales and 'marketing malpractices' (e.g. sale of power supplies, security devices);
- 'cowboy' builders.

Safety:

- the installation and maintenance of utilities (gas, plumbing, electricity);
- water pollution.

Quality of life:

- aggressive and invasive marketing practices; cold calling; SPAM.

The local neighbourhood

Financial:

- the indirect effects of corruption, tax evasion or public sector frauds.

Safety:

- chemical and noise pollution.

Quality of life:

- littering and fly posting.

The marketplace

Financial:

- consumer and sales frauds (short weight goods; deceptive packaging; bargain offers);
- 'cartels' and breaches of competition laws;
- counterfeit goods;
- food frauds and misleading descriptions of food.

Safety:

- sale of dangerous products (e.g. toys, counterfeit goods);
- food poisoning, food safety (e.g. additives, GM foods).

Quality of life:

- misleading sales practices and descriptions.

The workplace

Financial:

- offences involving pay and conditions.

(Continued)

Safety:

- breaches of health and safety regulations;
- occupationally related illnesses.

Quality of life:

- working conditions; bullying, intimidation, harassment.

Personal finance

Financial:

- frauds and misselling in relation to pensions, mortgages, investments etc; banks.

Safety:

- emotional trauma following severe losses.

Quality of life:

- sales practices; misleading advertisements; 'cold calling';
- damage to the legitimacy of financial institutions.

Health and welfare

Financial:

- frauds perpetrated on patients, clients and residents in institutions and on the NHS;
- misrepresenting the benefits of drugs, devices and test results on the part of pharmaceutical companies;
- 'quackery': the sale of bogus health foods, diets and other 'remedies'.

Safety:

- adverse effects of unsafe drugs and devices;
- physical and sexual abuse of the old and young in institutions (Peppin, 1996).

Quality of life:

- loss of health resources through fraud, tax evasion;
- loss of trust.

Transport

Financial:

- car sales and service frauds;
- pricing offences – airlines and bus companies.

Safety:

- transport 'disasters' such as the series of rail crashes in the UK;
- the safety of cars.

Quality of life:

- pollution from illegal exhaust fumes and the noise of air and other forms of commercial transport.

Leisure

Financial:

- marketing activities of holiday companies;
- crimes against tourists (e.g. overcharging in shops and restaurants; currency offences);
- offences (corruption, match fixing) in relation to sport.

Safety:

- 'adventure' centres; night clubs; pop concerts, sporting arenas.

Quality of life:

- environment, local amenities and pollution.

Gender and risks to consumers

While feminist victimology calls for the use of a 'gendered lens' (Walklate, 2003), analyses of white-collar and corporate crime have traditionally been 'gender blind' (Snider, 1996). Yet gender differences and assumptions of masculinity and femininity form a major part of the manufacturing and marketing of goods and services and the division of labour remains gendered (See Chapter 7). All of this creates differential risks of victimization – some examples of which are outlined below.

Female consumers are particularly at risk from the following:

- Pharmaceutical products and services aimed at altering women's bodies such as the case of the Dalkon Shield contraceptive device, marketed after its dangers were known, which caused deaths, septic abortions, miscarriages and long-term illnesses (Finlay, 1996). A wide range of cosmetics and particularly cosmetic surgery have been associated with many dangers and inadequate regulation. Silicone breast implants have been associated with long-term side effects and one company involved, Dow Corning was found to have acted with 'fraud malice and oppression' (Finlay, 1996). More recently, Botox or 'cosmetic' cowboys used illegal supplies of Botox (Hall, 2005) and revelations that private clinics had failed to carry out basic checks on surgeons led to proposed new regulations (Lister, 2005).
- Household products aimed primarily at 'housewives', some of which have been associated with allergies (Claybrook, 1996).
- Cosmetic products subject to pricing offences, misdescriptions of their effects and misleading packaging (Croall, 1995), particularly the use of 'meaningless' terms such as 'natural', organic or 'hypoallergenic'. As much as 50 per cent of the cost of a bottle of perfume can be taken up by packaging and advertising (www.wen.org.uk/cosmetics/facts.htm, accessed July 2005).
- Cultural and family pressures on women, particularly single parents, to purchase cheaper, substandard consumer goods.
- Assumptions of technical incompetence which may make them more likely targets of, for example, garage and car servicing frauds (Croall, 1995).

Male consumers also face risks from cosmetics and other products targeted at their bodies – from quite clearly bogus 'baldness' remedies to Viagra.

Crimes against workers

Female workers are particularly at risk from

- risks of miscarriage and respiratory ailments associated with the silicon chip industry (Simpson and Elis, 1996);
- illnesses due to high concentrations of food additives as in the food processing industry (Miller, 1985);
- exploitation of low paid and immigrant workers;
- exploitation in the 'sex industry';
- exposure to chemicals particularly, for example, in relation to food production (Miller, 1985) and beauty – hairdressers have been found to have higher rates of bladder cancer associated with hair dyes (Fletcher, 2003).

Male workers may be particularly at risk from

- deaths and injuries at work which occur in the 'risky' jobs associated with 'men's work' such as construction, transport and the oil industry.

Investors

Some investment frauds may adversely affect women – as mentioned above 'little old ladies' or 'Aunt Agathas' (Levi, 1987) are assumed to be financially ignorant. Though this may be a somewhat outdated notion, women were found to be more vulnerable to fraudulent doorstep sales and appliance repair frauds (Vaughan and Carlo, 1975).

Age and risk

Age is also related to crime and victimization although it is difficult to make generalizations as older people, often seen as particularly vulnerable to fraud, are not a homogenous group (Pain, 2003). Some are wealthier than others which may affect the likelihood of different forms of fraud, and Titus (2001) found lower rates of victimization among the elderly for telemarketing frauds as they had learnt to avoid them. Some examples of the risks faced by different age groups are indicated below.

Older consumers may be particularly vulnerable to

- food poisoning outbreaks, many of which have involved elderly people. The E.coli case in Scotland, for example, involved the deaths of 21 pensioners and one large outbreak in Canada caused the death of 19 residents of an old people's home in 1985;
- aggressive sales practices of security devices because they are 'easy to pressure, vulnerable, at home and living alone' and are seen as particularly vulnerable group;
- a variety of other forms of commercial or white-collar crime adversely affecting the elderly such as the sale of 'assistive products' for older people, and the activities of cowboy builders referred to above may have a disproportionate impact on the elderly with many press reports playing on vulnerable elderly victims (Croall, 2007).

The young, on the other hand, are more at risk of

- being harmed by toys, particularly cheap imitation versions of widely marketed toys which may cause injuries, as indicated by the many warnings around Christmas time from Trading Standards departments;
- being injured while engaging in physical and 'risky' activities;
- being the victim, in student accommodation, of landlords' failure to comply with electrical and fire safety precautions;
- purchasing substandard or counterfeit goods marketed at young people such as designer clothes, compact discs, DVDs and videos, designer trainers and football shirts. Mobile phone companies aggressively market products and services at young people and engage in misleading practices such as using tiny writing in contracts (Croall, 2007).

- being paid less than the minimum wage and exploited globally through child labour.

Other kinds of risks target both young and old simultaneously

- as residents of institutions, both the elderly, particularly those suffering from dementia, and the young are more at risk from physical abuse in care homes (Peppin, 1996);
- as savers and investors, the young may be more vulnerable as they are prepared to take more 'risks' (Titus, 2001), while older age groups are more vulnerable to pensions and investment frauds targeted at the need to provide for old age.

Socio-economic status and risk

Both gender and age are connected to socio-economic status in respect of which, as Levi (1995) comments, there is a 'complex moral arena' with both the rich and the poor being seen as vulnerable. Nonetheless, as was seen in relation to conventional crime in Chapter 3, the economic and cultural capital of the more affluent can protect them from some kinds of crime. Some of these relationships are summarized below.

Poorer consumers are more vulnerable to a range of crimes such as

- the sale of cheap and substandard goods;
- misleading 'bargain' offers;
- offences involving second-hand cars.

Regarding crimes involving workers, while those lower down the economic hierarchy are most at risk, employers are also vulnerable to the frauds and thefts of employees.

Lower level employees are more vulnerable to

- safety offences, including those leading to fatalities, which have a greater impact on manual, low level employees, often working on a casual basis in small, non-unionized companies who have less power to seek redress (Tombs, 1999);
- exploitation by low wages and poor working conditions.

Regarding investment and other financial frauds, the more affluent are more vulnerable to

- major investment frauds and risky investments which require large initial investments. As Levi (1995: 182) comments, the victims of many serious frauds are part of the same 'finance–capitalist' elite as offenders, thus Lloyd's of London 'happily skimmed profits from the nobility as well as from the *nouveaux riches* among syndicate members'.

In addition, poorer communities are more likely to suffer from *environmental* crime as they may be sited closer to polluting factories (South, 1998).

As is the case with conventional crime, offences may have a more severe impact on poorer victims as they can less easily remedy any problems. As seen above, many offences involve an abuse of occupational expertise which victims do not possess and rely on 'asymmetries of information' (Shapiro, 1990). This does affect employers, and the rich and poor alike may be vulnerable through their lack of medical, legal, financial or technological knowledge although the more affluent are more able to seek advice and information and, if victimized, to seek redress.

Economic and cultural capital also play a major role. In respect of consumer crime, the better off are more likely to be aware of many of the issues concerning the contents or quality of goods or food, are more likely to read consumer publications such as *Which?* and seek the help of advisers if they feel they have been victimized. On the other hand, poorer consumers, who can make fewer choices, are less likely to be in possession of appropriate information. A survey carried out for the OFT found that the elderly, the young and those on low incomes were more 'vulnerable' due to their greater difficulty in obtaining or assimilating the information needed to make 'informed' decisions. In respect of environmental crime, those living in more affluent areas, having already avoided living in more 'undesirable' areas, are more able to mount effective campaigns against the location of noisy or dirty factories and ensure that planning regulations are complied with.

QUESTION

Can you explain why Tombs and Whyte (2006a) claim that the economic and physical costs of corporate crime fall disproportionately on the disadvantaged and the poorest sections of society?

Global inequalities

A brief discussion of the global dimensions of white-collar and corporate crime victimization further illustrates its structural dimensions. Typical forms of global or transnational corporate crime, for example, involve avoiding the laws and regulations of more developed countries by siting production in countries with less stringent regulations (Croall, 2005). In this way, corporations exploit the 'spaces between laws' and have been involved in a corporate 'race to the bottom' (Passas, 2000; Gilbert and Russell, 2002). This has been associated with harmful activities such as

- 'dumping' toxic wastes and unsafe products;
- exploiting child labour;
- failing to pay a living wage;
- producing substandard or counterfeit products;
- exposing uninformed and unprotected workers to dangerous working conditions;
- using cheap and sometimes forced labour, including prison labour.

In general, these activities impact more severely on the most economically weak nations and within these on the poorest and most vulnerable workers (Gilbert and Russell, 2002). Wealthy individuals and corporations may also seek to evade tax laws by placing their money in offshore havens which has the effect of shifting a greater tax burden onto the least mobile, smaller businesses and lower income groups (Johnson and Holub, 2003).

White-collar, corporate or economic crime victimization does therefore reflect wider structures of inequality. While offences may appear random in their effect, and wealthy individuals and large organizations are also victimized, other activities have a more adverse effect on the least affluent. Women are particularly vulnerable to offences which, as feminist analyses indicate, seek to promote idealized notions of femininity, for example, by cosmetic improvement along with those which derive from wider inequalities in the workplace, thereby reflecting patriarchal structures of power (Szockyj and Fox, 1996). Ageist structures and stereotypes are reflected in the greater dependency of the old and young which makes them more vulnerable to some offences.

Reflections and future research directions

This chapter has selectively explored a wide range of information about the vast area of victimization from corporate and white-collar crime. In comparison to conventional crime, however, many questions remain unanswered and much research remains partial and restricted to case studies and individual crimes. Victims of many of these activities are not widely recognized as 'crime' victims and are excluded from most traditions of victimology, which have largely accepted conventional constructions of crime. As such, they are not included in victim surveys and the diffuse and indirect nature of victimization is often taken to prohibit their inclusion. Despite these difficulties, however, more research could be undertaken. Not all offences involve indirect victimization and victims are aware of some offences such as the sale of out-of-date food, breaches of safety regulations within workplaces or rented accommodation (Pearce, 1992), the activities of cowboy builders, the frauds of second-hand car dealers, misdescriptions of some goods, particularly those subsequently found to be substandard. A wide range of offences could, therefore be included within 'conventional' victim surveys and their numbers routinely compared with other forms of crime.

Other innovative forms of research could also be developed. More focused research could, for example, take place in workplaces,[1] or with focus groups of consumers, women, older or younger people to ascertain experiences of offences and attitudes towards issues of safety and quality, or within specific neighbourhoods in relation to environmental harms. Some valuable research, has been carried out by interest groups such as the CCA (see above), the Women's Environmental Network (WEN) or the National Consumer Council, although these studies focus on wider social issues rather than being focused narrowly on 'crime'. The 'mystery' shopping exercises carried out by Trading Standards Officers provide another example of the kind of research which has been carried out and which could, given more resources, be increased across a range of so-called regulatory areas.

It is necessary therefore to broaden the scope of victimology beyond the more narrow definition of crime employed by administrative criminology and victimology, tied as they are to conventional constructions of crime, and to incorporate yet more forms of victimization which are 'unseen'. The continuing neglect of these broader harms has led some critical criminologists to call for a move beyond criminology to the study of social harm, or *zemiology*, which would incorporate a much wider range of harms, exposing their structural nature and exploring different societal responses to them, rather than being restricted by the confines of criminal law and criminology (Hillyard and Tombs, 2004; Hillyard, 2006).

All this could, in addition to encouraging a wider recognition of the harms from fraud and other commercial activities, have an impact on criminal justice and other victim-centred policies. It could, for example, enhance the agenda of crime prevention and community safety programmes which, by taking account of a wider range of offenders and victimization, could become more inclusive. The anti-social behaviour agenda, for example, focuses almost entirely on the offences of lower-class youth – yet many of the activities described above could readily be seen as 'anti-social' and similar orders applied. In addition, as seen above, criminal justice policy could take more account of the victim's perspective in developing more innovative and reparative sentences for business offenders.

Summary

This chapter has demonstrated that victimology, particularly 'conservative' victimology, has failed to take account of a major area of victimization.

It has also demonstrated that victimization from white-collar and corporate crime is considerable and may well exceed that from so-called conventional crime and that individuals may suffer from many forms of white-collar and corporate victimization. The chapter concludes that many forms of white-collar and corporate victimization reflect wider patterns of social and economic inequality and that there is a need for victim-centred initiatives to include these forms of crime. Finally, further research is necessary to more fully understand the nature of victimization from economic crime and to compare it with that from conventional crime.

ANNOTATED BIBLIOGRAPHY

Croall, H. (2001a) *Understanding White-Collar Crime.* **Buckingham: Open University Press.** This includes a chapter introducing aspects of victimization from white-collar and corporate crime.

Croall, H. (2001b) 'The victims of white collar crime', in L. Sven-Ake (ed.), *White-Collar Crime Research. Old Views and Future Potentials: Lectures and Papers from a Scandinavian Seminar.* **National Council for Crime Prevention, Sweden Bra-Report 2001: 1. Croall, H. (2004)** *Cheated and Poisoned: Exposing Victimisation from Economic Crime.* **Swedish Council for Crime Prevention (English summary available on www.bra.se).** These references contain detailed analysis of the individual and structural dimensions of victimization.

Shover, N. and Wright, J.P. (eds) (2001) Crimes of Privilege: Readings in White-Collar Crime. Oxford: Oxford University Press. This text provides a good account of studies in the United States in the section on victims.

Tombs, S. and Whyte, D. (2007) *Safety Crime.* **Cullompton: Willan Publishing.** This text provides a good introduction to victimization from corporate crime, including an account of deaths and injuries resulting from safety crimes.

Note

1 I am grateful to the editors for this suggestion.

References

Adams, L. and Bannerman, L. (2005) 'Gas firm fined £15 million for the death of a family', *The Herald* 26 Aug. Available at: www.theherald.co.uk/news/45795, accessed 26 Aug. 2005.

Audit commission (1993) *Protecting the Public Purse: Ensuring Probity the Public Sector?* London: Audit Commission.

Braithwaite, J. (1995) 'Corporate crime and republican criminological praxis, F. Pearce and L. Snider leads, *Corporate Crime*. Toronto: University of Tornoto Press.

Blake, A. (2004) '300,000 homeowners "ripped off"', *Western Mail*, Cardiff, 23 Apr., p. 3.

Box, S. (1983) *Power, Crime and Mystification*. London: Tavistock.

Browne, A. (2001) 'Abused, threatened and trapped – Britain's foreign "slave nurses"', *The Observer,* 27 May 2001.

Calavita, H. and Pontell, K. (1995) 'Saving the Savings and Loans?, in F. Pearce and L. Snider (eds), *Corporate Crime: Contemporary Debates*. Toronto: University of Toronto Press.

Clarke, M. (1990) *Business Crime: Its Nature and Control*. Cambridge: Polity Press.

Claybrook, J. (1996) 'Women in the marketplace', in E. Szockyj and J.G. Fox (eds), *Corporate Victimization of Women*. Boston: Northeastern University Press.

Croall, H. (1995) 'Target women; women's victimisation from white collar crime', in R. Dobash, and L. Noaks (eds), *Gender and Crime*. Cardiff: Cardiff University Press.

Croall, H. (2001a) *Understanding White Collar Crime*. Buckingham: Open University Press.

Croall, H. (2001b) 'The victims of white collar crime', in L. Sven-Ake (ed.), *White-Collar Crime Research. Old Views and Future Potentials: Lectures and Papers from a Scandinavian Seminar*. National Council for Crime Prevention, Sweden Bra-Report 2001: 1.

Croall, H. (2004) *Cheated and Poisoned: Exposing Victimisation from Economic Crime.'* Swedish Council for Crime. Prevention (English summary available on www.bra.se).

Croall, H. (2005) 'White collar crime', in A. Wardak, and J. Sheptycki (eds), *Transnational and Comparative Criminology*, Cavendish: Glasshouse Press.

Croall, H. (2006a) 'Penalties for corporate homicide', Annex B to Scottish Executive (2005) ''The Findings and recommendations of the Expert Group Report on Corporate Homicide''', available at http://www.scotland.gov.uk/Publications/2005/11/14133559/35592.

Croall, H. (2006b) 'Sentencing companies and organisations: the need for significant reforms' unpublished paper delivered to CCA Conference, Glasgow, 6 October 2006.

Croall, H. (2007) 'White collar crime, consumers and victimization', in G. Geis and H. Pontell (eds), *International Handbook of White Collar Crime*. New York: Springer

Croall, H. and Ross, J. (2003) 'Sentencing the corporate offender', in N. Hutton, and C. Tata, (eds), *Sentencing and Society*. Aldershot: Ashgate.

Department of Trade and Industry (2002) *Car Servicing and Repairs: Mystery Shopping Research*, September. London: Department of Trade and Industry.

Dignan, J. (2005) *Understanding Victims and Restorative Justice*. Buckingham: Open University Press.

Finlay, L. (1996) 'The pharmaceutical industry and women's reproductive health', in E. Szockyj and J.G. Fox (eds), *Corporate Victimisation of Women*. Boston: Northeastern University Press.

Fletcher, V. (2003) 'Hair dye alert as study reveals risks to health: makers accused of insufficient testing', *Evening Standard*, 22 Apr., p. 15.

Fooks, G. (2003) 'In the valley of the blind the one-eyed man is king: corporate crime and the myopia of financial regulation', in S. Tombs, and D. Whyte, (eds), *Unmasking the Crimes of the Powerful*. New York: Lang, pp. 105–28.

Gilbert, M. and Russell, S. (2002) 'Globalization of criminal justice in the corporate context', *Crime, Law and Social Change*, 38: 211–38.

Hall, C. (2005) 'Health crackdown on beauty clinics and Botox parties', *The Daily Telegraph*, 29 Jan., p. 05.

Hillyard, P. (2006) 'Criminal obsessions: crime isn't the only harm', *Criminal Justice Matters*, 62: 26.7, 46.

Hillyard, P. and Tombs, S. (2004) 'Beyond criminology?' in P. Hillyard, C. Pantazis, S. Tombs and D. Gordon (eds), *Beyond criminology: Taking Harm Seriously*. London: Pluto Press.

Johnson, J. and Holub, M. (2003) 'Corporate flight: ''moving'' offshore to avoid US taxes', *Journal of Financial Crime*, Jan. 2003.

Journal of Financial Crime (2002) 'Serious fraud hits major European companies hard, crime survey shows', *Journal of Financial Crime* 9(2): 116.

Korsell, L. (2002) 'Economic crime', in *Crime Trends in Sweden 1998–2000*. Stockholm: National Council for Crime Prevention.

Lawrence, F. (2002) 'Customers find ever more "foreign objects" in food', *Guardian Unlimited*, 7 Feb. 2002.

Lawrence, F. (2004) *Not on the Label*. London: Penguin Books.

Levi, M. (1987) *The Regulation of Fraud: White Collar Crime and the Criminal Process*. London: Tavistock.

Levi, M. (1995) 'Serious fraud in Britain', in F. Pearce, and L. Snider, (eds), *Corporate Crime: Contemporary Debates*. Toronto: University of Toronto Press.

Levi, M. (1999) 'The impact of fraud', *Criminal Justice Matters,* 36 (summer).

Levi, M. (2005) *The Victims of Fraud*. Oxford: Clarendon Press.

Levi, M. and Pithouse, A. (1992) 'The victims of fraud', in D. Downes (ed.), *Unravelling Criminal Justice*. London: Macmillan.

Lindgren, S. (2002) 'Economic crime in Sweden: an essentially contested issue', *Criminal Justice*, 4(2): 363–83.

Lister, S. (2005b) 'Tighter facelift rules will tackle rogue practitioners', *The Times* 28 Jan., p. 11.

Miller, M. (1985) *Danger! Additives at Work*. London: London Food Commission.

National Consumer Council (2004) Press release.

Nelken, D. (2002) 'White collar crime', in M. Maguire, R. Morgan and R. Reiner, (eds), *The Oxford Handbook of Criminology*, 3rd edition. Oxford: Oxford University Press.

Pain, R. (2003) 'Old age and victimisation', in P. Davies, P. Francis and V. Jupp (eds), *Victimisation: Theory, Research and Policy*. Basingstoke: Palgrave Macmillan.

Passas, N. (2000) 'Global anomie, dysnomie and economic crime: hidden consequences of neo liberalism and globalization in Russia and around the world', *Social Justice*, summer: 16–35.

Peake, A. (2004) 'Cowboy builders take us for £1BN', *The Sun* 19 Oct., p.15.

Pearce, F. (1992) 'The contribution of "left realism" to the study of commercial crime,' in B. McLean and J. Lowman (eds), *Realist Criminology: Crime Control and Policing in the 1990s*. Toronto: University of Toronto Press.

Pearce, F. and Tombs, S. (1998) *Toxic Capitalism: Corporate Crime and the Chemical Industry*. Aldershot: Ashgate.

Peppin, J. (1996) 'Feminism, law and the pharmaceutical industry', in F. Pearce and L. Snider (eds), *Corporate Crime: Contemporary Debates*. Toronto: University of Toronto Press.

Powell, D. (2005) 'The posse: riding out to beat cowboy builders', *Daily Post*, 20 May, p. 2.

Prynn, J. (2004) 'Exposed: rip-offs of cowboy workmen', *Evening Standard,* 22 Jan., p. 1.

Punch, M. (1996) *Dirty Business: Exploring Corporate Misconduct*. London: Sage.

Scottish Executive (2005) 'The findings and recommendations of the Expert Group report on Corporate Homicide', available at: http://www.scotland.gov.uk/Publications/2005/11/14133559/35592.

Scraton, P. (2004) 'Death on the terraces: The contexts and injustices of the 1989 Hillsborough disaster', *Soccer and Society*, 5(2): 183–200.

Shapiro, S. (1990) 'Collaring the crime, not the criminal: re-considering the concept of white collar crime', *American Sociological Review,* 55: 346–65.

Shichor, D., Sechrest, D. and Doocy, J. (2000) 'Victims of investment fraud', in H. Pontell and D. Shichor (eds), '*Contemporary Issues in Crime and Criminal Justice: Essays in Honor of Gilbert Geis*'. Englewood Cliffs, NJ: Prentice Hall.

Shover, N. and Wright, J. P. (eds) (2001) *Crimes of Privilege: Readings in White-Collar Crime.* Oxford: Oxford University Press.

Simpson, S. and Elis, L. (1996) 'Theoretical perspectives on the corporate victimisation of women', in E. Szockyj and J.G. Fox (eds), *Corporate Victimisation of Women.* Boston: Northeastern University Press.

Slapper, G. (1993) 'Corporate manslaughter: an examination of the determinants of prosecutorial policy', *Social and Legal Studies*, 2: 423–43.

Slapper, G. and Tombs, S. (1999) *Corporate Crime.* London: Addison-Wesley Longman.

Snider, L. (1996) 'Directions for social change and political action', in E. Szockyj and J.G. Fox, (eds), *Corporate Victimisation of Women.* Boston: Northeastern University Press.

South, N. (1998) 'Corporate and state crimes against the environment: foundations for a green perspective in European Criminology', in V. Ruggiero, N. South and I. Taylor (eds) *The New European Criminology: Crime and Social Order in Europe.* London and New York: Routledge.

Sutherland, E. (1949) *White Collar Crime*, NewYork: Holt, Reinhart and Winston.

Szockyj, E. and Fox, J.G. (eds) (1996) *Corporate Victimisation of Women.* Boston: Northeastern University Press.

Titus, R.M. (2001) 'Personal fraud and its victims' in N. Shover and J. P. Wright (eds). *Crimes of Privilege: Readings in White-Collar Crime.* Oxford: Oxford University Press.

Tombs, S. (1999) 'Health and safety crimes: (in)visibility and the problems of "Knowing", in P. Davies, P. Francis and V. Jupp (eds), *Invisible Crimes: Their Victims and their Regulation.* London: Macmillan.

Tombs, S. and Whyte, D. (2003) 'Scrutinizing the powerful: crime, contemporary political economy, and critical social research', in S. Tombs and D. Whyte (eds), *Unmasking the Crimes of the Powerful.* New York: Lang, pp. 3–48.

Tombs, S. and Whyte, D. (2006a) 'Community saftety and corporate crime', in P. Squires (ed.), *Community Safety: Critical Perspectives on Policy and Practice.* Bristol: Policy Press.

Tombs, S. and Whyte, D. (2006b) 'From the streets to the suites: researching corporate crime', *Criminal Justice Matters*, 62(6): 24, 25–45.

Tombs, S. and Whyte, D. (2007) *Safety Crime,* Cullompton: Willan Publishing.

Vaughan, D. and Carlo, G. (1975) 'The appliance repairman: a study of victim-responsiveness and fraud', *Journal of Research in Crime and Delinquency,* 12: 153–61.

Walklate, S. (2003) 'Can there be a feminist victimology?' in P. Davies, P. Francis and V. Jupp (eds), *Victimization: Theory, Research and Policy.* Basingstoke: Palgrave Macmillan.

Wells, C. (1993) *Negotiating Tragedy: Law and Disasters.* London: Sweet and Maxwell.

Which? (2004) No to GM. *Online* Sep. 2004.

Whyte, D. (2004) 'Respectable yobs and corporate ASBOs', *New Law Journal*, 7142: 1293.

'Race', Ethnicity, Victims and Crime

Peter Francis

Chapter aims

- To describe patterns of victimization, risk and vulnerability by ethnic origin.
- To outline political and policy responses to violent racism.
- To situate and conceptualize violent racism.
- To discuss criminology's attempt to explain violent racism.

Introduction

Black and Minority Ethnic (BME) people experience a range of crimes and social harms. Since 1988, the British Crime Survey (BCS) has reported that BME groups have a higher risk of victimization than white people. It has also identified variations between and within BME groups as well as between different offence categories (Fitzgerald and Hale, 1995; Clancy et al., 2001; Salisbury and Upson, 2004). BME groups are likely to experience repeat and multiple victimization; perceive themselves more at risk of victimization; and are most likely to report being fearful of racially motivated crime (Chahal and Julienne, 1999; Bowling and Phillips, 2002). People from BME backgrounds also experience high rates of secondary victimization, as a consequence, for example, of insensitive criminal justice practices, and – as employees of criminal and social justice agencies and organizations – discrimination from colleagues and from members of the community (Home Office, 2006).

▶▶ **Black and Minority Ethnic (BME)** *refers to a person or group whose self-defined ethnicity is not 'White British'.*

It is violence fuelled by prejudice and racism that is perhaps the most pernicious of all of the crimes and social harms experienced by BME groups. **Violent racism** has always existed (Pearson, 1976; Fryer, 1984; Thompson, 1988; Panayi, 1993; Kahn, 2002). Nevertheless, it is only since the 1980s that it has reached the political and policy agendas and not until the 1990s that it came starkly to the public's attention with the murder of the black teenager Stephen Lawrence. Stephen Lawrence was murdered by a group of white racists in London in 1993 yet despite media and political interventions ever since, his killers have still not been brought to justice. Moreover it is debatable whether the public inquiry into the police investigation chaired by Sir William Macpherson (Macpherson, 1999) has had a transformative impact on the operation of the police (Foster et al., 2005; Docking and Tuffin, 2005). The Inquiry Report identified the police investigation as marred by professional incompetence, institutional racism and a lack of leadership among senior police officers (Macpherson, 1999: 317).

▶▶ **Violent racism** *is adopted here from Ben Bowling's (1999) book* Violent Racism. *In acknowledging the various terminologies used to describe 'racially motivated crime' and types of racial or racist 'incident', 'harassment', 'attack' and 'abuse', Bowling uses the term to describe 'racism in its various forms, especially its violent form' (Bowling, 1999: 13). For Bowling (1999: 13), the concept of violent racism is more relevant as it allows for connections between racist 'discourses, exclusionary practices and experiences of violence to be explored' (Docking and Tuffin, 2005). In summary, Bowling argues that violent racism should be regarded 'as a form of racism rather than a form of violence' (1999: 307), thus rooting the action in broader and more general forms of racist language and practice.*

Violent racism is deeply rooted within the towns and cities of rural and urban Britain (see, for example, Clancy et al., 2001; Connelly and Keenan, 2002). Between April and July 2001, the northern towns of Oldham, Burnley and Bradford erupted with racist gangs attacking Asian communities (Kundnani, 2001). The subsequent report into the riots (Cantle, 2001) identified polarities between communities, concluded that a national debate needed to be led by government with a 'view to developing a new compact, or understanding, between all sections of the community' (Cantle, 2001: 19 Para 5.1.5), and made 67 recommendations on the need for a more strategic approach to bridging the gaps between all citizens.

One of the most striking aspects of the events during the spring and early summer of 2001 was the depth of feeling between all involved. Such violent confrontations had not been seen since those in the London Boroughs of Handsworth, Brixton and Tottenham in 1985 and in Brixton in 1981. They were not isolated incidents but systemic outpourings of deep-rooted historical processes and contemporary realities. Violent racism has a history (Khan, 2002), but its contemporary manifestation must be understood within the context of late modern global change (Young, 2007). It is a consequence of the very real socio-economic, cultural and political changes that have taken place and the tensions and conflicts that these have given rise to globally and locally.

The aim of this chapter is to develop an understanding of 'race', ethnicity, victims and crime in England and Wales. The structure of the chapter is as follows. First, the chapter introduces the differential risk of victimization by BME groups. Second, the chapter explores the extent and nature of violent racism. Third, the chapter examines the political and policy response to racist victimization. Fourth, it highlights theoretical, conceptual and methodological weaknesses underpinning much political and policy discourse on violent racism. Finally, the chapter examines how racism actually results in racist victimization.

The focus throughout the chapter is on black and Asian victims of violent racism. This is in part due to my own research interests and in part the paucity of in-depth research on violent racism against, for example, 'Chinese and Other' BME groups (Garland et al., (2006) provide a useful discussion of issues in researching 'hidden' minority ethnic communities. See also Jansson, 2006).

'Race', ethnicity, risk and victimization

The majority of all crime committed against BME groups in England and Wales – estimated as much as 85 per cent – may not be racist in motivation (FitzGerald and Hale, 1996). Vulnerability to and risk and fear of crime are exacerbated by social, economic and political exclusion, and the risk of personal victimization is closely correlated with variables such as age, sex, "**race**" and **ethnicity**.

▶▶ **'Race'** *according to Bhavnani et al. (2005) 'race' is a changeable term that is not a 'real' or measurable quality, and hence the quotation marks to denote its social construction. They go on to state that '"Race" is a social relationship in which structural positions and social actions are ordered, justified and explained by reference to systems and symbols of beliefs which emphasise the social and cultural relevance of biologically rooted characteristics' (Bhavnani et al., 2005: 217).*

▶▶ **Ethnicity** *there is no universally agreed definition of ethnicity but the term is usually used as a means to describe attachment to a cultural group by birth, for example, English, Indian, African-Caribbean, Irish, and so on. Bhavnani et al. (2005) indicate that ethnicity is often used interchangeably with 'race', which can be problematic.*

In 2005/06 the BCS indicated a fall in reported crime in England and Wales since its peak in 1995 (Walker et al., 2006; Home Office 2006). Against this backdrop there is variation in the risks of victimization experienced by different BME groups as well as within groups and between offence categories. The BCS 2004/05 indicates that people of mixed ethnic origin (29 per cent) face significantly higher risk of being a victim of crime than white people (24 per cent). However, it reports that there were no other *statistically significant differences* between people of different ethnic backgrounds for the period 2004/05.[1] The 2004/05 BCS also suggests that levels of risk for white, mixed and Asian ethnic groups fell significantly between 2003/04 and 2004/05. In relation to worry, the 2004/05 BCS suggests that BME groups are significantly more likely than white people to worry about burglary, car crime and violent crime. In addition, it reports that people from black, Asian and 'Chinese and Other' backgrounds were more likely to worry about burglary than people from mixed ethnic groups.

Salisbury and Upson carried out an analysis of the 2001/02 and 2002/03 BCS. They found that people from BME backgrounds were at greater risk of experiencing crime overall than the white majority for 2002/03 and those aged 16–34 were at most risk of crime (Salisbury and Upson, 2004: 2). In addition, they note that BME groups were at greater risk of personal crime, including mugging, than white people, but not of household crime; that Asian people and those of mixed race backgrounds faced higher risks of being a victim of crime relative to 'Other' groups; and that people from BME backgrounds were more likely to have high levels of worry about burglary, car crime and violence than white people.

The higher risk of people from BME backgrounds to victimization is partly because they are more likely to be over-represented in social demographic groups associated with higher risks of victimization (Davies et al., 2003 and Chapter 3 in this volume). Zedner (2002) points out that BME communities are more likely to live in younger households of lower socio-economic status and generally to reside in socially disadvantaged communities. The BCS 2004/05 indicates that ethnicity was not independently associated with risk of victimization for either personal or all violent incidents (Home Office, 2006: 8). 'Instead other factors; age and sex, frequency of visiting pubs or bars, living in an area with high levels of perceived anti-social behaviour and marital status were the strongest predictors of risk of victimization' (Home Office, 2006: 8). However, as Fitzgerald and Hale (1996) also note, this is not to suggest that 'ethnicity plays no part in their victimization'. It should also be noted that people from BME groups are disproportionately represented at each stage of the criminal justice system from initial contact to sentence, and that this is not necessarily because people from black and minority ethnic groups are more likely to offend (Home Office, 2005: 7).

Defining and recording violent racism

Since 1988, the 43 police forces in England and Wales have recorded **racist incidents** separately from non-racist incidents.

▶▶ **Racist incident** *until 1999 the police in England and Wales used the Association of Chief Police Officers (ACPO) definition of a racist incident as 'any incident in which it appears to the reporting or investigating officer that involves an element of racial motivation; or any incident which includes an allegation of racial motivation made by any person' (cited in Holdaway, 1986). Since publication of the Stephen Lawrence Inquiry report in 1999, a racist incident has been defined by the police (and local government and criminal justice agencies) as an 'incident which is perceived to be racist by the victim or any other person' (Macpherson, 1999).*

Table 5.1 illustrates the increase in the number of incidents recorded by the police for the period 1997/98–2004/05. These figures must be interpreted with caution. Any increase (or, for that matter, decrease) will reflect the manner and sensitivity in which incidents are recorded by the police. For example:

- Victim reports may be considered too trivial, not believed, or deemed not to refer to a criminal offence (Maguire, 2002).
- The police may classify some racist incidents against the offence category rather than by the racial motivation.
- Recording and classification may also be affected by individual officer working rules, police organizational cultures and operational and strategic priorities.

Sections 28–32 of the Crime and Disorder Act 1998 (CDA 1998) as amended by the Police Reform Act 2002 introduced **racially aggravated offences**. The new offences came into force on 30 September 1998 and cover racially aggravated assault, criminal damage, harassment and public order. Burney and Rose (2002) provide an interesting review of the introduction of the new offences.

▶▶ **Racially aggravated offences** *An offence is racially aggravated ... if:*

(a) *At the time of committing the offence or immediately before or after doing so, the offender demonstrates towards the victim of the offence hostility based on the victim's membership (or presumed membership) of a racial group.*

(b) *The offence is motivated (wholly or partly) by hostility towards members of a racial group based on their membership of that group.*

(c) *'Membership', in relation to a racial group, includes association with members of that group. 'Presumed' means presumed by the offender.*

As a result of Section 39 of the Anti-Terrorism, Crime and Security Act 2001, this definition was extended to include religiously aggravated offences. Section 153 of the Powers of Criminal Courts (Sentencing) Act 2000, amended by the 2001 Act, imposes a duty on sentencers to treat evidence of racist and religious motivation as an aggravating factor. The

Table 5.1 Racist incidents for all police force areas 1997/8 to 2004/5[1]

Police force area	1997/8	1998/9	1999/00	2000/1	2001/2	2002/3	2003/4	2004/5	% Change 2003/4 to 2004/5
Avon & Somerset	409	626	887	956	940	1,125	1,474	1,765	20
Bedfordshire	75	134	300	301	289	293	410	471	15
Cambridgeshire	147	205	519	691	736	878	773	794	3
Cheshire	78	158	421	399	405	184	416	552	33
Cleveland	76	147	204	307	399	431	496	382	–23
Cumbria	46	45	85	97	155	162	197	289	47
Derbyshire	174	208	383	504	678	678	788	664	–16
Devon & Cornwall	90	116	538	776	874	852	944	1,072	14
Dorset	86	145	185	212	228	260	219	341	56
Durham	37	75	178	247	275	224	244	282	16
Essex	160	229	431	679	813	452	626	1,003	60
Gloucestershire	32	83	258	389	432	380	314	400	27
Greater Manchester	624	1,197	2,324	2,663	3,955	2,642	3,213	3,735	16
Hampshire	219	271	654	845	888	864	1,409	1,566	11
Hertfordshire	288	325	703	984	1,237	1312	1,463	1,343	–8
Humberside	72	111	215	422	477	422	432	477	10
Kent	276	273	914	1,278	888	986	869	1,041	20
Lancashire	311	450	917	1,274	2,178	1,521	1,923	2,103	9
Leicestershire	237	367	878	908	1,132	1,181	1,284	1,436	12
Lincolnshire	6	14	19	42	150	149	230	474	106
London, City of	6	28	55	91	72	103	32	57	78
Merseyside	241	324	822	761	690	763	951	1,168	23
Metropolitan Police	5,862	11,050	23,346	20,628	16,711	15,453	15,319	15,449	1
Norfolk	89	94	253	259	287	363	356	421	18
Northamptonshire	318	282	597	591	663	619	768	939	22
Northumbria	444	623	1,159	1,626	1,747	1,552	1,655	1,603	–3

(Continued)

Table 5.1 (Continued)

Police force area	1997/8	1998/9	1999/00	2000/1	2001/2	2002/3	2003/4	2004/5	% Change 2003/4 to 2004/5
North Yorkshire	41	64	96	128	228	214	151	201	33
Nottinghamshire	391	475	714	914	1,097	1,099	1,106	1,245	13
South Yorkshire	213	293	557	698	698	754	787	987	25
Staffordshire	214	220	202	500	1,138	466	948	918	–3
Suffolk	54	150	234	291	375	345	409	417	2
Surrey	45	126	338	573	607	648	853	941	10
Sussex	298	399	934	1,526	1,120	1,106	1,214	1,403	16
Thames Valley	279	486	999	1,088	1,470	1,445	1,772	1,935	9
Warwickshire	107	111	150	175	314	310	310	402	30
West Mercia	115	106	479	839	930	831	947	887	–6
West Midlands	632	988	1,548	3,321	4,058	3,009	3,256	3,072	–6
West Yorkshire	644	1,068	2,118	2,534	2,919	2,602	2,879	2,686	–7
Wiltshire	59	101	221	356	121	332	419	446	6
Dyfed-Powys	17	37	99	142	167	135	176	202	15
Gwent	45	98	213	269	191	232	261	314	20
North Wales[2]	12	36	80	248	301	369	337	354	5
South Wales	367	734	1,602	1,528	1,825	1,594	1,656	1,665	1
England & Wales	13,936	23,072	47,829	53,060	54,858	49,340	54,286	57,902	7

Note:
(1) Revised figures for all years shown.
(2) Estimated figure for 1997/8.

Source: Home Office (2006).

police recorded 37,028 racially or religiously aggravated offences in 2004/05. Of this figure, 61 per cent were classified as harassment, 15 per cent criminal damage, 14 per cent less serious wounding and 10 per cent common assault (Home Office 2006). Table 5.2 details the number of religiously and racially aggravated offences recorded by police forces in England and Wales for the period 2003/4 and 2004/5

Any increase or decrease in racist incidents or racially aggravated offences may also reflect a victim's predisposition to report their experiences to the police. Findings from victimization surveys carried out since the 1980s have indicated that BME groups are often unlikely to report their experiences to the police (Brown, 1984; Jones et al., 1986; Harris, 1987; Victim Support, 1991; Aye Maung and Mirrlees-Black, 1994; FitzGerald and Hale, 1996; Clancy et al., 2001; Salisbury and Upson, 2004). Analysis of BCS data has identified under-reporting as resulting from a victims:

- fear of communication due to language difficulties;
- fear of recrimination at the hands of the perpetrator;
- reluctance to having to admit experiencing a racist incident;
- belief that the incident was too trivial to report;
- lack of confidence and/or fear of the police and other statutory agencies;
- belief that the police and other statutory agencies are unresponsive to their needs;
- lack of understanding of the bureaucratic process.

Witnesses may also under report violent racism. The BCS records people's experiences and perceptions of crime including whether a victim perceived it to be racist. The BCS estimates that the total number of **racially motivated incidents** for 2004/05 stood at 179,000 compared with a total of 206,000 incidents reported in 2002/03 (Salisbury and Upson, 2004). However, these figures include incidents directed at white people. Taking only the racially motivated incidents reported by BME groups for 2002/03, the figure stood at 107,000 (Salisbury and Upson, 2004). As a consequence of the adoption of the new Census classifications in the 2001/02 BCS onwards, comparisons prior to this date are limited. Nevertheless, looking further back in time, the number of racially motivated incidents directed at BME groups increased from 130,000 to 143,000 between 1991 and 1995 and then fell to 98,000 in 1999 (Bowling and Phillips, 2002: 112).

▶▶ **Racially motivated incidents**   *the BCS uses the term racially motivated incidents to refer to those incidents reported by victims as involving a racist element. It is often used interchangeably in the BCS literature with racially motivated crime, racially motivated victimization and racially motivated offences (see, for example, Salisbury and Upson, 2004).*

The first two BCSs carried out in 1982 and 1984 (Hough and Mayhew, 1983; 1985) attributed little attention to racially motivated offending, and

Table 5.2 Racially or religiously aggravated offences recorded by police forces by offence type, 2003/4 and 2004/5, with clear-up rates for England and Wales

Police force area	Harassment		Less serious wounding		Criminal damage		Common assault		Total	
	2003/4	2004/5	2003/4	2004/5	2003/4	2004/5	2003/4	2004/5	2003/4	2004/5
Avon & Somerset	868	906	128	192	178	200	82	133	1,256	1,431
Bedfordshire	127	136	42	67	18	37	20	26	207	266
Cambridgeshire	248	234	90	73	17	54	29	37	384	398
Cheshire	273	294	22	25	71	81	34	38	400	438
Cleveland	129	167	23	47	58	51	41	23	251	288
Cumbria	93	142	11	14	7	22	5	8	116	186
Derbyshire	354	297	99	95	126	62	21	20	600	474
Devon & Cornwall	350	399	117	131	44	82	77	82	588	694
Dorset	58	109	51	81	28	28	29	36	166	254
Durham	107	125	14	10	5	9	12	10	138	154
Essex	393	441	134	141	161	158	72	67	760	807
Gloucestershire	122	149	19	32	10	25	16	9	167	215
Greater Manchester	1,608	1,779	467	538	618	674	171	212	2,864	3,203
Hampshire	265	377	43	53	67	77	40	63	415	570
Hertfordshire	424	536	77	101	140	145	89	77	730	859
Humberside	293	366	67	51	49	32	29	39	438	488
Kent	206	274	105	123	93	131	76	81	480	609
Lancashire	714	802	138	139	142	153	91	89	1,085	1,183
Leicestershire	465	636	101	123	133	119	110	102	809	980
Lincolnshire	84	91	41	41	37	24	17	13	179	169
London, City of	40	30	8	6	2	2	10	10	60	48
Merseyside	478	601	101	133	303	257	61	70	943	1,061
Metropolitan Police	5,469	5,720	782	982	1,291	1,080	1,926	1,563	9,468	9,345
Norfolk	170	196	40	37	32	65	26	35	268	333
ANorthamptonshire	210	171	82	70	91	114	30	34	413	389
Northumbria	690	645	107	104	106	81	71	56	974	886
North Yorkshire[1]	12	40	6	11	5	15	5	2	28	68
Nottinghamshire	463	400	53	66	62	57	41	30	619	553
South Yorkshire	124	289	43	50	69	74	23	58	259	471

(Continued)

Table 5.2 (Continued)

Police force area	Harassment		Less serious wounding		Criminal damage		Common assault		Total	
	2003/4	2004/5	2003/4	2004/5	2003/4	2004/5	2003/4	2004/5	2003/4	2004/5
Staffordshire	239	353	146	114	141	124	74	55	600	646
Suffolk	198	174	46	45	24	6	29	19	297	244
Surrey	284	286	71	89	72	85	55	50	482	510
Sussex	266	379	127	89	86	62	73	45	552	575
Thames Valley	647	682	121	159	212	196	124	117	1,104	1,154
Warwickshire	94	143	26	36	41	30	26	13	187	222
West Mercia	456	433	85	79	83	68	50	29	674	609
West Midlands	1,177	1,239	719	645	449	424	134	125	2,479	2,433
West Yorkshire	1,218	1,430	298	304	257	307	101	99	1,874	2,140
Wiltshire	147	138	35	37	36	32	26	13	244	220
Dyfed-Powys	91	123	17	10	11	12	7	9	126	154
Gwent	186	186	25	24	18	17	11	6	240	233
North Wales	144	175	35	72	85	58	14	28	278	333
South Wales	576	530	78	76	103	87	37	42	794	735
England & Wales[1]	20,560	22,623	4,840	5,315	5,581	5,417	4,015	3,673	34,996	37,028
% racially aggravated[2]	11.9	10.4	1.1	1.1	0.5	0.5	1.7	1.7	1.8	1.8
% cleared-up										
Racially-aggravated	37	40	41	39	19	20	29	35	34	36
Non-racially aggravated[3]	58	66	50	49	13	14	38	43	27	30

Note:
(1) Revised figures for 2003/4
(2) Percentage of the overall total of the racially and religiously aggravated offence and the equivalent non-aggravated offence.
(3) Numbers of non-aggravated offences are not shown in this table.

Source: Home Office (2006)

the third in 1986 (Mayhew et al., 1989) attempted only to measure 'ethnic minority risk'. Aye Maung and Mirrlees-Black (1994) and Fitzgerald and Hale (1996) analysed data from the 1988 and 1992 BCSs, Clancy et al. (2001) analysed data from the 1994, 1996 and 2000 BCSs and Salisbury and Upson (2004) analysed data from the 2001/02 and 2002/03 BCSs. Although the findings vary by publication, and comparison cannot be easily made, a number of themes can be identified. These include:

- Risk of racially motivated incidents is higher for people from each of the BME groups than for white people.
- Experiences vary by and within group, by offence category and other factors including age and sex.
- Many incidents are cumulative (form part of a series of related incidents). It is for this reason that Clancy et al. (2001) argue that incidence rates (racist incidents per 10,000 adults) as opposed to prevalence rates (the percentage of all of the people that have experienced at least one racially motivated incident in the reference period) give a better indication of the extent of racially motivated incidents.
- Racially motivated incidents are more commonly personal offences (violence and threats). The majority of racially motivated household offences are incidents of vandalism.
- Although the use of racist language and threat constitute the main form of abuse, serious racially motivated victimization is commonplace.

Box 5.1 provides evidence that over recent years victims are more willing to report racist incidents to the police and that the police are more likely to record them as such.

Box 5.1   Changes in police recording of racist incidents

Changing government strategies directed at tackling racist incidents – such as the Code of Practice introduced in 2000 in response to the Lawrence Inquiry – have led to more consistent police recording of racist incidents across England and Wales (Docking and Tuffin, 2005). Docking and Tuffin draw on evidence from the Crown Prosecution Service (2004) which suggests that the number of incidents identified by the police for CPS attention for the period 1998/99–2003/04 increased, while over the same period the number of additional incidents identified by the CPS remained fairly steady. In addition, Clancy et al. (2001) suggest that the very steep increase in police figures between 1997/98 and 1999/00 (see Table 5.1) is not reflected in the BCS figures for reported incidents. They suggest that the rise in racist incidents recorded by the police reflects a greater willingness among victims to report incidents, and better recording by the police of incidents reported to them.

How are risk and fear of crime connected to the vulnerability of BME groups?

What factors may affect whether BME groups report their experiences to the police and to victimization surveys?

Are the definitions used by the police and the British Crime Survey able to adequately capture the experiences of BME groups?

List the major qualitative methods of social research. Review your list and answer the following question: What research methods, other than the victim survey, might be used to research violent racism?

Political and policy responses

Violent racism was officially acknowledged by central government and the statutory agencies as a problem in need of a strategic and operational response in 1981. Publication of the Home Office report *Racial Attacks* (Home Office, 1981) (see Box 5.2) signalled a formal change in official attitudes on the issue (Bowling, 1993: 233–4). Indeed, for Khan, the 'period between the first Home Office report and the publication of the Stephen Lawrence Inquiry Report saw an increasing official response as well as public recognition of violent racism' (Khan, 2002: 35).

Box 5.2   Home Office (1981) *Racial Attacks*

The study was based upon a survey and analysis of inter-racial incidents defined as 'An incident, or alleged offence by a person or persons of one racial group against a person or persons or property of another racial group, where there is indication of racial motive' (Home Office, 1981: 7) recorded by 13 police forces over a two-month period, and interviews with police representatives, local community organizations and local officials. The report identified Afro Caribbean and Asian persons as being 36 and 50 times more likely respectively to suffer racially motivated attacks than white people. The report concluded, 'the incidence of racial attacks presents a significant problem. The frequency of such attacks, often of an insidious nature, and the depth of feeling and concern which they generate in the ethnic minority communities are a matter of fact and not of opinion' (Home Office, 1981: 35).

Paul Gordon (1990: 168–9) suggests three reasons for the intervention by the Home Office in the 1980s. First, a political belief that violent racism was escalating in size and seriousness. The publication of reports by Bethnal Green and Stepney Trades Council (1978), the Commission for Racial Equality (1979) and the Institute of Race Relations (1979) during the late 1970s gives credence to this view. Second, BME groups across England and Wales were taking action against perpetrators in the shadow of perceived inaction by the criminal justice system. Third, the presentation of a report by the Joint Committee Against Racialism to the Home Secretary in February 1981. The convergence of these factors, for Gordon, meant that 'Violent racism ... was no longer a marginal issue that could be ignored' (1993: 169). The Home Office report placed violent racism 'on the political agenda for the first time' (Home Office, 1989a: Para 1), and paved the way for political and academic responses to it (Bowling, 1993: 8).

The police response

Given the tense and sometimes volatile nature of police–race relations in the early 1980s (see, for example, the Scarman Report 1981), numerous changes were introduced by the police following publication of the Home Office report (see Holdaway, 1996). The Metropolitan Police Service (MPS), for example, introduced recording and monitoring procedures, and identified racist incidents as force priorities and the subject of several MPS Orders. Guiding Principles, including, as noted above, a definition of a racist incident were issued by the Association of Chief Police Officers in 1985. Moreover, the number of police forces recording racist incidents increased from 15 in 1984 to 40 in 1988. By 1990, many police forces had introduced specialist squads whose sole purpose was the policing of violent racism (Holdaway, 1996: 61–2).

However, throughout the 1980s and 1990s, much of the police response remained piecemeal and fragmented – a consequence perhaps of the tensions between the Home Office, chief police officers and central government (see Holdaway 1996: 58–61). Victimization surveys and research studies (Greater London Council, 1984; Gordon, 1990, 1993; Hesse et al., 1992; Saulsbury and Bowling, 1991; and Sampson and Phillips, 1992) carried out during this time reported an inadequate police response to victims of violent racism and BME groups' perceptions that police officers often fail to take their experiences, fears and concerns seriously. A 1987 Home Office study reported that although much of the operational police response across England and Wales was adequate, more could be done (Home Office, 1989a) (see Box 5.3).

Box 5.3 Home Office (1989a) *Racially Motivated Incidents Reported to the Police*

The Home Office replicated the 1981 study in 1987 and suggested that, while the overall figure for recorded racially motivated offences had declined (these obviously may be attributed to reporting levels and recording practices), there was an increase in incidents which 'fall into the broad categories of harassment and nuisance behaviours - incidents that the police and the white population overall do not encounter in their day-to-day lives, and so may not regard them with the same degree of concern as ethnic minority groups' (Home Office 1989a: 2–30).

A decade later, Maynard and Read (1997), in a survey of all police forces for the Home Office, identified a large degree of variation in what was recorded and counted as racially motivated crime. Evidence of the failure of the police response was confirmed when the Stephen Lawrence Inquiry report concluded that 'The investigation was marred by a combination of professional incompetence, institutional racism and a failure of leadership by senior officers' (Macpherson, 1999: 317, Para 46.1).

Other statutory responses, multi-agency working and victim support

Following publication of the Home Office report in 1981, other statutory organizations, including local authority departments, introduced policies to tackle racially motivated offending. Concomitantly, these organizations experienced increasing scrutiny with regards to their operational practices. For example, education and housing departments received damning criticisms from the Commission for Racial Equality (1987, 1989) for their limited policies, poor monitoring arrangements and lack of awareness of the problem. During the 1990s, however, much progress was made by local government. Taking housing as an example, it is now commonplace for housing departments and organizations responsible for the provision of social housing to local authorities to have policies and procedures prohibiting racist and other forms of harassment, with sanctions, including eviction, for repeat perpetrators. The Housing Act 1996 strengthened the power of local authorities to respond to anti-social behaviour often associated with racist harassment and victimization (Rowe, 2004).

During the 1980s and 1990s, police and local government responses were also enhanced by multi-agency working (see Neyroud 1992, 1993). The lever for closer agency working was the inter-departmental Governmental Racial Attacks Group (RAG) established in 1987. The first RAG report (Home Office, 1989b) gave advice on the development of a coordinated response that brought together criminal and social justice agencies and organizations, recommending strategies for each individual agency complemented by multi-agency arrangements. The second RAG report, published in 1991, concluded that 'Further considerable co-ordinated action is required before the reports findings will have been fully implemented nationally' (Home Office 1991: 32). The third RAG report (1996) identified that the practical work which was being done locally had to be supported by a clear appreciation of the problems which those local groups faced in seeking to resolve those issues (Macpherson, 1999).

It was also during this period that crime prevention measures were promoted as having the potential to tackle racist victimization. Sampson and Phillips (1992) provide a good review of the types of measures and initiatives that were introduced at this time, and report their own research findings on the development and implementation of a multiple victimization project on an east London estate. A year earlier Saulsbury and Bowling (1991) (see also Bowling and Saulsbury 1993) reported their findings of an evaluation of a multi-agency approach to violent racism in the east London Borough of Newham. They identified a number of strengths, weaknesses, opportunities and constraints associated with the development of closer working between the police, local government and voluntary sector organizations. They also described and evaluated the implementation and impact of a range of single agency and joint initiatives to tackle racist victimization.

Racial harassment support projects were also introduced to complement these preventative measures. Chahal (2003), offers a useful review and discussion of their development and operation (a detailed discussion of the work of Chahal can be found later in this chapter).

The Stephen Lawrence Inquiry

The murder of Stephen Lawrence and the subsequent publication of the report of the inquiry into his murder and the police investigation (Macpherson 1999) politicized the official response to racist victimization. Stephen Lawrence was murdered on the evening of 22 April 1993 in Eltham, South London, while walking home with his friend Duwayne Brooks. Nearing a bus stop at 10.30 p.m., the two teenagers were approached by a group of five or six white youths, and Stephen was fatally stabbed. He was 18 years of age. Three witnesses were at the bus stop but none were able later to identify any of those involved (Cathcart, 1999).

What followed led to a public inquiry set up in 1997. Stephen Lawrence and Duwayne Brooks were investigated for alleged gang membership. In May 1993, five suspects – Jamie Acourt, Neil Acourt, Gary Dobson, Luke Knight and David Norris – were taken into custody. In July 1993, the Crown Prosecution Service (CPS) dropped charges against two of the suspects and two years later, with little progress made, the Lawrence family brought a private prosecution against the five suspects which was withdrawn when the judge indicated that eye witness evidence would not be admissible. In 1997, an inquest jury, attended by the same five suspects, returned a unanimous verdict that Stephen Lawrence was unlawfully killed in a completely unprovoked racist attack and the police investigation was deemed to be fundamentally flawed.

To date, despite the *Daily Mail* publishing photographs of those suspected of the murder of Stephen Lawrence on 14th February 1997 under the headline 'MURDERERS', with the strap line 'The Mail accuses these men of killing. If we are wrong let them sue us' and a BBC documentary programme in 2006 alleging that one of the police officers involved in the case was in the pay of one of the suspect's families, no one has been convicted for Stephen's murder (see also Chapter 2 in this volume).

Box 5.4 provides a brief overview of the Stephen Lawrence inquiry report and recommendations.

Box 5.4   Macpherson (1999) *The Stephen Lawrence Inquiry. Report of an Inquiry by Sir William Macpherson of Cluny*

The Stephen Lawrence Inquiry was initiated in 1997 by Home Secretary Jack Straw. It was chaired by Sir William Macpherson of Cluny, a high court judge. It first sat in March 1998, took evidence for six months from 88 witnesses and received 148 written submissions. It produced approximately 100,000 pages of evidence. The subsequent report, 340 pages in length states that 'Stephen Lawrence's murder was simply and solely and unequivocally motivated by racism' (Macpherson, 1999: 2 Para. 1.11) and lists 70 recommendations grouped under the following headings:

(Continued)

- Definition of a racist incident
- Reporting and recording of racist incidents and crimes
- Police practice and the investigation of racist crime
- Family liaison
- Victims and witnesses
- Prosecution of racist incidents
- Training
- Employment, discipline and complaints
- Stop and search
- Recruitment and retention
- Prevention and the role of education.

Under the heading 'Openness, accountability and the restoration of confidence', the report calls for the establishment of a ministerial priority to ensure that the police service 'increase trust and confidence in policing amongst ethnic minority communities' (Macpherson, 1999: 327).

It is hard to underestimate the significance of the Stephen Lawrence Inquiry report. It

- confirmed the insidious and horrendous impact violent racism has on BME communities in England and Wales;
- defined racist incidents and recommended the use of this definition across all police, local government and voluntary and community groups and organizations;
- acknowledged the systemic nature of **institutional racism** within the police organization, and by association, criminal justice and other statutory organizations;
- highlighted the inadequate and the incompetent nature of the police response to violent racism and the need for more direct and effective measures to be implemented;
- pointed towards the need for a more informed and strategic government response to violent racism.

▶▶ **Institutional racism** *there have been numerous attempts to define institutional racism (see, for example, Bowling and Phillips, 2002: 40–1). In general terms, institutional racism refers to the way in which organizations operate in racist ways and racist actions inform decision-making, irrespective of the attitudes of individuals and the presence of anti-discriminatory polices. Macpherson defined institutional racism as 'The collective failure of an organization to provide an appropriate and professional service to people because of their colour, culture, or ethnic origin. It can be seen or detected in processes, attitudes and behaviour which amount to discrimination* *through unwitting prejudice, ignorance, thoughtlessness and racist stereotyping which disadvantage minority ethnic people' (1999: 28 Para. 6.34).*

For critical and thought-provoking pieces on the Lawrence Inquiry report, consult *Sociological Review* Online http://www.socresonline.org.uk 4(1) 1999.

The post-Macpherson landscape

In the shadow of the Stephen Lawrence Inquiry, there have been a number of key legislative and policy developments. The 1976 Race Relations Act was amended in 2000 to meet one of the key recommendations from the Lawrence Inquiry report that placed a duty on public authorities to 'actively promote race equality and – to avoid race discrimination before it occurs'. The Act was further amended in 2003, to include discrimination and harassment on the grounds of race or ethnic origins. Other key legislative developments include the Human Rights Act 1998, the Local Government Act 2000, the National Strategy for Neighbourhood Renewal (NSNR) 1998 and the Crime and Disorder Act 1998 (CDA 1998) as amended by the Police Reform Act 2002.

Policy developments have continued to support partnership working. The Crime and Disorder Act 1998 required the police and local authorities to work in partnership with other relevant local agencies and the Lawrence Inquiry highlighted the need for greater cooperation between agencies especially in the gathering and sharing of information:

- All racist incidents should be reported, recorded and investigated.
- Police services should cooperate closely with local agencies and local communities to encourage reporting of racist incidents.
- Local education authorities, schools, housing authorities and other agencies should record racist incidents.

In response, multi-agency working has continued to develop in many local authority areas. In 2000, the Home Office produced a Code of Practice which sought to establish effective and consistent procedures on reporting and recording racist incidents. The Code aimed to build community trust and confidence in the police and other agencies, to increase victim satisfaction with the handling of racist incidents, and to aid in their prevention. The findings of research carried out by Maria Docking and Rachel Tuffin (Home Office, 2005) on the Code of Practice are detailed in Box 5.5.

Box 5.5 The Code of Practice on Reporting and Recording Racist Incidents

Research carried out by Maria Docking and Rachel Tuffin (Home Office 2005) identified that:

- Although the code had impacted on reporting and recording procedures, improvements could be made particularly in relation to the recording of less serious incidents.
- Under-reporting by victims continues and their satisfaction as to the police response was contingent upon individual officers and did not suggest a consistent approach.
- Multi-agency working had increased.
- More work is required to understand perpetrators' views in order to help understand the problem and aid its prevention.

In a major study of the impact of the Lawrence Inquiry on the police in England and Wales, led by Janet Foster, Tim Newburn and Ann Souhami and published in 2005, it is reported that substantial improvements have been made in relation to the recording, monitoring and response to violent racism; the organization, structure and management of murder investigations; liaison with families of victims of murder; consultation with local communities and the general excision of racist language from the police service. However, they also report that there remain important caveats to these findings. For Foster et al. there remains inconsistency across police force areas; for example, forces tend to focus attention on those changes that were most obviously identifiable and achievable, and certain groups continue to receive an inappropriate or inadequate service because of their culture or ethnic origin (Home Office, 2005: ix).

QUESTIONS

How effective are the police in responding to racist incidents and the needs of victims of violent racism?

To what extent has the Stephen Lawrence Inquiry report had a transformative effect on the philosophy and operation of the police and criminal justice system?

What are the advantages and disadvantages of the police, criminal justice agencies, local authorities and voluntary and charitable organizations working together in partnership to tackle violent racism?

For a good review of the types of action taken to tackle violent racism, consult Lemos, G. (2000) *Racial Harassment: Action on the Ground*. Plymouth: Lemos and Crane.

Violent racism as a social process

Since 1981 political and policy response to violent racism have tended to be reactive, 'one-off' and police and local authority led rather than community based, preventative and fully responsive to the needs and lived experiences of BME communities (Chahal 2003; see also Lemos 2000 and Bowling, 1999).

In order to shed light on why this is the case it is necessary to revisit and review two of the most significant documents of the last 30 years, namely the Home Office Racial Attacks report of 1981 and the Macpherson report of 1999. Both reports say very little about the historical processes and contemporary realities that have shaped relations between the white population, the police and BME communities; offer little detailed discussion of the meanings and motives that underpin much violent racism; present little evidence as to the cumulative nature of much racist violence and harassment; and provide little evidence of 'what works' in tackling violent racism and supporting victims. Simply put, they do not adequately explain why violent racism occurs and thus do not identify the most appropriate and effective mechanisms for tackling it.

The situated nature of violent racism

The Home Office report and the Macpherson report present violent racism as no more than inter-racial conflict between one or more people. Both fail to situate the nature of racism within historic and contemporary social, political, economic and cultural processes and do not acknowledge the uneven power relations that exist between groups based upon 'race', ethnicity, and so on. Writing about the definition used in the 1981 Home Office Report, for example, Paul Gordon (1993: 170) argues that 'in no meaningful sense can such incidents be regarded as racist ... not if by racism we understand hostility towards people because of their skin colour, or ethnic or national origins in the context of a system of unequal power relations'. Similarly, Kusminder Chahal (1999) argues that the Lawrence Inquiry definition of a racist incident fails to locate the racist motivation behind the behaviour:

The Macpherson definition is 'business as usual' in its misunderstanding of what racist harassment is and why racist incidents occur, and a definition which cannot adequately locate the motivation behind a racist incident is of little practical use to clarifying meaning. The paradox is that the Macpherson Report openly discusses 'racism', and 'institutional racism', particularly with regard to it disadvantaging minority ethnic people, and yet locating racism as a motivation for suffering a racist incident and its prime target being black and minority ethnic people is generally ignored by the Inquiry Report. In attempting to clarify what institutional racism is, the Inquiry should have also attempted to clarify what a 'racist incident' is, who it is aimed at and why. (Chahal, 1999: Para. 1.6)

Research broadly suggests that violent racism is related to wider and deeply embedded racist ideologies (Solomos, 1999; Hewitt, 2006). Gordon argues that perpetrators of violent racism are acting out a particular form of white identity and recognizes the causal links between the racist actions of individual perpetrators and institutionalized racist practices of the state. Violent racism for Gordon should be seen as a crime against communities rather than the individual *per se*. Individuals, buildings, properties and institutions may all be attacked because they are perceived to represent or symbolize 'foreign or strange' communities or their interests (Witte, 1996).

The cumulative nature of violent racism

A further set of problems of the Home Office report and the Macpherson report arise from their failure to acknowledge the role violent racism plays in the everyday lives of many BME groups. In defining violent racism as 'incidents' both reports, and much of the political and policy responses that have arisen from them have failed to prioritize the cumulative nature of racist victimization. Bowling argues that violent racism cannot be reduced to 'incidents' as they do not occur 'in a moment' but are an 'on-going dynamic embedded in time, space and place' (Bowling, 1999: 285). They involve 'a number of social events, each of which is inextricably bound up with the other(s)' (Maclean, 1986: 4–5). As such, Bowling has contended that violent racism is a cumulative **social process** which the police and other criminal justice agencies respond to by dealing with 'it' as discrete incidents.

▶▶ **Social process** *the use of the term social process presents violent racism not as static, fixed and discrete, but as an ongoing, dynamic, and fluid set of interconnecting* *events. For Maclean (1986: 8), 'It is impossible for us to understand crime or any other process by looking at an individual event or moments'.*

Indeed, Bowling insists that this tension explains why victims of violent racism feel unprotected and continue to voice dissatisfaction with the police response, despite apparent improvements in policy and practice over recent years; 'policies have tended to emphasise reactive police and local authority responses rather than community-based preventative measures' (Bowling, 1993: 243). Where community based preventative measures have been developed, Chahal (2003) reports that:

- They exist unevenly across the country and have been set up in response to local needs (political, organizational, community).
- The nature of the work delivered by them is broad ranging from outreach work with schools and young people to training and challenging racism.
- Case work is delivered to victims of violent racism and can have a positive impact upon a victim's life.
- The support sector could be strengthened by adequate funding streams, through mechanisms of support for caseworkers and by developing community based solutions to providing support and assistance.

Researching violent racism

The failure of many political and policy responses to violent racism is also a consequence of the primacy placed upon the victimization survey. While not denying its ability to capture some parts of the process of victimization, survey research has difficulty in capturing repeat victimization, is descriptive rather than dynamic, and only focuses upon the victim in the crime process. For Bowling (1993: 241–4), surveys have indicated little about alternative responses to victimization, such as self-defence and retaliation – they focus on the process after reports have been made to an agency, and most surveys are never presented within their social, geographical and historical context – creating descriptions of victimization and its patterning divorced from wider social processes. The BCS, for example, is unable to qualify the unequal power relations between BME groups and the white majority population. For Bowling, a more holistic approach to researching violent racism is required. When such an approach has been used, it has contributed to an in-depth understanding of the lived experience and unequal patterning of racist victimization; of the impact violent racism has on families and communities;

of high rates of multiple and repeat victimization, suggesting that racist crimes are not random one-off incidents; of the impact of community-based responses to violent racism; and of the failure of many statutory-based responses (Hesse et al., 1992; Hewitt, 2006). Box 5.6 provides a discussion of the findings of qualitative research carried out by Chahal and Julienne (1999).

Box 5.6   Research by Chahal and Julienne

Chahal and Julienne (1999) carried out research on the experiences of 74 people in Belfast, Cardiff, Glasgow and London using focus groups and in-depth interviews and identified that:

- Racism is routine. It is part of everyday experience in a variety of social situations, not just in and around the home, but in shops, in the street and at school. Violent racism can include a wide range of actions, experiences and behaviours, including racist abuse, harassment, insulting behaviour and violence. The home was a prominent target for attacks. Some respondents had experienced unprovoked assault and threats.
- Violent racism is a social process. It has a profound effect beyond the actual event or incident. Family relations between spouses can be affected, the health and well-being of individuals are compromised, and there is a sense of social isolation because relatives and friends are less likely to visit because of the threat and fear of racist harassment and families seldom venture out at night. A harrowing common experience for those with children was the fear and experience of racism when the children were travelling to and from school, at school or playing outside. Racist victimization did not create victims but strategists who acted on the basis of creating normality within an oppressive environment.
- The experience of racist victimization does not fit with the policies and procedures that are in existence to tackle it and offer support. Racist motivation is often questioned or not taken seriously by reporting agencies. Such agencies gave limited information on which victims could approach them for help and guidance. Many respondents did not report their experiences to an agency with a professional obligation to investigate the complaint.
- There was limited feedback and no support infrastructure to help those making complaints of racist victimization. Support is often sought from within the family experiencing the victimization.

Racist offenders and perpetrators

In order to develop our understanding of violent racism, this chapter will take a closer look at three studies that examine the motives and motivations of racist offenders and or perpetrators. These studies are by Sibbitt (1997), Webster (2001) and Ray and Smith (2001, 2004) and Ray et al. (2003, 2004).

The essentially qualitative and descriptive research carried out by Sibbitt (1997) in two London boroughs suggests that racism and violent racism may provide perpetrators with a sense of identity which they otherwise feel to be absent. She argues that 'communities, with their own entrenched problems of socio-economic deprivation and crime, appear to "spawn" violent perpetrators' through a mutually supportive relationship between the individual perpetrator and the wider community' (1997: 101). Sibbitt uses Allport's (1954) theory of scapegoating to explain that the racist attitudes held by some members of the perpetrator community serve a particular function by providing an external focus for their personal dissatisfaction, frustration and alienation. This may help ameliorate the perception of being a victim of contemporary British society whereby white people are treated as second-class citizens and black people receive preferential treatment. Given that perpetrators may regard themselves as acting out the collective racist views of a community, responsibility for violent racism extends beyond the individual to the wider community. Sibbitt constructs a typology of perpetrators ordered by age.

- *The pensioners* have lived in an area a long time; have witnessed a worsening of conditions and financial and physical insecurity; and view black people as suitable scapegoats for all their problems. They see their views reinforced by politicians and central government which maintains immigration controls. While friendly with immediate black neighbours whom they see as 'different' from most black people, they are racist to those they don't know.
- *The people next door* are adults who latch on to their parents' racialization of problems (e.g. unemployment, housing shortages, crime, and financial insecurity). They have little respect for the local authorities which they see as remote institutions failing to provide necessary resources, and biased in the allocation of resources towards ethnic minorities. The people next door may engage in racism, especially against those they deem obtain unfair advantage, e.g. larger accommodation.
- *The problem family* experiences poor physical or mental health and sees the authorities as persecuting them. Parents behave abusively towards their children and the children behave abusively towards others. Like their parents, they are low achievers educationally. The family tends to act as a unit, encouraging and reinforcing each other's behaviour, and engages in many forms of anti-social behaviour. In areas where

racism among local white people is the norm, the family may be virulently racist towards ethnic minority neighbours.

- *15–18-year-olds* have grown up with parents and grandparents with racist views in an area where such attitudes are generally prevalent. In school, they may have had black friends – some close – who they did not see as black. Out of school, they will have hung around with older youths who were particularly racist, and will have engaged in anti-social behaviour, racial harassment or violence carried out by these older youths, seeing it as 'fun', and as accepted by the older youths.
- *11–14-year-olds* have also grown up in an area where racist views are prevalent and regularly expressed. They receive little educational input from their parents who are also likely to have been low achievers. They have low self-esteem and bully children they perceive as weaker than themselves, in order to gain prestige among their peers whom they are unable to impress in other ways. Where the other child is of ethnic minority origin, the bullying will include racist abuse.
- *4–10-year-olds* see racism as part of the language that they have grown up with. Their grandparents, parents, relatives, elder siblings and friends' families hold, and regularly express racist views. An integral part of the young boys' or girls' language is the notion that people who are not white 'do not belong here' and should 'go back to their own country'. They perceive it as normal to hold such views and to voice them to others without fear of contradiction.

Colin Webster (2001; see also 2007) argues that violent racism is embedded in social relationships and the drawing of boundaries around real or imagined 'colour-coded' areas. Such areas, based on racialized territories, define for each ethnic group – minority and majority – the formation of racial and ethnic identity. In studying adolescent perpetrators of racist harassment and violence, Webster suggests that it is possible to delineate three levels of violent racists:

- *Normal racists* were individuals least involved in violent racism. Racism was not directed at those ethnic minority individuals the group knew personally. The group differentiated normal and routine abuse, fighting and violent racism.
- *Aggressive racists* were young men aged between 14–15 years who had been involved in violent racism during their time in school. After leaving school attitudes continued to be hostile while they appeared to be less overtly violent in their behaviour.
- *Violent racists* were aged 12–13, apart from a couple of older boys, and the majority were from a socially disadvantaged and feared housing estate, with a disproportionate number of the group likely to have experienced acute family pressures, conflicts and loss. Their aggressive racism was palpable, shown whenever the group were in proximity to Asians or Asian areas.

Webster identifies a number of analytical themes which, he argues, can help explain different individual and group expressions of racism and violent racism. These include:

- *The continuum of criminality, violence and violent racism.* Although the three groups displayed different levels and intensities of racial violence, it was found that likely predictions of criminal careers and the likelihood of persistent violent racism were influenced by the same factors.
- *The continuum of normal, aggressive and violent racists.* It is important to recognize that the three groups did not form three strict categories of racist behaviours. Instead, the different groups overlapped and were interdependent because the existence and acceptance of a large youth population of 'normal' racists gave legitimacy to a group of hard-core violent racists.
- *The influence of locality.* Tending to be the territory of aggressive racists, this theme refers to specific regions in the community becoming territorial due to conflict and violence between ethnic groups.
- *Processes of inclusion and exclusion.* These processes relate to the often competitive relationship between poor white communities with poor Pakistani/ Bangladeshi communities in the distribution of resources, housing and political influence.
- *Family.* This theme draws attention to the influence of personal loss and family breakdown experienced by a number of young people, which may exert a negative influence upon their behaviour. Another important finding from Webster's study is that both Asian and White young people shared aspirations to marry, settle down and have children themselves.
- *Work and the economy.* Demographic issues of joblessness in northern mill towns have a strong potential to impact upon young people's perception and identity of community.
- *Fear of crime and violent racism.* Asian and White young people were found to have 'more fears in common than they believed but spoke about these fears through the prism and at the boundary of racial and ethnic difference'.

Drawing upon work by Scheff and Retzinger as a basis for understanding the views and motivations of racist offenders, Ray and Smith (2001, 2004) and Ray et al. (2003, 2004) argue that violent racism can be understood in terms of unacknowledged shame and its transformation into fury. They interviewed 36 offenders (and accessed 28 case files) (30 had committed previous violent offences with a racist element) who were predominantly male, of whom half were unemployed, two-thirds had left school with no educational qualifications, and two-thirds had other convictions. Many reported disrupted and unhappy family backgrounds. In the research sample, all offenders: knew their victims, though not that well; were very rarely specialists in violent racism; and tended to live in outlying parts of Greater Manchester, on poor, virtually all-white and environmentally run-down estates, with high levels of unemployment, poor transport links and few material or cultural resources. Contact with ethnic minority groups was mostly commercial – in shops, taxis, and garages, which were mostly owned and run by south Asians.

Most, but not all of the sample of offenders interviewed, disavowed racist views and attitudes, showing an awareness that they were widely regarded as unacceptable. Many spoke openly about their use of violence, for some a routine strategy of domination or survival, yet few spoke about the racist motivation and showed very little interest in the activities of such racist organizations as the British National Party and the National Front. While the offenders did not deny using violent racism, they sought to justify it by some perceived provocation and many offenders showed powerlessness and a sense of exclusion.

Ray and Smith (2004) argue that the nature of violent racism needs to be understood in terms of emotion rather than as rational cognitive processes, and that the key emotion is shame. Interviews with offenders revealed a sense of grievance, victimization, unfairness and powerless when comparing their situation with that of neighbouring Asians. The authors identify that the victims of these offenders were mostly Asians and that the offenders were predominantly living in nearly all-white estates and were more likely to encounter Asians than other black and minority ethnic groups.

QUESTIONS

How and in what ways do macro-economic and social policies and micro-lived realities interplay and impact on the experiences of BME groups in England and Wales?

What factors combine to create the conditions within which particular white individuals carry out violent racism in England and Wales?

How would you tackle violent racism?

Summary

Three inter-related themes run through the chapter. The first relates to the problem of under-reporting and under-recording of racist and non racist incidents. What is recorded by the police and BCS is the tip of an iceberg and does not easily capture iterative, multiple and secondary forms of racist victimization. Second, it is suggested that the political and policy response to racist victimization has failed to fully meet the needs of BME communities. It is the failure to situate, conceptualize and understand violent racism as a social process that lies behind much of the inadequacies of the political and policy response. Third, it is acknowledged that over recent years criminologists have attempted to examine the motives and motivations of offenders and perpetrators of violent racism.

ANNOTATED BIBLIOGRAPHY

Bowling, B. (1999) *Violent Racism: Victimisation, Policing and Social Context.* **Oxford: Clarendon Press.** Drawing upon a case study in east London in the late 1980s and early 1990s, and a critical review of political, policy and academic documentation and literature, this book documents the very nature of violent racism within local and global contexts, and highlights the very real deficiencies in the police and policy response.

Cathcart, B. (1999) *The Case of Stephen Lawrence.* **Harmondsworth: Viking.** Written by esteemed journalist Brian Cathcart, this book provides a wonderfully honest and frank account of the circumstance surrounding the murder of Stephen Lawrence and the police response.

Gordon, P. (1990) *Racial Violence and Harassment.* **2nd edition. London: Runneymede Trust.** Although dated, the central organizing theme of this book is as relevant today as it was when it was published – that violent racism must be understood within the wider context of socio-economic and political change.

Ray, I. Smith. D. and Wastell, L. (2004) 'Shame, rage and violent racism', *British Journal of Criminology 44(3): 350–68.* There is a developing interest in the motives and motivations of racist perpetrators and offenders. Ray et al. have produced some of the most thoughtful analyses of violent racism, and this article, published in the *British Journal of Criminology*, offers possibly the most accessible introduction to their work.

Note

1 Home Office (2006) define statistically significant as an observed difference between variables that is unlikely to have occurred by chance.

References

Allport, A. (1954) *The Nature of Prejudice*. Cambridge, MA: Addison-Wesley.

Aye Maung, N. and Mirrlees-Black, C. (1994) *Racially Motivated Crime: A British Crime Survey Analysis*, Home Office Research and Planning Unit Paper 82. London: Home Office.

Bhavnani, R., Mirza, H.S. and Meetoo, V. (2005) *Tackling the Roots of Racism: Lessons for Success*. Bristol: The Policy Press.

Bethnal Green and Stepney Trades Council (1978) *Blood on the Streets*. London: Bethnal and Stepney Trades Council.

Bowling, B. (1993) 'Racial harassment and the process of victimisation: conceptual and methodological implications for the local crime survey', *British Journal of Criminology*, 33(1): 231–50.

Bowling, B. (1999) *Violent Racism: Victimization, Policing and Social Context*. Oxford: Clarendon Press.

Bowling, B. and Phillips, C. (2002) *Racism, Crime and Justice*. London: Home Office.

Bowling, B. and Saulsbury, W. (1993) 'The North Plaistow Project: a multi-agency approach to racial harassment', in P. Francis and R. Matthews (eds), *Tackling Racial Attacks*. Leicester: Centre for the Study of Public Order.

Brooks, D. and Hattenstone, S. (2003) *Steve and Me*. London: Abacus.

Brown, C. (1984) *Black and White Britain: The Third PSI Survey*. London: Heinemann.

Burney, E. and Rose, G. (2002) *Racist Offences – How Is the Law Working? The Implementation of the Legislation on Racially Aggravated Offences in the Crime and Disorder Act 1998*, Home Office Research Study 244. London: Home Office.

Cantle, T. (2001) *Community Cohesion: A Report of the Independent Review Team*. London: Home Office.

Cathcart, B. (1999) *The Case of Stephen Lawrence*. Harmondsworth: Viking.

Chahal, K. (1999) 'The Stephen Lawrence Inquiry report, racist harassment and racist incidents: changing definitions, clarifying meaning?' *Sociological Review* Online 4(1). Available at: www.socresonline.org.uk/soresonline/4/lawrence/chahal.html: accessed 23 September 2006.

Chahal, K. (2003) *Racist Harassment Support Projects: Their Role, Impact and Potential*. York: Joseph Rowntree Foundation.

Chahal, K. and Julienne, L. (1999) *We Can't All Be White: Racist Victimization in the UK*. York: Joseph Rowntree Foundation.

Clancy, A., Hough, M., Aust, R. and Kershaw, C. (2001) *Crime, Policing and Justice: The Experience of Ethnic Minorities. Findings from the 2000 British Crime Survey*, Home Office Research Study 223. London: Home Office.

Commission for Racial Equality (1979) *Brick Lane and Beyond: An Inquiry into Racial Strife and Violence in Tower Hamlets*. London: Commission for Racial Equality.

Commission for Racial Equality (1987) *Living in Terror*. London: Commission for Racial Equality.

Commission for Racial Equality (1988) *Learning in Terror: A Survey in Eight Areas of Britain.* London: Commission for Racial Equality.

Commission for Racial Equality (1989) *Race Relations Code of Practice for the Elimination of Racial Discrimination and the Promotion of Equal Opportunity in the Field of Rented Housing.* London: Commission for Racial Equality.

Connolly, P. and Keenan, M. (2002) 'Racist harassment in the white hinterlands: minority children and parents experiences of schooling in Northern Ireland', *British Journal of Sociology of Education,* 33(2): 341–35.

Davies, P., Francis, P. and Jupp, V. (eds) (2003) *Victimisation: Theory, Research and Policy.* Basingstoke: Palgrave.

Docking, M. and Tuffin, R. (2005) *Racist Incidents: Progress Since the Lawrence Inquiry,* Home Office Online Report 42/05. London: Home Office.

FitzGerald, M. and Hale, C. (1996) *Ethnic Minorities, Victimisation and Racial Harassment: Findings from the 1988 and 1992 British Crime Surveys.* Home Office Research Study 154. London: Home Office.

Foster, J., Newburn, T. and Souhami, A. (2005) *Assessing the Impact of the Stephen Lawrence Inquiry,* Home Office Research Study 294. London: Home Office.

Fryer, P. (1984) *Staying Power: The History of Black People in Britain.* London: Pluto Press.

Garland, J., Spaler, B. and Chakraborti, N. (2006) 'Hearing lost voices: issues in research-ing "hidden" minority ethnic communities', *British Journal of Criminology,* 46(3): 423–37.

Gordon, P. (1990) *Racial Violence and Harassment,* 2nd edition. London: Runnymede Trust.

Gordon, P. (1993) 'The police and violent racism in Britain', in T. Bjorgo and R. Witte (eds), *Violent Racism in Europe.* London: Macmillan.

Harris, J. (1987) *Report of a Survey of Crime and Racial Harassment.* London: London Borough of Newham.

Hesse, B., Rai, D.K., Bennet, C. and McGilchrist, P. (1992) *Beneath the Surface: Racial Harassment.* London: Avebury.

Hewitt, R. (1986) *White Talk Black Talk: Inter-racial Friendship and Communication Among Adolescents.* Cambridge: Cambridge University Press.

Holdaway, S. (1996) *The Racialization of British Policing.* London: Macmillan.

Home Office (1981) *Racial Attacks.* London: HMSO.

Home Office (1989a) *Racially Motivated Incidents Reported to the Police,* Research and Planning Unit Paper 54. London: Home Office.

Home Office (1989b) *The Response to Racial Harassment and Attacks: Guidance for the Statutory Agencies,* Report of the Inter-Departmental Racial Attacks Group. London: HMSO.

Home Office (1991) *The Response to Racial Attacks and Harassment: Sustaining the Momentum,* Second Report of the Inter-Departmental Racial Attacks Group. London: HMSO.

Home Office (1996) *Taking Steps: Multi-Agency Responses to Racial Attacks and Harassment,* Third Report of the Inter-Departmental Racial Attacks. Group. London: HMSO.

Home Office (1998) *The Crime and Disorder Act: Guidance on Statutory Crime and Disorder Partnerships*. London: Home Office Communications Directorate.

Home Office (2005) *Race and the Criminal Justice System: An Overview to the Complete Statistics 2003–2004*. London: Home Office.

Home Office (2006) *Statistics on Race and the Criminal Justice System – 2005: A Home Office Publication Under Section 95 of the Criminal Justice Act 1991*. London: Home Office.

Hough, M. and Mayhew, P. (1983) *The British Crime Survey First Report*, Home Office Research Study 76. London: HMSO.

Hough, M. and Mayhew, P. (1985) *Taking Account of Crime: Key Findings from the 1984 British Crime Survey*, Home Office Research Study No. 85. London: HMSO.

Institute of Race Relations (1979) *Evidence to the Royal Commission*. London: Institute of Race Relations.

Jansson, K. (2006) *Black and Minority Ethnic Groups' Experiences and Perceptions of Crime. Racially Motivated Crime and the Police: Findings from the 2004/05 British Crime Survey*. Home Office Online Report 25/06 London: Home Office.

Jones, T., Maclean, B. and Young, J. (1986) *The Islington Crime Survey: Crime Victimisation and Policing in Inner London*. Aldershot: Gower.

Khan, O. (2002) *Perpetrators of Violent Racism and Harassment*. London: Runnymede Trust.

Kinsey, R., Lea, J. and Young, J. (1986) *Losing the Fight Against Crime*. London: Basil Blackwell.

Klug, F. (1982) *Racist Attacks*. London: Runneymede Trust.

Kundnani, A. (2001) 'From Oldham to Bradford: the violence of the violated', available at: www.irr.org.uk, accessed 23 September 2006.

Lemos, G. (2000) *Racial Harassment: Action on the Ground*. Plymonth: Lemos and Crane.

Maclean, B. (1986) 'Critical criminology and some limitations of traditional inquiry', in B.D. Maclean (ed.), *The Political Economy of Crime: Readings for a Critical Criminology*. Scarborough, Ontario: Prentice Hall.

Maclean, B. (1991) 'In partial defence of socialist realism: some theoretical and methodological concerns of the local crime survey', *Crime, Law and Social Change*, 15: 213–54.

Macpherson, W. (1999) *The Stephen Lawrence Inquiry*. London: The Stationery Office.

Maguire, M. (2002) 'Crime statistics patterns and trends: changing perceptions and their implications', in M. Maguire, R. Morgan and R. Reiner (eds), *The Oxford Handbook of Criminology*. 3rd edition Oxford: Oxford University Press.

Marlow, A. and Loveday, B. (2000) *Policing After Macpherson*. Lyme Regis: Russell House.

Mayhew, P., Maung, N.A. and Mirrlees-Black, C. (1989) *The 1986 British Crime Survey*, a Home Office Research and Planning Unit Report. London: HMSO.

Mayhew, P., Maung, N.A. and Mirrlees-Black, C. (1993) *The 1992 British Crime Survey*, a Home Office Research and Planning Unit Report. London: HMSO.

Maynard, W. and Read, T. (1997) *Policing Racially Motivated Incidents*, Home Office Crime Detection and Prevention Series paper 84. London: Home Office.

Neyroud, P. (1992) 'Multi-agency approaches to racial harassment: the lessons of implementing the RAG Report', *New Community*, 18(4): 567–78.

Neyroud, P. (1993) 'Multi-agency approaches to racial harassment: The lessons of implementing RAG', in P. Francis and R. Matthews (eds) *Tackling Racial Attacks*. Leicester: Centre for the Study of Public Order, University of Leicester.

Panayi, P. (ed.) (1993) *Racial Violence in Britain: 1984–1950*. Leicester and London: Leicester University Press.

Pearson, G. (1976) 'Paki-Bashing in a north eastern Lancashire cotton town: a case study and its history, in J. Mungham and G. Pearson (eds), *Working Class Youth Culture*. London: Routledge.

Ray, L. and Smith, D. (2001) 'Racist offenders and the politics of "hate crime"', *Law and Critique*, 12: 203–21.

Ray, L. and Smith, D. (2004) 'Racist offending, policing and community conflict', *Sociology*, 38(4): 681–99.

Ray, L. Smith, D. and Wastell, L. (2003) 'Understanding violent racism', in B. Stanko, (ed.), *The Meanings of Violence*. London: Routledge.

Ray, R. Smith, D. and Wastell, L. (2004) 'Shame, rage and violent racism', *British Journal of Criminology*, 44(3): 350–68.

Rowe, M. (2004) *Policing, Race and Racism*. Cullumpton: Willan.

Salisbury, H. and Upson, A, (2004) *Ethnicity, Victimisation and Worry about Crime: Findings from the 2001/02 and 2002/03 British Crime Survey Findings 237*. London: Home Office.

Sampson, A. and Phillips, C. (1992) *Multiple Victimisation: Racial Attacks on an East London Estate*, Crime Prevention Unit No 36. London: HMSO.

Saulsbury, W. and Bowling, B. (1991) *The Multi-Agency Approach in Practice*: *The North Plaistow Racial Harassment Project*, Research and Planning Unit Paper 64. London: Home Office.

Scarman, L. (1981) *The Scarman Report*. London: Home Office.

Sibbitt, R. (1997) *The Perpetrators of Racial Harassment and Racial Violence*, Home Office Research Study 176. London: Home Office.

Solomos, J. (1999) 'Social research and the Stephen Lawrence Inquiry', *Sociological Review* Online, 4(1): available at: www.socresonline.org.uk/ soresonline/4/lawrence/ solomos.html accessed 23 September 2006.

Thompson, K. (1988) *Under Siege: Racial Violence in Britain Today*. Harmondsworth: Penguin.

Victim Support (1991) *Racial Attacks in Camden, Southward and Newham*. London: Victim Support.

Walker, A., Kershaw, C. and Nichols, S. (2006) *Crime in England and Wales 2005/06*, Home Office Statistical Bulletin. London: Home Office.

Webster, C. (2001) 'Qualitative career research on perpetrators of violent racism', Paper Presented to the ESRC Violence Seminar, University of Lancaster.

Webster, C. (2007) *Understanding Race and Crime*. Buckinghamshire: Open University Press.

Witte, R. (1996) *Violent Racism and the State*. Harlow: Longman.

Yarrow, S. (2005) *The Experiences of Young Black Men as Victims of Crime*, Criminal Justice System Race Unit and Victims and Confidence Unit. London: Criminal Justice System.

Young, J. (2007) *The Vertigo of Late Modernity*, London: Sage.

Zedner, L. (2002) 'Victims', in M. Maguire, R. Morgan, and R. Reiner, (eds), *The Oxford Handbook of Criminology*, 3rd edition. Oxford: Oxford University Press.

Men, Victims and Crime

Sandra Walklate

Chapter aims

- To problematize the victim and crime victimization.
- To examine the relationship between men and criminal victimization.
- To assess the extent to which work of radical feminism and masculinities theories have contributed to an understanding of men and victimization.

Introduction

In 1959, Barbara Wootton made the observation that 'if men behaved like women, the courts would be idle and the prisons empty' (Wootton, 1959: 32). Some 30 years later Cain commented that 'the criminological gaze cannot see gender, the criminological discourse cannot speak men and women' (Cain, 1989: 4). Both of these writers in their different ways were drawing attention to the maleness of crime and crime-related activity, as well as the inability of criminology to see and take account of this. Indeed, as Braithwaite (1989) was to observe, the maleness of crime is one of the 'facts' that any theory of crime should fit. If all these commentators are correct in their analysis, then how, if at all, has criminology (or victimology) responded to these observations?

The aim of this chapter is to examine men and their relationship with criminal victimization. First, it will briefly consider the nature of victimology, that is the study of victimization, as a sub-discipline of criminology, and examine how the knowledge that this study generates structures who might be considered to be a victim of crime and who might not. This section will also consider the extent to which the work of **radical feminism** has contributed to these considerations. Second, it will offer a review of recent developments within masculinity studies and examine their relevance to understanding criminal victimization. This section will be particularly concerned to examine the question of whether or not men can be victims. Third, three studies of male victimization will be examined as a way of demonstrating the different directions that a consideration of particular forms of male victimization might take. Finally, by way of conclusion, this chapter will consider what questions remain to be answered in the light of this review of the relationship between men, victimization and crime. However, before we can address these questions, it is important to consider what the term 'victim' means.

▶▶ **Radical feminism** *is a systematic analysis of the nature of women's oppression. It seeks to understand, respond to, campaign against and end male dominance and control of women and children, focusing, in particular, upon sexual violence (Radford, 2001). For further explanation and illustration of radical feminism, see Chapter 7 in this volume.*

What does the term 'victim' mean?

For many people working with victims of crime either as a practitioner or as an academic, the term 'victim' is highly problematic. It is particularly problematic for those working within the feminist movement. So, what are these problems?

When the word 'victim' is gendered, as in French for example, being la victime, it is denoted as female. If the genealogy of the word 'victim' is examined, it is connected to processes of sacrifice in which again the victim was more often than not female. The links between the word victim and being female implies that the passivity and powerlessness associated with being a victim are also associated with being female. It is this link that is problematic for those working within the feminist movement who prefer to use the term 'survivor' to try to capture women's resistance to victimization. At the same time the tension between being a victim or being a survivor is also problematic for others interested in criminal victimization since this either/or distinction fails to capture the *processes* of victimization. In other words, it is possible that an individual at different points in time in relation to different events could be an active victim, a passive victim, an active survivor, a passive survivor, or at a point on a whole range of experiences in between. The label 'victim', as a consequence, seems quite sterile when considered in this way.

There is, however, another problem associated with the word 'victim' that is derived from appreciating the process whereby an individual becomes identified as a victim. This problem is connected with what Nils Christie (1986), a Norwegian criminologist, called the 'ideal victim'. In other words, there are certain assumptions attached to the label 'victim' that means not everyone actually acquires the label of victim. For Christie, the 'ideal victim' is the Little Red Riding Hood fairy story victim: a young, innocent female out doing good deeds who is attacked by an unknown stranger. Indeed, this 'ideal victim' fits all the common-sense stereotypes of the 'legitimate' victim of rape. In other words, some people are 'deserving' victims, that is, they acquire the label of victim very readily and easily, and other people are 'undeserving' victims and may never acquire the label of victim at all. This distinction between deserving and undeserving victims and how it impacts upon people's experiences of the criminal justice process is one of the issues that has preoccupied criminologists interested in the victim of crime.

Awareness of this problem has led Carrabine and others (2004: 117) to talk of a 'hierarchy of victimization'. This hierarchy is most readily visible in media constructions of criminal victimization, and especially graphic in the coverage often given to the elderly female as the victim of violent crime (see Chapter 2 in this volume). Such coverage persists despite the consistent evidence that the group of people most likely to be the victim of violent crime are young males who go out drinking two or three times a week.

This observation sensitizes us to the third problem intrinsically associated with the term victim. It is highly gendered. Understanding the gendered nature of this concept and how it has become so gendered is the central concern of this chapter. In order to develop this understanding it will be of value to reflect upon the way in which both victimology, as a sub-discipline of criminology, and in its own way (radical) feminism, have contributed to ways of thinking about who might legitimately claim the label victim, that have fuelled taken for granted (and gendered) assumptions about criminal victimization.

Domain assumptions and the victim of crime: victimology

The term 'domain' is intended to draw attention to the deeply embedded assumptions that ways of thinking reflect in what they establish as being problematic or not. In order to unpick what such assumptions look like, it is necessary to reflect upon the origins of their concerns. The origins of victimology are usually located in the work of Von Hentig and Mendelsohn. They were two émigré lawyers-cum-criminologists who worked in the United States in the late 1940s. In common with many other like-minded intellectuals of the late 1940s and the 1950s who found themselves in the United States as a consequence of the Second World War, they were perplexed by the events that had happened in Germany during that time. That perplexity led Von Hentig and Mendelsohn to think about the dynamics of victimization, though being lawyers how they understood those dynamics was very much at the level of the individual and very much informed by their legal training. However, in addition to the influence of their legal training, it is also possible to see the influence of early criminological thought in their ideas.

Both were concerned to develop ways of thinking about the victim that would enable the victim to be differentiated from the non-victim. In other

Table 6.1 Typologies of Victimization

Von Hentig's typology of victim proneness	Mendelsohn's typology of victim culpability	Hindelang, Gottfredson and Garofalo's propositions of likely violent victimization in relation to lifestyle
Young people, females, the elderly	The completely innocent	Time spent in public places especially at night
The mentally defective, 'dull' normals, the depressed	Those with 'minor' guilt	Levels of interaction between people with similar lifestyle
Immigrants, members of minority groups	Those as guilty as the offender	Shared demographic characteristics
The acquisitive, the wanton, the lonely and heartbroken	Those more guilty than the offender	Amount of time spent with non-family members
The tormentor, the 'fighting victim'	Those who are the most guilty	The desirability and vincibility of an individual as a target

words, both were clearly suggesting that there is a normal person against whom the victim is measured and the victim somehow falls short. In order to achieve this kind of understanding they each developed **victim typologies**. Von Hentig's typology worked with a notion of **victim proneness**. He argued that there were some people, by virtue of their socio-economic characteristics, who were much more likely to be victims (in this case of crime) than other people. He identified 13 categories in all, and these are outlined in Table 6.1. Thinking about victim proneness critically, it is possible to see that Von Hentig thought the normal person against whom the victim was to be measured was the white, heterosexual male. Von Hentig does not suggest that there is a 'born victim'. However, there are clear parallels with the ideas of Lombroso, especially in respect of the concern to mark out the differences between victims and non-victims as Lombroso did with offenders, understood as the principle of differentiation. Von Hentig's work has been very influential and is perhaps most keenly identified in the concept of **lifestyle** that has informed much criminal victimization survey work.

▶▶ **Victim typologies**   *refers to a classification scheme that aids in the understanding of what different types of victims have in common and how they differ from others. Identifying and distinguishing between different kinds of victims is a means of generating an understanding of the victim/offender relationship.*

▶▶ **Victim proneness**   *suggests that some people are much more prone to victimization than others or, put another way, that some people are much more likely to be victims of crime than other people.*

▶▶ **Lifestyle**   *as a victimological concept, refers to the idea that there is a link between routine daily activities and exposure to circumstances in which there are greater risks of, or possibilities for victimization. In this view the key to understanding the process of victimization is to study routine patterns of behaviour.*

Mendelsohn adopted a more legalistic framework in developing his typology. His underlying concept was the notion of **victim culpability**. Using this concept, he developed a six-fold typology from the victim who could be shown to be completely innocent, to the victim who started as a perpetrator and during the course of an incident ends as the victim. Arguably his typology is guided by what might be considered a reasonable or rational way of making sense of any particular incident, given the nature of the law. Moreover, given this as the starting point from which these ideas are derived, it is possible to suggest that his understanding of 'reasonable' also equates with that which the white, heterosexual male would consider to be reasonable. This is especially demonstrated in the work that was generated from Mendelsohn's ideas, in which victim culpability is translated into **victim precipitation**.

▶▶ **Victim culpability**   *is the extent to which the victim can be held responsible for the events that occurred. Victim culpability is similar to the concept of victim precipitation and linked to the notion of 'lifestyle' in that these concepts are used to try to explain the process of victimization.*

▶▶ **Victim precipitation**   *refers to actions by the victim that encourage a response in the offender that increases the chance of victimization. The extent to which crime is 'precipitated' by victim behaviour was used as a way of explaining criminal homicide as well as cases of rape where the assumption that 'she's asking for it' became prevalent. Such explanations, where the victim is considered to have contributed towards their own victimization, are controversial and are connected to the concept of victim-blaming and victim-provocation and suggestions that women can be blamed for their attack.*

From these beginnings the concepts of lifestyle and victim precipitation have formed the core of much traditional victimological work and illustrate what Miers (1989: 3) has called a positivistic victimology. The parallels with criminology are clear. Within positivistic victimology there is a similar emphasis on measuring differences, seeing those differences as being somehow abnormal, and looking for explanations of those differences that lie outside of individual choice. In all of this, the development of the concept of lifestyle has been of central importance in perpetuating certain assumptions about criminal victimization. Key to those assumptions is the implicit acceptance of the view that the chances of personal victimization vary in relation to the amount of time spent in public places. This assumption does two things simultaneously. First, it reflects a very male view of what constitutes a problematic arena for people: the public. As a result it hides the world of the private (all that goes on 'behind closed doors') as an arena in which personal victimization might occur. In other words this assumption hides the world of women and children. Second, in focusing on what goes on in public, it implicitly accepts the view that this is the context in which legitimate criminal victimization might occur as per Christie's articulation of the 'ideal victim'.

Of course, typologies and propositions such as these, while reflecting the context in which they were produced, raise a number of questions, for example:

- Who is included and excluded in the various propositions about victimhood?
- To whom or what is the victim being compared in order to create these ways of thinking about victimization?
- What criteria are being used to differentiate the victim from the non-victim?
- How valuable and legitimate are these criteria?
- And, perhaps most interesting of all, to what extent is the kind of thinking that lies behind these ideas still articulated contemporarily, especially in respect of who is considered to have a legitimate claim to victim status and who does not?

In some respects, it is possible to argue that the concept of lifestyle reflects an interesting twist in the domain assumptions of victimology. No longer is the white, male exempt from victim status but arguably is placed at the centre of victimhood with women and children placed in the background as a result of the lifestyle focus on public space. However, despite the potential of this twist, the early criminal victimization work that emanated from this conceptual development did little to build on the centring of maleness reflected in this assumption and the consequences that this might have in understanding criminal victimization in general. It was not until the early 1990s, and arguably as a consequence of the input of radical feminism in criminology, that the conundrums that this work generated (for example, the empirical finding that while men were most at risk from criminal victimization, they expressed the least concern about it) were subjected to closer (gendered) scrutiny.

So, as this discussion has intimated, early victimologists followed a similar line of thinking to that of the early criminologists. They tried to find ways of marking out the differences between victims and non-victims. In doing this, both Von Hentig and Mendelsohn used different kinds of measuring sticks but each in their different ways drew implicitly on the idea that the white, heterosexual male was the norm (i.e. the non-victim) against which victims were to be measured. Moreover, as these ideas were developed, largely through the concept of lifestyle, the maleness inherent in victimological ideas remained unchallenged. As a result the presumptions of the 'ideal' victim were perpetuated, leaving untouched the reality of criminal victimization both for men and for women.

These assumptions went largely unchallenged until the publication of Amir's work *Patterns of Forcible Rape* in 1971. In this work, Amir applied the concept of victim precipitation, derived from the work of Mendelsohn, to the crime of rape, and came to the conclusion, that 19 per cent of the recorded rapes that formed part of his study could be deemed 'victim-precipitated'. This conclusion did not go down well with the growing feminist movement of the 1970s which was vociferous in its criticism of Amir's work, arguing that his use of the concept of 'victim precipitation' was not too far removed from saying that 'women asked for it'. It is at this juncture that it is worth reflecting on the contribution that feminism has made to the domain assumptions of criminal victimization.

Domain assumptions and the victim of crime: feminism

It is important to note that the feminist movement encapsulates a range of different views on the position of women in society. Indeed, it is possible to identify four main strands of feminist thought:

- *Liberal feminism* – a position that argues for equality of opportunity between men and women.
- *Socialist feminism* – a view that argues for the need to appreciate the complex interaction between social class and women's position in society.
- *Post-modern feminism* (sometimes also referred to as French feminism) – a view that argues for the importance of valuing the 'other position', the difference that women's lives represent.
- *Radical feminism* – a view that clearly sees women's position of powerlessness in society as a direct result of male dominance, **patriarchy**.

Given the voice that radical feminism has had in relation to crimes of violence against women in particular, and the relevance that this view has for understanding criminal victimization, I shall only be referring to radical feminism in this discussion.

▸▸ **Patriarchy** *is the systematic expression and maintenance of male power and control over women and children which permeates all social and political and economic institutions.*

But, first, it is important to recognize that the critique of Amir was, of course, connected to the wider discomfort that many feminists also felt (and still do feel) with the use of the term 'victim' in relation to women in general. The concept of 'survivor' is much preferred by feminists since this captures the positive strategies women employ to live their day-to-day lives, given their inherent structural powerlessness rather than the passive acceptance implied in the concept of victim. This is the starting point of the relationship between feminism and victimology that has always been one full of tension. However, the incursion of the feminist challenge to victimology (and, it has to be said, criminology) has been an important source of development for both disciplines.

What feminist work did was not only to offer a different conceptual apparatus, informed by the concept of patriarchy, with which to understand women's lives in general, but also it applied that apparatus to the crimes that affected women's lives: those crimes that occurred in private, behind closed doors – mainly rape and 'domestic' violence. Much of the focus for understanding the nature and impact of this kind of crime was generated by radical feminism. Radford (2001: 232) defines radical feminism in *The Sage Dictionary of Criminology* in the following way:

> Radical feminism offers a systematic analysis of the nature of women's oppression; including the ways in which it is sustained through law and the criminal justice processes. Its aim is not only to understand male dominance and control of women and children but also to end it.

So radical feminist analysis focuses on the ways in which men oppress women (and children) and how the structure of society helps sustain that oppression. This structure and its impact are what is referred to as patriarchy. The key variable in understanding women's experiences including their experiences of criminal victimization is, therefore, men's power over women. This power is reflected in all aspects of social life and at its centre for the radical feminist lies the question of sexuality. Tong (1989), a North American feminist, puts the issues that concern radical feminism in this way: Who rapes whom?; Who batters whom?; For whom does pornography exist?; For whom does prostitution exist?; For whom does female sexuality exist? The answer in each case is men. So put simply, radical feminism clearly focuses attention on all those criminal victimizations that go on in private between people who are for the most part known to each other. This means rape, sexual assault, and domestic violence. In focusing attention on these kinds of criminal victimizations, radical feminism also emphasized that the offenders are men.

Of course, in the 1970s the understanding of 'domestic' violence looked somewhat different than it does contemporarily, and it has to be said that both criminology and victimology as academic areas of study have benefited greatly as a result of feminist work that clearly put these issues on these respective academic agendas. There have, however, also been other gains and losses in this process. A clear gain has been that, in addition to putting particular crimes on the academic agenda, feminism also contributed to making visible the extent to which crime was predominantly a male occupation. And moreover, that much male crime was committed against women. Herein lies a loss. The equation, male – criminal, female – victim, became a double-edged sword resulting in hiding male victimization and to a certain extent female criminality. Arguably this resulted in an additional construct to the white, heterosexual male as the victimological other: that which cannot be spoken.

Of course, neither the criminological nor the victimological gaze are quite so simplistic. The pictures they create are compounded by the additional variables of age, class, ethnicity and sexuality. However, before it is possible to consider their compounding effect, it is important to appreciate how the challenge posed by feminist work was responded to within the disciplines of criminology and victimology. This response was largely constructed from an appreciation of work being generated by studies in masculinity. For the purposes of this discussion we shall focus on the application and relevance of the concept of hegemonic masculinity.

QUESTIONS

Early victim studies concentrated on the role of the victim in the causes of crime and focused on the victim in the precipitation or perpetration of crime.

What are the consequences of this for our understanding of men as victims?
What are the consequences of this for our understanding of women as victims?

What are the implications for the gendering of victimology?

Challenging the domain assumptions on the victim of crime: hegemonic masculinity, crime and criminal victimization

▶▶ **Hegemonic masculinity**   *Jefferson (2001: 138), a UK sociologist, defines hegemonic masculinity in The Sage Dictionary of Criminology in the following way:*

The set of ideas, values, representations and practices associated with 'being male' which is commonly accepted as the dominant position in gender relations in a society at a particular historical moment.

Given the maleness of the crime problem and the dominance of men within the criminal justice professions, some criminologists, most notably James Messerschmidt in North America and Tony Jefferson in the UK have explored the extent to which an appreciation of the dominance of men in society as a whole is the starting point for understanding the dominance of men within criminal behaviour. Much of the focus of this work owes a good deal to the work of Connell (1987, 1995), an Australian social scientist.

According to Connell (1987), the ways in which men express their masculinity in contemporary society is connected to the powerful position held by the presumption of normative heterosexuality. In other words, it is expected and considered normal for men to see themselves as different from women and at the same time to desire women. This deep-rooted expectation of what it is to be a man is reflected in all kinds of social relations. So, for example, it is found in the idea of the man being the breadwinner, in the criminalization of homosexuality, and in making women the objects of pornography. **Normative heterosexuality** underpins all of these examples and for Connell this presumption defines the structure and the form of manhood that any individual man is constrained to live up to. If the question of ethnicity is added to this framework, it indicates that it is the white, heterosexual male who is in a position of power and at the same time indicates that other forms of manhood are downgraded in relation to this (like, for example, the homosexual male, or the ethnic minority male), as are forms of femininity.

▶▶ **Normative heterosexuality**   *refers to the 'ideal type' of manhood; that is the white, heterosexual male. This form of manhood commands a greater degree of power and is privileged over and above other forms of manhood which are are downgraded, marginalized and subordinated.*

The powerful position of this version of masculinity is maintained and sustained by consent, that is, by common agreement of all members of society. This occurs since, as we are all gendered subjects, we all benefit as existential individuals to a greater or a lesser degree by the framework of hegemonic masculinity. So far, maybe so good; but how does this relate to crime?

Messerschmidt (1993, 1997) relates these ideas to crime in three key locations: the street, the workplace and the home. In each of these locations he provides a detailed account of the variety of ways in which masculinity is given expression; from the pimp on the street to the sharp business practice of the rising white-collar executive, to expressions of male proprietary in the forms of various violences in the home. All of these can be understood as different ways of doing manhood within the framework of dominance highlighted by Connell. They all demonstrate the ways in which men display their manliness to others and themselves. So while the business executive might use his position and power to sexually harass his secretary in perhaps more subtle ways than the pimp controls his women, the effects are the same. In this particular example, the women are 'put in their place' and the men are confirmed as men.

This way of thinking about crime and criminality certainly brings to the fore the maleness of crime and the criminal justice industry. It has even been used to facilitate an understanding of how men deal with victimization, an experience that men often struggle with since the demands of masculinity would suggest that being a victim is something highly contradictory for them (see below). However, as a way of thinking, it has not proceeded without its critics, and while it is not necessary for such a critique to be explored in detail here, the following question from Hood-Williams (2001: 44) captures the essence of the problem: 'The question remains, however, why it is that only a minority of men need to produce masculinity through crime rather than through other, non-criminal means?' Therefore, questions remain regarding the contexts in which the notion of hegemonic masculinity clarifies the nature of the crime problem or renders it more opaque. However, what remains to be more fully explored here is the extent to which this concept helps clarify an understanding of men's experiences of victimization.

While much victimological work leaves us with the impression that victims are not likely to be male, this is empirically not the case. Much male violence is committed against other men. Any examination of criminal statistics, and/or criminal victimization statistics reveals that from crimes of murder, through to street robbery, gun-related crime, and even terrorist activity, the perpetrators of such acts are most frequently male and so are the victims. It is only in the arena of sexual violence and other sex-related crimes that women appear as the most frequent victims of male criminal acts. However, in recent years there has been an increasing awareness that much male violence against other men is also sexual violence (see, for example, McMullen, 1990; Lees, 1997). So quite clearly men can be victims, even if they have been relatively hidden from the victimological gaze. What is problematic, however, lies in understanding how they experience that victimization and the impact that it has. Increasingly, criminologists and victimologists have used the concept of hegemonic masculinity to understand this experience. In other words, they have used this concept to develop an appreciation of how men see themselves as men.

Goodey (1997), for example, a UK criminologists, in researching male reaction to violence, used the phrase 'big boys don't cry' to help explain how it was that young men struggled with being victimized. Put simply, it contradicted their understanding of them as men. The following quote is taken from Etherington (2000), a UK social scientist who has worked with men who were sexually abused as children. One of his respondents said about his experiences of being abused by his mother:

> Apart from being my mother, she was a woman. I'd been educated by my father that women were there for the cooking, cleaning and sex. They were put on earth for our benefit and every man should have several. They were not the abusers they were abused upon. So how could she abuse me when I was the man?

This quote captures some of the confusions that can be identified as existing for men when the concept of hegemonic masculinity is employed to understand how they experience victimization. Of course, not all men will experience victimization in the same way. Criminal victimization survey data suggest the general unwillingness of men to identify themselves as a victim and the greater likelihood of men reporting anger at being criminally victimized. This unwillingness to report victimization and the kinds of emotional response that men experience to it, is only just beginning to be understood by criminologists and victimologists, but may go some way to help us understand the relative invisibility of men in the patterning of reported criminal victimization. Box 6.1 identifies some of the methodological issues associated with researching male victimization, and identifies some key findings.

Box 6.1   The nature and extent of male sexual victimization. A. Coxell, M. King, G. Mezey and D. Gordon (1999)

This study is one of the few that have been conducted within the UK that has endeavoured to offer an understanding of the nature and extent of non-consensual sexual relations between men. It extends earlier exploratory work conducted by Mezey and King (1992) in a hospital setting. The 1999 study aimed to identify the lifetime non-consensual sexual experiences of men, and to explore the impact that such experiences had on them as a child or an adult and to ask questions about the kind of help they received. In order to do this men were asked whether or not they were willing to participate through accessing 18 general medical practices in England and those who

---

were willing to take part did so via the use of a computerized interview in a private room. Some 2474 men agreed to take part. This sample had a mean age of 46; 92.6 per cent were white, 3.4 per cent were black, 3.9 per cent were from other ethnic minority groups: 35.3 per cent were manual workers, 58.2 per cent were non-manual workers, and 6.5 per cent were either unemployed or retired; 3.15 per cent identified themselves as gay, bisexual or as heterosexual but sometimes having sex with men. The key findings from this sample are reported as:

- Almost 3 per cent of these men reported non-consensual sexual experiences as adults.
- Over 5 per cent of these men reported sexual abuse as children.
- Non-consensual sexual experiences as a child are predictive of non-consensual experiences as an adult.
- Medical professionals should be aware of the potential range of psychological difficulties found in men who have had these experiences. These range from psychological and alcohol abuse problems to other forms of self-harm.

Researching male victimization

As the previous discussion has intimated, getting men to talk about victimization (which by implication means getting them to talk about how, where and when they feel vulnerable) is neither an easy nor a straightforward process. Stanko (1990) was one of the first researchers to try this and she suggested that it is important to ask men questions in relation to a context with which they could resonate, for example, perhaps feeling 'under threat' at a big football match or other similar circumstances. However, since her first foray into exploring men's relationships with the experience of victimization, much has been made of them, as a group, as being hidden by criminological research, by presuming, for example, that it is women who are the victims of domestic violence and not men, or that they experience a 'hidden' level of sexual violence from other men. Indeed, and as the research reported below suggests, much work has endeavoured to raise the visibility of men as victims in both these domains. However, before we go on to discuss the findings and the pertinences of those studies it will be useful to be aware of some of the limitations associated with exploring this particular topic. Many of those limitations can still be understood by reference to the concept of hegemonic masculinity but it is worth spelling some of them out in a little more detail.

Gadd et al. (2003) suggest that quantitative studies of men as victims of domestic violence tend to assume that male and females are victims of this kind of behaviour in the same way and to the same degree. However, if you explore men's responses in a little more depth Gadd et al. suggest that men are less likely to be repeatedly victimized, are less likely to be seriously injured with only a third of them in their study considering themselves to be abused. In other words, the 'typical' male victim of domestic violence has somewhat different experiences than the 'typical' female victim. Of course, as Gadd et al. indicate, it is possible to interpret these findings in one of two ways: either men are not as systematically abused as women and as such do not live in fear in the same way as women do, or their responses reflect a denial of abusiveness that they experience. The problem of denial in the male use of abuse is also evident in the problems experienced in trying to get men to talk about their own abusive behaviour, and as Gadd (2004) goes on to point out, the role of the researcher, and their understanding of what is being said to them and how it is being said, are crucial in this process.

Thus, the research process in relation to accessing an understanding of male victimization is not a simple one and neither is the process of understanding the findings. Graham (2006) argues that the presumptions that are found in much of the research in the area, especially in relation to men's experiences of 'male rape', is fundamentally framed by presumptions of sexual difference (of there being essential differences between males and females), normative heterosexuality, along with understandings of what counts as sexual harm. All of which are embodied in the law and legal understandings of who can be penetrated by what and where. This results in some bodies, and some physical bodily attributes, being privileged over others, frequently leaving the homosexual male (and female for that matter) out of the equation. From the point of view of the power and influence of hegemonic masculinity, perhaps such latent invisibilities are to be expected. Nevertheless they are important when thinking about in relation to how research on these issues is framed and understood.

QUESTIONS

Why is it important to ask men questions in contexts with which they resonate?

What issues need to be taken account of when researching male victimization?

Men, masculinities and sexual victimization

In order to develop our understanding of the relationship between men, maleness, and criminal victimization further, this chapter will take a closer look at three studies that each take a different position in relation to this issue and in fact are also quite different ways of researching this issue too. These studies are the epidemiological work of Coxell et al. (1999) on non-consensual sex between men, the in-depth interviewing work with male victims of rape reported by Allen (2002), and the psychoanalytical approach taken by Jefferson (1996, 1997, 1998) in his work on Mike Tyson. Each of these studies will be considered in turn before reflecting on the questions that have yet to be addressed in understanding the relationship between men, maleness and criminal victimization.

While other studies in the UK, most notably those conducted by Lees (1997), have considered the experiences that male victims of rape have of the criminal justice system, that is, when 'their' crime has been reported, the study by Coxell et al (1999: see box 6.1) stands out as being unique in its efforts to establish the nature and extent of non-consensual sexual experiences between men from a general sample of the male population. Moreover, while it is a prevalence study, that is, it offers a picture of such experiences over an individual's lifetime and thus makes estimates as to how many men per year might be subjected to such experiences, it is clearly indicative that such experiences are not rare. This study then certainly provides empirical support with regard to

- challenging the victimological stereotype about who can and cannot be a victim;
- understanding the potential impact that such experiences might have on men;
- identifying further areas of investigation to enable more detail to be put in the picture;
- the need for other large-scale survey studies of the male population in order to test the hypotheses generated by this study a little further.

However, this study, despite its importance in documenting the prevalence of men's experiences, helps little in developing the understanding of the impact of those experiences. As the report on these findings clearly indicates, there is important scope for further work here. For example, this study can make few claims about the relationship between the severity of the non-consensual experience and subsequent problems experienced by the victim and it makes no claims about non-consensual sexual experiences between under-age males and older females. These are clearly areas for further research. This is much more central to the focus of the next study to be considered here (Box 6.2).

Box 6.2   Male victims of rape: responses to a perceived threat to masculinity. S. Allen (2002)

This study is based on 50 in-depth interviews with biographically diverse men conducted with a view to providing 'thick descriptions' of their experience of rape and the impact it had on them. Using men's own definitions of rape and sexuality, the interviews were intended to gather a picture of whether or not sexual victimization undermines a man's sense of their identity and when this is likely to occur; what implications this has, if any, for their understanding of what had happened to them and whether or not all men experience such events in the same way. On the basis of this interview data, Allen argues, that while men experience rape as a threat to their autonomy in rather the same way that women talk about such experiences, for men this has the added dimension of constituting a direct challenge to the sense of themselves as men. In order to deal with this, Allen identifies different strategies that the men in her sample used to cope with this challenge. These are:

- I was overpowered: this strategy gels most readily with the common conception of rape as occurring in a secluded place and being committed by a stranger or a brief acquaintance.
- I was overridden: this strategy was used most often by men who had agreed to a level of sexual intimacy but whose resistance was subsequently ignored.
- I was intimidated: this coping strategy was used by those men who felt that the consequences of non-participation may have been worse than participating.
- I was entrapped: this was voiced by those for whom the rape occurred subsequent to them being drugged or otherwise incapacitated.

The importance of understanding the significance of each of these coping strategies lies in understanding what they enable the men to keep intact. As Allen (2002: 48) states,

> [they] help explain why male victims find it difficult to accept that 'normal' men can be raped. When confronted with this reality they seek alternative explanations for what has happened, thereby ensuring that the powerful stereotype of masculinity remains unchallenged. This protects the masculine stereotype that 'real' men are powerful and thus also protects the 'normality' of masculine power that continues to pervade the existing social order.

As Allen herself concludes, this study illustrates very well the uneasy relationship that exists between being male and being a victim; a relationship that has been of central concern to this chapter. In making sense of the tensions within this relationship, men who experience victimization clearly engage in different kinds of coping to keep their sense of themselves as men whole. This is a process that women who have been sexually assaulted do not have to subject themselves to; so understanding the differences and similarities here are important. However, the question remains as to how men deal with these processes in relation to their psyche. This question has led some researchers influenced by masculinity studies to engage with psychoanalysis as a way of making sense of what men 'do' in relation to their internal psyche.

In this vein, Jefferson (1996, 1997, 1998) has done some interesting and provocative work on the boxer Mike Tyson. In this context, Tyson as an offender is constructed and reconstructed as a victim and masculinity theory is the tool that is used to achieve this. For the purposes of the discussion here I shall be referring to only one of the papers written by Jefferson on Mike Tyson (Box 6.3).

Box 6.3   From 'little fairy boy' to 'the compleat destroyer': subjectivity and transformation in the biography of Mike Tyson. T. Jefferson (1996)

Jefferson's problematic in trying to make sense of Mike Tyson is to understand how a passive and bullied boy turned into a world champion boxer and then engaged in behaviours that were to ensure his downfall. Perhaps put more colloquially and in terms closer to Tyson's own; how was being good, bad (the 'little fairy boy') and how was being bad (in the boxing ring: the 'compleat destroyer') considered to be good? In order to make sense of Tyson's experience of this disjunction, Jefferson employs the psychoanalytic concept of anxiety. Put very simply, Jefferson's argument is that it was only through his success as a boxer that Tyson was able to resolve the psychic anxiety that was provoked by the contradictions of being both good and bad and being black in a white world. Through boxing, he could be all of these things at the same time. Of course, his success story was always a tentative one as he lost people close to him, found it difficult to deal with his emotional life and subsequently served six years for rape. The argument is that boxing provided both the social and psychic outlet for the rage produced by his constant state of anxiety.

The extent to which this is an accurate portrayal of Tyson is, as Jefferson admits, not without its problems. In addition, it must be remembered that what has been presented here is only a very small part of Jefferson's work on Tyson and the reader is advised to follow his analyses through the following references:

Jefferson, T. (1997) 'The Tyson rape trial: the law, feminism and 'emotional' truth', *Social and Legal Studies* 6(2): 281–301.

Jefferson, T. (1998) '"Muscle", "hard men" and "iron" Mike Tyson: reflections on desire, anxiety and the embodiment of masculinity', *Body and Society* 4(1): 77–98.

The point of presenting this work, however, is to illustrate both the importance of understanding personal biography as a mediator of masculinity and to demonstrate the way this has been developed within criminology and victimology. It is no great surprise that a superficial conclusion that might be drawn from Jefferson's work on Tyson is that Tyson was a victim of the complex interactional process that occurred within his personal social and psychic processes. Those personal social processes placed him within a deprived, predominantly black, neighbourhood in which pressures to be tough as a mechanism of survival were necessary but frowned upon by the wider society in which he was located and then when his toughness won him wealth and fame, his own success as a boxer did not permit him to leave either his toughness or blackness behind, thus adding to his already powerful rage. In this respect Tyson could be seen as a multiple victim: of his background, of his success, and of a white society that made all kinds of assumptions about being tough and being black. While this might be a superficial conclusion to draw, it is nevertheless a thought-provoking one. It should at least return us to the question of what does the term victim mean, with which this chapter began. It should also point to the questions that still remain about the relationship between men, crime and criminal victimization.

QUESTIONS

How has radical feminism influenced the way in which research has recently been conducted on men as victims?

Explain and illustrate the obstacles to exposing and explaining gendered experiences of criminal victimization.

What's so difficult about getting men to talk about their own victimization?

Are men still the 'Victimological Other' or can men now be 'real' victims?

Summary

This chapter has explored through particular illustrations what has been made visible and invisible in studies that address the relationship between men, victimhood and criminal victimization. In so doing, it has recognized that while the concept of the victim is problematic, much work conducted under the auspices of victimology in its various forms has contributed to a presumption that to be male is to be a non-victim. This chapter has explored studies that have challenged this presumption not only demonstrating that men can be victims but also providing a way of thinking about men's experiences of victimization that results in them being perpetually constrained by hegemonic masculinity.

The attempts by criminologists and victimologists to employ the concept of hegemonic masculinity to explain not only men's criminal behaviour but also their response when victimized is an interesting one. At one level, it is possible to suggest that the recourse to this conceptual framework facilitates the perpetuation of what Scraton (1990) has called the pervasive hegemonic masculinity of the discipline and what Hearn (2004) has described as the hegemony of men. Both these observations reflect a concern with the way in which those issues that concern men have retained the centre stage in academia and thereby have contributed to the marginalization of other issues. Put another way: not everything may be explicable by reference to masculinity. There are (at least) two issues to think about here. The first is, when is masculinity the key variable in understanding the relationship between men, crime and victimization and when might other variables be more important? Messerschmidt (1997: 113) expresses this problem in this way: 'Gender, race and class are not absolutes and are not equally significant in every social setting where crime is realized. That is, depending on the social setting, accountability to certain categories is more salient than accountability to other categories.'

The same might also be said about when criminal victimization is realized. Indeed, the complex ways in which different variables interact with each other in determining the structural conditions for action and the biographical responses of action demand critical reflection and examination. This means not only exploring masculinity(ies) and femininity(ies) but also blackness and whiteness, ageness and classness. It also means challenging normative heterosexuality (Collier, 1998). Moreover Kersten's (1996) comparative study of male violence against women in different socio-economic circumstances is a valuable exception that proves the rule for this kind of work. So the question is: when does gender matter?

The second issue raised by thinking critically about the value of the concept of masculinity concerns sex. The crimes that have been the focus of attention in this chapter have for the most part been sexual crimes. These seem to be the kinds of crimes that when perpetrated by a man on a man, pose the greatest challenge to men's sense of their masculinity. However, what is left out of our understanding of this challenge is sex. Some time ago Cameron and Fraser (1987) and Scully (1990) endeavoured in their different ways to bring sex back into their analyses of male sexual crime on females, recognizing its relationship with power. Apart from Jefferson's (1997) attempt to explore the issue of desire in his analysis of the Tyson rape case, little sociological work has so far attempted to bring sex back in a similar way in exploring men, victims and crime though it is possible to point to the evolutionary psychological work of Wilson and Daly (1998) that attempt this in the context of murder.

So important questions remain: how are men's experiences of crime mediated by age, class, ethnicity, and sexual orientation? How do these different variables structure not only men's experiences of criminal victimization but also how they express those experiences? What might they fear and how might they express that fear? How do they manage their feelings in relation to what has happened to them and does all of this vary according to the variables mentioned above? In addition, what kind of conceptual apparatus might help to make best sense of the questions that an exploration of men, victimization and crime leaves us with?

ANNOTATED BIBLIOGRAPHY

Collier, R. (1998) *Masculinities, Crime and Criminology*. London: Sage. This book offers a thorough going critique of the inherent heterosexism implied by how maleness is considered.

Connell, R.W. (1987) *Gender and Power*. Cambridge: Polity Connell, R.W. (1995) *Masculinities*. Cambridge: Polity and Connell, R.W. (2002) *Gender*. Cambridge: Polity. These books offers an appreciation of the importance and development of an understanding of masculinity. Connell's work has been extremely influential across all the social sciences but particularly in relation to criminology. His ideas have been applied to an understanding of masculinity and crime in the work of Messerschmidt.

Hoyle, C. and Young, R. (eds) (2002) *New Visions of Crime Victims*. Oxford; Hart Publishing. It is more difficult to find the same kind of thorough application of masculinity theory to male experiences of victimization as opposed to their propensity for offending behaviour. This in itself speaks volumes about the inherent domain assumptions of both criminology and victimology that this chapter has been concerned to unpick. However, the above edited collection, as well as including the work of Allen – commented on in this chapter – also covers some other interesting issues. In particular, the chapter by Grady on men as victims of female violence raises some interesting questions.

Kersten, J. (1996) 'Culture, masculinities and violence against women', in T. Jefferson and P. Carlen (eds), *Masculinities, Social Relations and Crime.* **Special issue of the** *British Journal of Criminology,* **36(3): 381–95.** This article usefully situates an understanding of masculinity and propensity for violence within its wider socio-economic setting. It would be of great value to see similar work on masculinity and propensities for experiences and understandings of criminal victimization.

Walklate, S. (2004) *Gender, Crime and Criminal Justice,* **2nd edition. Cullompton: Willan.** This book offers a comprehensive overview of the general issues that pertain to an appreciation of the relationship between gender and crime. It does this in relation to both criminology and victimology.

References

Allen, S. (2002) 'Male victims of rape: responses to a perceived threat to masculinity', in C. Hoyle and R. Young (eds), *New Visions of Crime Victims.* Oxford: Hart Publishing.

Amir, M. (1971) *Patterns of Forcible Rape.* Chicago: University of Chicago Press.

Braithwaite, J. (1989) *Crime, Shame and Reintegration.* Cambridge: Cambridge University Press.

Cain, M. (1989) 'Feminists transgress criminology', in M. Cain (ed.), *Growing Up Good.* London: Sage.

Cameron, D. and Fraser, E. (1987) *The Lust to Kill.* Oxford: Polity.

Carrabine, E., Iganski, P., Lee, M., Plummer, K. and South, N. (2004) *Criminology: A Sociological Introduction.* London: Routledge.

Christie, N. (1986) 'The ideal victim', in E.A. Fattah (ed.), *From Crime Policy to Victim Policy.* London: Macmillan.

Collier, R. (1998) *Masculinities, Crime and Criminology.* London: Sage.

Connell, R.W. (1987) *Gender and Power.* Oxford: Polity.

Connell, R.W. (1995) *Masculinities.* Oxford: Polity.

Coxell, A., King, M., Mezey, G., and Gordon, D. (1999) 'Lifetime prevalence, characteristics and associated problems of non-consensual sex in men: cross-sectional survey', *British Medical Journal* 318, 27 March.

Etherington, K. (2000) 'When the victim is male', in H. Kemshall and J. Pritchard (eds), *Good Practice in Working with Victims of Violence.* London: Jessica Kingsley.

Gadd, D. (2004) 'Making sense of interviewer–interviewee dynamics in narratives about violence in intimate relationships', *International Journal of Social Research Methodology,* 7(5): 383–401.

Gadd, D., Farrall, S., Dallimore, D., and Lombard N. (2003) 'Male victims of domestic violence', *Criminal Justice Matters,* 53: 16–17.

Goodey, J. (1997) 'Boys don't cry: masculinities, fear of crime and fearlessness', *British Journal of Criminology,* 37(3): 401–18.

Graham, R. (2006) 'Male rape and the careful construction of the male victim', *Social and Legal Studies,* 15(2): 187–208.

Hearn, J. (2004) 'From hegemonic masculinity to the hegemony of men', *Feminist Theory,* 5(1): 48–72.

Hood-Williams, J. (2001) 'Gender, masculinities and crime', *Theoretical Criminology,* 5(1): 37–60.

Jefferson, T. (1996) 'From 'little fairy boy' to 'compleat destroyer': subjectivity and transformation in the biography of Mike Tyson', in M. Mac an Ghiall (ed.), *Understanding Masculinities.* Buckingham: Open University Press.

Jefferson, T. (1997) 'The Tyson rape trial: the law, feminism and 'emotional' truth', *Social and Legal Studies* 6(2): 281–301.

Jefferson, T. (1998) 'Muscle', 'hard men' and 'iron' Mike Tyson: reflections on desire, anxiety and the embodiment of masculinity', *Body and Society,* 4(1): 77–98.

Jefferson, T. (2001) 'Hegemonic masculinity', in E. McLaughlin and J. Muncie (eds), *The Sage Dictionary of Criminology.* London: Sage.

Kersten, J. (1996) 'Culture, masculinities and violence against women', in T. Jefferson and P. Carlen (eds), *Masculinities, Social Relations and Crime.* Special Issue of the *British Journal of Criminology,* 36(3): 381–95.

Lees, S. (1997) *Ruling Passions.* London: Sage.

McMullen, R.J. (1990) *Male Rape: Breaking the Silence on the Last Taboo.* London: Gay Men's Press.

Messerschmidt, J. (1993) *Masculinities and Crime.* Lanham, MD: Rowman and Littlefield.

Messerschmidt, J. (1997) *Crime as Structured Action.* London: Sage.

Mezey, G. and King, M. (eds) (1992) *Male Victims of Sexual Assault.* Oxford: Oxford University Press.

Miers, D. (1989) 'Positivist victimology: a critique', *International Review of Victimology,* 1(2): 3–22.

Radford, J. (2001) 'Radical feminism', in E. McLaughlin and J. Muncie (eds), *The Sage Dictionary of Criminology.* London: Sage.

Scraton, P. (1990) 'Scientific knowledge or masculine discourses? Challenging patriarchy in criminology', in L. Gelsthorpe and A. Morris (eds). *Feminist Perspectives in Criminology.* Buckingham: Open University Press.

Scully, D. (1990) *Understanding Sexual Violence.* London: Unwin Hyman.

Stanko, E.A. (1990) *Everyday Violence.* London: Virago.

Tong, R. (1989) *Feminist Thought: A Comprehensive Introduction.* London: Unwin Hyman.

Wilson, M. and Daly, M. (1998) 'Sexual rivalry and sexual conflict: recurring themes in fatal incidents', *Theoretical Criminology,* 2(3): 291–310.

Wootton, B. (1959) *Social Science and Social Pathology.* London: George, Allen and Unwin.

Women, Victims and Crime

Pamela Davies

Chapter aims

- To engender a discussion on women, victims and crime.
- To review and illustrate the nature of women as victims.
- To explore how women negotiate and are helped to survive social harm and criminal victimization.
- To consider women as real offenders and criminal victimizers.

Introduction

The social relations of gender in the study of victims have slowly been exposed during the past 30 years. In the UK, one of the ways in which this can be appreciated is in the context of feminism and voluntarism. The confluence of **feminism** and voluntarism was particularly evident in the decade of the 1970s when feminist pressure groups together with pro-victim lobbies within the voluntary sector shared a number of ideals and principles. Against this backdrop, political impetus was provided to the victim movement producing practical responses to the problems faced by women victims of crime and abuse. This, in turn, provided much space for empirical research, methodological and epistemological developments. This chapter considers some of these developments as they specifically relate to women, victims and crime. Unless otherwise noted, it draws upon literature and evidence from England and Wales. It focuses upon three substantive areas: women as victims, women as survivors and women as victimizers. By way of a historical and contextual preamble the chapter begins by discussing the notion of **the gendered victim**.

▶▶ **Feminism**   *concerned with advocating the claims of women and with bringing a woman-centred or 'feminist' perspective to analyses.*

▶▶ **Gendered victim**   *that female/male victimhood is interconnected materially, culturally and structurally.*

Gendering the victim

While the context of voluntarism and feminism is a useful starting point for a discussion on women, victims and crime, this confluence of ideas and principles is not ideologically unproblematic. As Walklate argues, various strands of feminism have impacted differently on both victimology and criminology (2004b: 94). However, in some respects, feminism challenges the very heart of the conventional victimological agenda (Walklate, 2000) and there are some common features across feminist positions regarding the female victim of crime, one of which is asking the woman question and this means doing research for example, *for* rather than *on* women (Smith and Wincup, 2000). The key characteristics of liberal, radical, socialist and post-modern feminisms are illustrated in Table 7.1.

For liberal feminists, the woman question might include the investigation of sexism; to radical feminists, it includes analysis of men's power over women; to socialist feminists, the compounding of social class and patriarchy is crucial to understanding social justice and victimization; while post-modern feminists problematize the notion of 'the other' and celebrate difference (Walklate, 2002, 2004b) acknowledging that different women have different needs (Williams, 2004). The influence of radical feminism has perhaps been the most enduring and influential in the study of victims.

Radical feminism, through its critique and reaction to the failures, omissions and partiality (Davies et al., 2004) of the early positivists fuelled debates about the notion of the gendered victim and the salience of gender to the study of victims more generally. It contested positivism and brought gender issues, men's and women's victimization to the fore in understanding social justice. The woman question has since been considered amidst realist criminology and interpretivist victimologies (Marsh et al., 2004, Wright and Hill, 2004) while the critical perspective claims to more broadly incorporate the concerns of feminism (Mawby and Walklate, 1994).

Among victimologists it is now generally acknowledged that:

- Crime and the experience of victimization occur on a gendered terrain.
- Gender relations impinge on the experience and recovery from crime and victimization.

The reminder of this chapter explicitly prioritizes the social relations women have to victimization.

Women as victims

Constructing women as victims is complex and problematic at a number of levels. To start with, victimization is artificially and socially constructed

Table 7.1 Feminism and victimology

Key hallmarks	Liberal feminism	Radical feminism	Socialist feminism	Post-modern feminism
Argues against…	inequality and discrimintion	men's oppression and controlling power over women, the neglect of structural analyses	the neglect of structural analyses	the uncritical and the universal, phallocentrism and assumptions of unity
Argues for…	'fair play' and equal opportunities between the sexes	women's knowledge, women suffering violent and sexual abuse	women's knowledge, the interplay between patriarchy and capitalism, intersectionalities of class–race–sex/gender–age	woman as 'the other' and celebrates difference
In the context of victimological: theory	challenges masculinist assumptions – white, male middle-class, heterosexual views in relation to victimization, prioritizes women as a disadvantaged group	challenges men's sexual power over women and raises questions about men, masculinity and sexuality	focuses on the social system and socio-structural conditions as an explanation for victimization, draws on 'transgressive' debates outside of criminological and victimological domains	focuses on difference, plurality and gives voice to diversity, challenges main stream thinking and concerns about victims and victimization
In the context of victim: policy	challenges sexism in theory, policy, practice and research and promotes equality	focuses on sexual violence and harassment, rape, domestic violence, child abuse, intimate and domestic relations	campaigns for social justice	no policy agenda, challenges conventional links between science, rationality and policy-making

(Continued)

Table 7.1 (Continued)

Key hallmarks	Liberal feminism	Radical feminism	Socialist feminism	Post-modern feminism
Methodology	focuses on empirical methods of data gathering and 'adds women in' as victims	includes women and strives to allow women to speak for themselves as victims	'standpoint knowledge' admits to 'whose side we are on' and elevates women as victims, research done 'by women, with women, for women'	challenges and critiques feminist science and feminist victimology, deconstructs ideas, language and structures
Political strategy	focuses on the discriminatory practices of the legal and criminal justice system on equal legal rights, the implementation of 'correct' (PC), unbiased procedures	at one extreme they challenge positivist notions of victim precipitation, at the other they ask, are all men-potential rapists? to reconstitute sexuality, promotes women as survivors	to explore social justice and expose how there is a compounding effect of, for example, racism, sexism and classism which impacts upon women's experiences of victimisation	gives voice to the silenced: emphasizes diversity in women's experiences

Sources: Carlen (2002); Walklate, (2000, 2001, 2004a, 2004b)

(Heidensohn, 1989) and this gives rise to problems of defining 'a victim' or categories of victim. In constituting 'women as victims', value judgements are implied. For radical feminists in particular, viewing women as victims rather than survivors is especially counterproductive. Such views are close to those that challenge the notion that all women are always afraid and are fearful of crime (Gilchrist et al., 1998; Pearce and Stanko, 2000; Walklate, 2001). The concept of surviving victimization is more thoroughly explored in the section 'Surviving victimization'.

While the sub-title used here is acknowledged as problematic, it nevertheless allows for a naming of activities experienced mostly by women and of harms perpetrated predominantly by men. It also opens up debates about male domination and power, patriarchy and masculinist modes of researching and theorizing victimization in society. I begin by illustrating the nature and extent of our knowledge of women as victims and show how understanding women as victims is generally hampered by 'invisibility'.

What we do and don't know about women as victims

Similar to the way in which invisible crimes and our understanding and appreciation of the crime problem suffer from various combinations of these features (Davies et al., 1999), victim awareness, victim policies, and victimological scholarship suffer from a distinct lack of statistics, research, knowledge, theory, politics, panic and control. This device or headline template of seven 'features of invisibility' helps us to better appreciate and understand how some victimizations are rendered invisible and how some victims – in this case female – remain more invisible than others. To help illustrate this in Table 7.2 I make use of the template of seven features of invisibility and apply it to women as victims.

The Table articulates what we do know. However, when considered in proportional terms to what we know about crime and victimizations more generally, it also implies that any understanding of women as victims is less well developed. To help illustrate this, I use the first four features of invisibility above to show how these combine to help explain why many aspects of women's experience of victimization remain under explored.

Table 7.3 considers what we don't yet know about women as victims.

Table 7.2   What we currently know about women as victims

Feature of invisibility	What we know[1]
Statistics	• victimization is generally higher for males than females. The exception to this pattern is rape • for some victimizations, age combined with sex renders women more at risk • black males have the highest rate of violent victimization and white females the lowest • single, divorced or separated women show higher rates of victimization than those who are married or widowed
Research	• more detailed knowledge is gained from specific case studies (see Szockyj and Fox, 1996), local and subject specific surveys and empirical research (see Hester et al., 1996; Lees, 1997), critical (Mooney, 2000, Walklate, 2000) and qualitative research (Chigwada-Bailey, 2003; Dobash and Dobash, 1980)
Knowledge on risk/vulnerability	• risks to victimization are gendered • divorced/single, poor women have higher risks • women are more vulnerable to domestic violence from current or former partners • women-on-women incidents are more common in acquaintance violence than in any other type • young homeless women are more likely to be sexually assaulted • female consumers are particularly at risk from some specific pharmaceutical products and services, household and cosmetic products, pressures to purchase substandard goods, assumptions of technical incompetence (see Chapter 4 in this volume)
Knowledge on workplace victimization	• women and men suffer from high levels of criminal victimization • welfare workers, nurses, office managers (women) are three times more likely than 'average' to suffer from violence at work • female workers are particularly at risk from miscarriage and respiratory ailments, other illnesses and exploitation in certain industries (see Chapter 4 in this volume)
Knowledge on fear	• gender and age structure social experiences of fear of crime and victimization • women are more worried and fearful about crime despite having lower chances of victimization than men and young people • fear of sexual violence and harassment from men underpins women's higher fear

Table 7.2 (Continued)

Feature of invisibility	What we know
Knowledge on impact	• high impact of criminal victimization on women • violence and sexual abuse are major reasons for young women running away from home
Knowledge on levels	• large numbers of crime committed by non-strangers against women are not reported to the police • levels of violence against women are far higher than the BCS and other national surveys show

Theory	• different types of feminisms (liberal, radical, socialist and post-modern) have impacted upon our understanding and appreciation of women as victims (see Table 7.1)
	• recent feminist concerns centre on:
	  • deconstructing women's irrational and rational fears of crime and victimization (Stanko, 1987)
	• recent gender concerns centre on:
	  • the ways in which violence and abuse against men and boys have been marginalized within victimology
	• Walklate (2004a) has debated whether or not there can be a feminist victimology

Politics	• the women's movement and the second wave of feminism had a significant political impact resulting in:
	  • women's Refuge provision
	  • Rape Crisis and Women's Aid
	  • struggle for women's rights and
	  • notion of 'survivorship'
	• the voluntary sector has also been instrumental in supporting women victims of domestic and sexual abuse

Panic	• women are often portrayed as particularly fearful of crime and victimization as well as 'irrational' to due 'misplaced' fears of crime • the media reproduces women as vulnerable and reinforces and fuels women's fears of crime
Control	• fear and experience of crime and victimization impact upon women's lifestyles and day-to-day activities • women do control for themselves • they perceive and deal with risk via different types of coping strategies and constraints

Note:
[1] Specific sources and references include: Budd and Mattinson, (2000); Crawford et al. (1990); Jones et al. (1986); Mayhew, (1983); Mirrlees-Black and Byron, (1999); Simmons and Dodd, (2003); Upson, (2004); Walby and Allen et al. (2004a).

Table 7.3 What we don't yet know about women as victims

Feature of invisibility	What we don't know
Statistics	• the nature, extent, impact and effects of victimization upon individual women and upon different groups of women
Research	• much research remains partial and restricted to case studies and individual crime (see Chapter 4 in this volume and Table 7.2)
Knowledge	• the real extent of crime committed by non-strangers and strangers against women • the impact of victimization upon women suffering from violence at work • immigrant women's experiences of victimization • the effects and impact of different types of consumer crimes • how global dimensions of white-collar and corporate crime impact upon women as mothers, carers and workers • how they experience and survive disasters, human rights abuses and atrocities • how and why gender and age structure social experiences of fear of crime and victimization
Theory	• there is a growing body of work seeking to theorize the gendered nature of crime, much of which focuses on masculinity and crime (see Chapter 6 in this volume and also Connell, 1987, 1995; Messerschmidt, 1993) and some of which focuses upon femininity and crime (see e.g. Joe-Laidler and Hunt, 2001; Miller, 1998) • there is a less well-developed body of work on the gendered nature of victimization • Walklate has asked 'Can there can be a feminist victimology'? (Walklate, 2001, 2004a)

Reflecting on what we do and do not know about women's victimization

Consider the answers listed under each of the questions in Box 7.1.

Box 7.1   What is victimization?

Q: What is victimization?
A: Mugging, theft, disorder and violence, murder.
Q: Where does victimization happen?

(Continued)

A: Streets, close to football stadium and public city/town centre spaces –
      outside.
Q: Who victimizes?
A: Hooligans, youth.
Q: Who is victimized?
A: The weak and vulnerable, the elderly and the innocent.

The answers presented rely upon obvious manifestations, features and characteristics of victimization and illustrate the legacy of positivist traditions in victimology. However, there is much misleading information and indeed missing data in these answers which denote only partial and limited knowledge about victimization generally, and the gendered nature of victimization in particular.

At face value, the answers are **gender-blind** but, on closer reading, **gender-bias** is implied. These common-sense answers play down the fact that much crime and victimization exists on a gendered terrain and that a rather different set of answers can be provided to the same set of questions. For example, now consider different answers listed under each of the same questions.

Box 7.2   What is victimization?

Q: What is victimization?
A: Murder/manslaughter, injury, maiming, monetary and financial, disfigurement, exploitation.
Q: Where does victimization happen?
A: Corporations, workplaces, institutions, industries.
Q: Who victimizes?
A: Corporations, workplaces, institutions, industries.
Q: Who is victimized?
A: Workers, employees, investors, women, consumers.

This new set of answers illustrates that victimization also includes injuries, maimings, monetary and financial harms to workers, employees, investors and consumers and these are perpetrated by employers and the trusted. As with the first set of answers, at face value the answers are gender-blind but on closer reading once again gender bias is implied, for example, that the victims of disfigurement are women.

In terms of a gendered approach to the study of victimization, gender-specific victims are implied (female elderly pensioners, women as mothers, young and older women seeking to emulate fashion industry perfection). Other features relating to the social and spatial patterning of victimization appear **gender-neutral,** i.e. types of victimization, places where victimization takes place, who victimizes, when victimization occurs. However, this is supposition and there are several grounds on which to argue that where the victimization of women is concerned, gender-blindness operates. For example, in the home, women experience violent forms of victimization disproportionately.

▶▶ **Gender-blind** *women/men are indistinguishable. A failure to consider gender at all.*

▶▶ **Gender-bias** *masculinist/feminist, male/female, man/woman.*

▶▶ **Gender-neutral** *woman/man question is absent – androgenaeity. There is no acknowledgement of the significance of being male/female.*

Women, work and the environment

While there is some evidence to suggest that traditional male workplaces are risky environments and the mining industry, unsafe building sites and the construction industry generally are classic examples where men are at risk of victimization at work (Croall, 2001), the gendered nature of victimization across workplaces has been little researched (Davies and Jupp, 1999). Yet, using data from the 1992–96 National Crime Victimization Survey, Fisher and Gunnison found that specific types of jobs place females more at risk of experiencing a violent incident (robbery and assault) than males in the same types of jobs (Fisher and Gunnison, 2001). As Croall has stated, it cannot be argued that women or men are more at risk to victimization in the workplace, risks are affected by the gendered division of labour (Croall, 2001).

As Marsh has recently noted, 'it is still the case that a neglected area of victims of corporate crime is that of women as victims' (Marsh et al., 2004: 126). This statement, made more than a decade after Gerber and Weekes (1992) continues to highlight that the corporate victimization of women requires feminist theorizing. It suggests the continued **androcentricity** of victimological work generally and the corporate victimization of women more specifically as well as the absence of gynocentric approaches that see the world from a female perspective. There has been only one significant publication on this very subject in 1996 (Szockyj and Fox, 1996).

▶▶ **Androcentricity** *being centred upon the male. From a male perspective. Parallel to this is gynocentricity – seeing the world from a female perspective.*

With respect to the victimization of women workers, the edited volume referred to above notes how Imperial Foods has been implicated in the killing of black women workers (Szockyj and Fox, 1996). More recently, and linked to economic globalization, there has been an apparent reappearance of sweatshops where 90 per cent of all workers are young – and in the West immigrant – women, working in the garment industry and where 'operators are notorious for avoiding giving maternity leave by firing pregnant women and forcing women workers to take birth control or to abort their pregnancies' (Feminist Majority Foundation 2001). There are also indications from other case studies of corporate crime that the pharmaceutical, cosmetics, health and medical industry have harmed women as consumers on a mass basis (Finlay, 1996; Mintz, 1985; Peppin, 1995; see also Croall, 1995, 2001; Perry and Dawson, 1985; Slapper and Tombs, 1999; Swasy, 1996).

Other evidence supports the understated nature and extent of victimization of women. Tombs and colleagues have concerned themselves with exposing the subject of corporate victimization and with raising the profile of toxic crimes and harms in particular. They have estimated that as many as 20 million women's jobs entail toxic risks (Pearce and Tombs, 1997, 1998; Slapper and Tombs, 1999). Certainly there is evidence of hundreds of polluting companies in England and Wales involving emissions of cancer-causing chemicals (Brown, 1999: 5). Dramatic but rare exposures of such hazards have spawned pockets of empirical research into the effects of toxic chemicals including pesticides, dioxin, and hazardous waste on the public. Lynch and Stretesky's (2001) review notes a Norwegian study that evidences birth defects linked to exposure to environmental toxins. There have also been some high profile and recurrent attempts to expose scandals affecting women and their babies. Switzerland's largest industrial company Nestlé – the world's largest artificial baby milk producer – has been targeted for its unethical marketing and its part in causing malnutrition among infants in the global South and an estimated 1.5 million infants to die each year (Corporate Watch, 2004a). The same industrial giant has also been the focal point for pollution incidents and the target of feminist opposition groups in relation to its sponsoring of beauty contests and thereby its perpetuating of sexism (Corporate Watch, 2004a). Monsanto has similarly been the focus of Corporate Watch. This body claims Monsanto has an impressive history of committing corporate crimes, several of which have a direct bearing on the health of women, including their marketing of a genetically engineered hormone BST where evidence suggests BST milk may cause breast cancer (Corporate Watch, 2004b).

Women, violence and abuse

Watts and Zimmerman (2002) have pointed out an increasing amount of research is showing violence against women in a global context. This includes intimate partner violence; sexual abuse by non-intimate partners; trafficking; forced prostitution; exploitation of labour and debt bondage of women and girls; physical and sexual abuse against prostitutes; sex selective abortion, female infanticide; the deliberate neglect of girls; and rape in war. A variety of recently reported incidents are beginning to impact upon the global victimological landscape. From a UK perspective, there is now a particularly well-developed body of work addressing the nature and extent of rape, sexual and domestic violence and abuse as experienced by women and predominantly perpetrated by men dating back to the influence of radical feminist activists in the decade of the 1970s. These forms of victimization are staggeringly high:

- A man has physically or sexually abused one in five women at some time in women's lives (Venis and Horton 2002).
- The BCS estimates 13 per cent of women had been subject to domestic violence, sexual victimization or stalking in the twelve months prior to interview and states that 'women are the overwhelming majority of the most heavily abused group' (Home Office, 2004).
- Women's Aid claims that every week two women are killed in domestic violence situations (Women's Aid, 2003).

Feminist commentators generally agree that we fail to adequately capture women's real experiences or approximate the real extent of their suffering and that an unquantifiable number of such victimizations often remain or are rendered invisible. Some have argued the term 'domestic violence' renders women's experiences invisible by hiding the gender of the perpetrator (Morley and Mullender, 1994) and the gendered nature of the offence and victimization generally. Other research has recently uncovered how women do not always classify their experiences as rape (Kahn et al., 2003) and cultural issues appear to militate against those women from diverse social and ethnic groups publicly admitting their victimization or seeking out help (Chigwada-Bailey, 2003).

Women and multiple victimization

What is also insufficiently emphasized is the extent to which women in particular suffer from several or multiple forms of victimizations. Women are direct as well as indirect victims of criminal acts and omissions, but they also suffer secondary, repeat, multiple and serial forms of criminal and non-criminal victimizations. Their direct victimization can take visible and less visible forms and those most likely to be officially recognized are those that can be read off in the Criminal Injuries Compensation Scheme (2001) booklet. The booklet lists and describes 14 injuries in its tariff

(Home Office, 2001: 25). It also lists 25 levels of compensation (Home Office, 2001: 21). If we were to read the tariff from a feminist perspective and ask what is does for women, the tariff notes 'loss of foetus' – level 10, standard amount £5,500. Other women-specific victimizations in the tariff fall within the three categories: 'Physical abuse of adults', 'Sexual assault/abuse of victims (if not already compensated as a child)' and 'Sexual assault/abuse – additional awards'. However, many of the harms and hazards and criminal victimizations including the compounded nature of women's victimizations fail to be adequately recognized in these formulaic, strict and rigid categorizations of harms. The Criminal Injuries Compensation Scheme not only fails to deal with the gendered nature of victimization as it specifically harms and impacts upon women but also in some instances it may inflict further harm, adding insult to injury and re (or secondary) victimization (Dignan, 2005 and see below).

In terms of secondary victimization, let us focus for a moment on the serious crime of rape. In the UK, the adversarial system assumes innocence on the part of the accused and attempts to establish guilt. In terms of police interviewing of rape victims Roger Graef's pioneering 'fly on the wall' *Police* film in 1982 of Thames Valley Police treatment of women reporting rape was to force a change in police practice, so poor was their treatment of women accusing men of rape. While the adversarial system might appear to encourage re-victimization as might hostile police interrogations and similar approaches from defence solicitors and barristers and members of the judiciary whose questioning, cross-examinations and judgements assume the woman is an 'alleged victim', this does not excuse the treatment some women have been subjected to by the various institutions and personnel of the criminal justice system. Thus the reality of the rape victim's experience in court is that she has often been forced to relive her ordeal in the witness box – almost as if to prove her innocence in the crime (see, for example, R v Allen 1982, Ipswich Rape Case) or as in 1989 the judge has suggested that she precipitated or caused her rape (Williams, 2004). Following the ordeal of rape and other forms of sexual victimization women and girls must cope with the longer-term aftermath and this includes psychological damage and the suffering of stigmatization or ostracization (Human Rights Watch, 2004).

In terms of repeat victimizations, for women, domestic violence is the most obvious example and for female (and male) children child sexual abuse. In relation to domestic violence, victim blaming is also in evidence. Gilchrist and Blisset (2002) report victims being blamed for the perpetrator's behaviour in the courts. Additionally for women, multiple or serial victimization is often a feature of their overall experience of victimization.

Radical scholars refer to women's multiple disadvantages and women's complex cultural heritage and identity in order to demonstrate women's particular relationship to various criminal and non-criminal forms of victimization, they point to how women's victimization is complex and multi-layered, and how ungendered definitions of multiple victimization render much of our experience invisible.

Social change, women and victimization

Victimization can embrace a wide range of anti-social experiences and many alternative labels that might justifiably constitute victimization include abuse, atrocity, disaster, accident, scandal and exploitation, all of which can be employed to deny official harm and victim status as well as obscure the gendered terrain of victimization.

Evidence is emerging in relation to women's suffering following the consequences of economic globalization and during and in the wake of military violence. These derive initially from journalistic reports and are followed by academic interest. Newspaper journalism has commented upon war crimes against women, 'Bosnian Serbs jailed for rape and sexual slavery' (Bishop, 2001). Since the break-up of the former Soviet Union and in the wake of relaxed border controls, there have been increased opportunities for freedom of movement and there has been a proliferation of research focusing upon human trafficking of women and girls, often for the purpose of sexual exploitation in the form of prostitution, pornography, escorts (CWASU, 2002; Hughes and Denisova, 2002; US Department of State, 2003; Goodey, 2004). Smuggled migrants suffer in similar ways to those subjected to trafficking and violence against immigrant workers has also been apparent (Raj and Silverman, 2002). Europol, the European police agency, has recently confirmed that culturally sensitive 'honour killings', in which young women who are often fleeing forced marriages have been murdered, remain well hidden but appear to be increasing in Europe (Bennetto and Judd, 2004).

While there has been a limited research agenda devoted to the gendered nature of victimization, key case studies suggest the victimization of women warrants further research. With respect to war crimes against women, while this is not a new phenomenon (Askin, 1997), there has been recent interest on the part of some criminologists (Ruggiero, et al., 1998; Cohen, 2002) to bring the crimes and victimizations of war within the remit of that discipline. Jamieson (1998) has acknowledged the ways in which feminists, for example, have focused upon rape as expressions of the gender order and how although gender features in our understanding of war crimes, there are limits to and gaps in our knowledge. Those that pertain to women include the need to identify the processes which produce the intensification of the sexual victimization of women in wartime (Jamieson 1998: 496). There are others who have similarly argued that gender matters in understanding militarism and violence and that sexual violence against women and girls as a weapon of war is a serious human rights issue (Caiazza, 2001). Askin (1997) argues that while women are subject to the same atrocities as men, they are also victims of additional crimes – rapes and enforced pregnancies, forced maternity – because of their gender. This is supported by Ristanovic's investigations of wartime victimization of refugees in the Balkans (Ristanovic, 1999, 2004).

Women and social harm

The impact of victimization on women includes women as wives, as mothers, as single parents, as workers and employees, as consumers, as citizens, as investors, as passengers, as residents and tenants, as female youths, children and babies (Croall, 1998; Sheley, 1995). Spaces, places and venues for women's victimization include public and private places, the street, the home, and care home, the institution, the workplace, the battlefield and the war zone, the shopping mall and public transport. As women, and as indirect victims, we feel the pains, harms and victimizations of those close to us. This suggests a bias in the gendered nature of victimization where women appear to bear the brunt of harm and suffering and victimization. One of the commonly shared characteristics of victimization is the notion of being harmed (Miers, 1989). Harm can be physical, emotional and/or psychological and financial. Harms can involve very many forms of suffering, including exploitation, mental abuse, violence, disease, deformity and deprivation. Harms can be multiple and serious as well as long-lasting and debilitating. The British Crime Survey has shown that those victimizations that remain relatively invisible are not always or necessarily the least serious forms. Vast amounts of financial hardship remain un-criminalized and while men and women suffer, there are indications that there is a gendered impact here too. Smith (2001) has pointed out how the privatization of retirement income affects men and women differently. Due to women's employment patterns during their life course, their low wages are replicated in low retirement incomes, resulting in many women living in poverty in retirement. As the many examples provided here demonstrate, serious forms of financial, physical, sexual, abuse and assault, corporate victimizations at home, at work, in peace and in wartime, are experienced in very specific ways by women.

Feminist scholars and philosophers have persuasively argued that women are differently connected to the social world to men, that women's needs and experiences differ greatly from men's. Women's social existence is connected, dependent and interdependent (Nelson, 1996) and more orientated towards an ethic of care and responsibility towards others in relationships (Gilligan, 1982). For women, the family, the home, emotions, nurturing and caring are central to social life and these are generally considered feminine characteristics. Women's suffering, as wives, partners, (single) mothers, carers, sisters, and daughters is intricately connected to these. Even when ostensibly victimizing others – doing property and acquisitive crimes particularly shoplifting and prostitution – we do so ostensibly and in the main for others benefits, for families, partners, neighbours and friends (Davies, 2003a, 2003b). Following feminist criminological theorizing (Carlen, 1988; Worrall, 1990) on criminal women, this leads to a victimological dilemma for women, who find themselves doubly victimized and doubly suffering, as opposed to doubly deviant and doubly suffering (Carlen, 1988).

While those who more closely approximate characteristics typically associated with femininity are likely to feel others suffering more readily and easily than those who don't, it does not follow that *women* necessarily bear the brunt of harm and suffering. Nor does it imply that *women* have a monopoly on suffering and hardship. A fully gendered approach to the understanding and appreciation of victimization in society should not allow for *women* to hijack harm and suffering for themselves. While harm, suffering and victimization occurs on a gendered terrain, men can exhibit so-called feminine characteristics and women can similarly exhibit those characteristics most commonly and routinely associated with men and traditional notions of masculinity. Women can do female or male gender; men can do female or male gender.

QUESTIONS

How have different feminisms impacted upon our knowledge about women who experience social harm and criminal victimization?

What is the significance of 'location' to understanding the criminal victimization of women?

How has feminism shaped the victimological gender agenda?

Negotiating and surviving victimization

> Not everyone who suffers victimization likes to think of themselves or to be called, a victim. Feminists including those involved with Rape Crisis centres prefer to speak of survivors, for a number of reasons. First, using the term 'survivor' makes clear the seriousness of rape as, often, a life-threatening attack. Second, public perceptions are shaped by terminology and the word 'victim' has connotations of passivity, even of helplessness. In the context of a movement which aims to empower people who have been victimised, this is clearly inappropriate: using the word 'victim' to describe women takes away our power and contributes to the idea that it is right and natural for men to 'prey' on us. (London Rape Crisis Centre, 1984: iv)

The notion of survivorship is significant for women. Miers (1989) has pointed out that being a victim is an accorded status, which carries with it a set of expectations. A female victim might have expectations that the criminal justice system – from the police though to the CPS, the courts, the judiciary and the prison system – treat her with respect, dignity and due process. There may also be expectations that others will have of her. Family, friends, colleagues and criminal justice personnel might expect female victims to be dependent, passive, inert, fatalistic and tolerant. When women have appeared in court as defendants and have not conformed to the expectations others have of them as a victim, they have been described as not subscribing to the 'gender-deal' (Carlen, 1988). When women have appeared in court as victims and witnesses and have failed to do the gender-deal and strike a gender-specific bargain, they have been treated less than sympathetically and have experienced 'secondary victimization' often through 'victim blaming'. Through being gender-deviant and failing to enter into the gender-contract (Worrall, 1990), women have found themselves treated more punitively than had they conformed to a more respectful and respectworthy stereotype of the dutiful wife/partner and caring mother.

As defendants and victims in contact with the CJS and facing the courts particularly, women present a complex paradox for feminists. Conforming to the ideal-type female victim presents a double-bind situation. There are positive connotations attached to the term victim as well as negative ones (Williams, 2004). Women can capitalize on these associations or they can suffer from them. In terms of surviving victimization, on the one hand, it is important for women not to accept, collude and through surrendering to victimhood help reproduce gendered stereotypes of femininity and prescriptive notions of the victim. On the other hand, if women fail to toe the line of doing gender through victimization in traditional CJS settings, if we appear to resist and deny labels and victimhood as understood by the justice system that judges us all, we risk incurring harsher treatment and penalties, and in the case of victims, 'rough justice'.

There are several levels at which we might approach the problem of women suffering harms and victimizations and several ways of tackling the problems they face in the short, medium and longer term. At one level, women actively and routinely engage with and negotiate their own safety in their daily social life (Stanko, 1990b). At another level they have recourse to formal and legal remedies and there are also provisions and assistance generally available to crime victims – and some very specifically offered to women – from the voluntary sector.

Rational negotiation of safety

The level at which women 'do it for themselves' by negotiating their own safety and minimizing risks connects strongly to the ways in which victimization, fear and risk are mediated through gender. The first British Crime Survey (Hough and Mayhew, 1983) and virtually all fear of crime surveys since have reported women as more fearful of crime and victimization than men (Pain, 2001). This holds true in the home, in the workplace (Upson, 2004) and the city. Since 1983, when the debate about irrational fears was sparked, feminists have offered counter-responses to the claims that women's fear of victimization from men is irrational (Stanko, 1988). More sensitive research tools used in the local measurement of crime and victimization since 1982 (see Hanmer and Saunders, 1984; Hall, 1985; Jones et al., 1986; Crawford et al., 1990) have produced results that help to support these arguments. Feminist research in the area of domestic violence has explained the reasons why women stay in violent relationships, revealing women's rationalism rather than their irrationality and irresponsibility (see Walklate, 2004b; and Mooney, 2000). Another example is in the area of youth violence and community safety. Pearce and Stanko (2000) note the complexity of women's relationship to fear creation and alleviation. Contrary to finding young women as always in need of protection from young men, they find young women often take an active role in either disrupting or stabilizing the feeling of safety and order within communities.

The ways in which women do rationality are as mediated by gender as any area of social activity. Walklate has argued that what a man may consider rational, may not be considered so by a woman (Walklate 1995: 63). Women's negotiation of risk points to their understanding of risk as gendered (Chan and Rigakos, 2002) but that does not imply that risk is universalized in sex/gender terms. Recent research has reported fearful men and fearless women (Gilchrist et al., 1998).

As well as women doing survivorship for themselves, they do so on behalf of others too. The ways in which women help other women are evident in the voluntary and mutual support work carried out under the auspices of Women's Aid (see below). Other ways in which women are instrumental and pro-active in encouraging and promoting survival from victimization and disaster are often less self-evident, indeed, women's valuable contributions often remain invisible and incalculable. As the edited collection by Enarson and Marrow shows, women are in fact present in every disaster response 'as mitigators, preparers, rescuers, caregivers, sustainers and rebuilders' (1998: 6) and women's survival assets stand them in good stead as resource managers with specialized knowledge of coping and survival strategies during and after disasters. Women not only feel and experience victimization on behalf of others but they help in reconstructing lives and communities shattered by disaster and rioting (Campbell, 1993).

Criminal justice and public policy

Although women have formal equal access to justice, their experiences of criminal justice have been signalled as problematic and 'rough justice' for women can manifest itself at various stages of the criminal justice. Women also have formal equal access to criminal injuries compensation, the mainstay of the State's form of redress for victims of crime. However, it too has been shown to adopt discriminatory criteria for selecting in and selecting out 'innocent' as opposed to 'culpable', 'blameworthy' or 'deserving' victims (Dignan, 2005).

An article entitled 'When crime doesn't pay' written by Mullin for *The Guardian* in 1995, refers to one example of a female victim of robbery and rape who was denied criminal injuries compensation on grounds related to her character, conduct and lifestyle. Three years later in 1998, Women Against Rape London wrote to the Chief Executive of the Criminal Injuries Compensation Authority to complain about similarly discriminatory policies. Having initially refused to award compensation to the applicant who had suffered rape, beatings and robbery, on grounds related to her work as a prostitute, on appeal the tariff for rape (£7,500) was awarded with an imposed reduction of 25 per cent (£5,625) with the implication that she was acting immorally and that her work was provocative. In April of

2004, the Criminal Injuries Compensation Authority again failed a female victim of a stabbing and a rape. The headline in the *Daily Telegraph* reads 'I am more angry at the system than at my rapist' (Stewart, 2004: 21). The article conveys the outrage the victim feels at her application for compensation being considered in the context of 'value for money', at the distastefulness and 'surreality' of the tariff and seriousness scales and of the notion of compensation being contentious as well as the bureaucracy of the 'expensive, cumbersome system'. Such views and criticisms of awards echo previous cases in 1993 and 1995 (Kennedy, 1998; Nuttall, 1998).

Nevertheless, formal legal approaches to enlisting the help of victims in securing justice have changed significantly during the past 30 years or so and have been important legislative and other criminal justice-related landmarks for women facing the criminal justice system as complainants, defendants and witnesses, most notably those affecting women as victims of rape and domestic violence (see Chapter 10 in this volume).

In 1975, the police issued the first public policy on domestic violence, which led to domestic violence-related legislation in 1976, 1978 and 1983 and Circular Instructions for police in 1986 and 1990 (Marsh et al., 2004). As regards victims of rape, theoretically there have been some improvements for victims. In 1976, limited protection of the identity of raped women was introduced in courts in England and Wales. In 1999, the Youth Justice and Criminal Evidence Act excluded most evidence about the complainants' previous sexual history. Rape suites, 'sympathetic units' (Williams, 2004) were also introduced in many police command areas. In Scotland, in 1989, the CHANGE programme was established followed in 1990 by Lothian Domestic Violence Probation Project; both examples of court-ordered re-education programmes for men who are convicted of violence towards their partners. In 1992, a 'Zero Tolerance' publicity campaign against male violence was launched in Edinburgh (Williams, 1999).

Initiatives relating to violence against women coincided with the spread of good practice from elsewhere, notably the Duluth, Minnesota Domestic Violence Abuse Intervention Project, as published in 1986. The impact of feminist scholarship encouraged tackling violence against women on a number of fronts (Dobash and Dobash, 1998) and this includes those arguing 'the progressive potential of the law' (Lewis, 2004). There was further legislation in 1997 and 1999 that impacted upon women as victims and the most recent legislative activity is the *Domestic Violence, Crime and Victims Act*, 2004 introducing a Code of Practice for Victims of Crime (Home Office, 2005), a Commissioner for Victims and Witnesses and Victims' Advisory Panel. The Code governs services provided in England and Wales by 11 organizations connected to the criminal justice process (see Home Office, 2005).

Voluntary sector support

Although there are some major differences between the various provisions arising from within the voluntary sector, most voluntary bodies in the UK that provide support to women have a general commitment to voluntarism and along with this go several other key common features. There is usually a common agreement on the philosophies of self-government, self-help, mutual support and power-sharing secured through encouraging 'speaking out', 'thinking positive' and through 'good friend' and 'supportive partner' methods (Madge, 1997). These ideas clearly connect to the notion of women doing it for themselves. To some extent the voluntary sector also encourages its clients to take control of their lives as opposed to conforming to a submissive and fatalistic victim image.

It would be impossible to list and discuss the full range of services provided by the voluntary sector. Some voluntary groups and networks are listed in Table 7.4. While each bears a commitment to the notion of voluntarism and they have different historical roots, they represent a diverse range of provision and some are more woman-oriented than others. Charities and not-for-profit organizations such as Victim Support and other bodies such as the NSPCC rely upon voluntary workers as do the variety of telephone helplines run by, for example, Childline, the NSPCC, Rape Crisis and Victim Support. Some provisions are born of 'grass roots' movements – where victims and activists often combine their efforts and organize and mobilize together, for example, Aftermath, a self-help and counselling organization (Howarth and Rock, 2000). Some groups form in connection with specific events. Some have an educational role. Others have a lobbying role as with Women's Aid, while others again are less politically orientated as with the National Association of Victim Support Schemes (Rock, 1990). Some connect on a global level and world victim movements have emerged such as that in Brazil where on Mother's Day 2001 a campaign was launched for women to force the men of Brazil to give up their guns (Carrabine et al., 2004). Non-governmental organizations (NGOs) have also mobilized at local, national and international levels in response to the trafficking in women and in order to develop more effective solutions in the relative absence of government initiatives and assistance for trafficking victims (Tzvetkova, 2002).

In the future, restorative justice models of victim-focused reforms (these include victim–offender mediation, family group conferencing, police-led conferencing and reparation boards) (Dignan, 2005) may allow for the expansion of voluntary contributions to support provisions. However, it will be a challenge to effectively incorporate racial and sexual violence

Table 7.4 Voluntary/charitable support groups/networks

Name of group	Supporting activity
Victim Support	offers advice and practical assistance for crime victims, also seeks to influence government policy and advance victim's rights
Witness Support	provides support services to victims and witnesses throughout the criminal courts in England and Wales
Women's Aid	the national domestic violence charity, campaigns to protect abused women and children and to keep them safe
Rape Crisis	provides a variety of services including information, support and counselling, a 24-hr telephone hotline, raises awareness, provides training and outreach work, contributes to policy initiatives on child sexual abuse, rape and sexual and violent assault
Refuges	emergency and temporary accommodation and other services, including emotional and practical support, counselling and advocacy
Women only Organisations WAVAW	Women Against Violence Against Women
NCASA	National Coalition Against Sexual Assault
NOW	National Organisation of Women
WPC	Women's Political Causes
Victim Lobby/Single Issue Groups	exist to support and promote the cause of certain victims
SAMM	Support After Murder and Manslaughter, for those bereaved as a result of murder or manslaughter, provides emotional support and victim advocacy
MADD	Mothers Against Drink Driving
Zito Trust	Highlights issues related to mental illness

in any restorative justice framework (Hudson, 1998). In the UK today, voluntary sector provisions can trace their roots to the decade of the 1970s and those connected to the feminist movement include Rape Crisis, Refuges and Women's Aid. In terms of specialist and specific support for women, Women's Aid has been supporting women and children who are victims of domestic violence for over 30 years and this particular national charity incorporates the ethos and vision of believing women and promoting empowerment (Women's Aid Federation of England and Wales 2004). It is perhaps the largest most pro-feminist body.

Women's Aid

In 1972, the first UK Women's Aid refuge was set up in Chiswick, London, two years prior to the establishment of the Women's Aid Federation. This charity co-ordinates and supports local projects, provides over 500 refuges, runs helplines and outreach services. In terms of the extent of their work-load and demand for services, statistics show that over 40,000 women and children stay in refuges each year. Women and children's use of all the services offered by Women's Aid is growing year on year. In 2004/2005, 196,205 women and 129,193 children were supported.

The strain on these services is best illustrated by focusing on the local level of provision, see Box 7.3. In Newcastle upon Tyne, this translates into six calls every day and for the period April 2003-March 2004 they helped 827 women and 1,039 children (Citylife, 2004).

Box 7.3 Women's Aid in North Tyneside, South Tyneside and Newcastle

South Tyneside

Numbers of families helped locally over a period of a year = 104 women (families) and 125 children staying during 2002/03 (South Tyneside Women's Aid, 2002/03).

North Tyneside

For the same year in North Tyneside, they helped 93 women (families) and 109 children and received a total number of 720 calls for accommodation and/or advice.

NB: This does not take account of personal visits made to the refuge by women calling in for advice, and ex-residents who come back to visit and who often need continuing support.

Staff complement = 1 full-time Project Manager, 2 full-time refuge workers, 1 full-time administrative staff, 1 full-time Floating Support worker, 1 part-time finance worker, 1 part-time cleaner and 4 part-time night staff (personal communication 2004).

Floating Support Scheme

North and South Tyneside Women's Aid project also run a Floating Support Scheme where support is provided for women moving into new tenancies after leaving supported housing. This support can range from six weeks to two years (North Tyneside Women's Aid, 2002/2004).

Newcastle upon Tyne Freedom Programme

Examples of local projects supported by the Women's Aid Federation, in Newcastle includes a 12-week 'Freedom Programme'. This programme recognizes that women who have been victims of abuse can be very vulnerable and the programme helps women to protect themselves in the future.

Probation Partnership

Many local Women's Aid branches have partnerships with the Probation Service. Refuge workers from North Tyneside Women's Aid have previously taken referrals from Northumbria Probation Service whose male clients had been placed on a DIVERT Programme, a programme intended to address their violent behaviour towards their partners.

While at a national and local level, Women's Aid statistics are testament to the need to provide safe emergency accommodation and support to families suffering from domestic violence, and while many women and children benefit from the support and assistance offered, the service is unable to accommodate many others and demand outstrips available provision. South Tyneside (in Tyne and Wear in the North-East) Women's Aid report that from the 345 referrals received in the year 2002/03 they were unable to accommodate 49 per cent due to a full house or the rooms were too small to accommodate the size of the family (South Tyneside Women's Aid, 2002/03). Research has also uncovered some interesting anomalies between urban and rural demands upon services (Davies et al., 2001). This points towards the unmet needs of many hundreds of women and children across the country every year and re-confirms the general under-provision of refuge places and a need to develop services in line with those needs. While the notion of victims,' needs is a controversial one (Zedner, 2003), there is no doubt that women's immediate and longer-term needs in surviving domestic violence include the need for safe accommodation and refuge provision and these women's needs are surely among the more serious unmet needs of victim groups.

The brief illustration of some aspects of provision and assistance for female victims of crime from the voluntary sector, together with a snapshot of the demands made upon local Women's Aid projects, illustrates the enormous and continuing demand for such services from women striving to become survivors of domestic violence. While the assistance and support provisions that have emerged from within the voluntary sector are diverse and often compete with one another for funding, staffing and clientele, they do share some key hallmarks of pro-feminist support networks. They tend to empha-size survival aspects in both their formal and informal means of support and encourage women's recovery through status passage from victim to survivor through giving women more access through self-help to personal power (Stanko, 1990a,b). All of this is in stark contrast to the core philosophies and ideals enshrined and observed in the formal criminal justice system towards victims of crime and female victims in particular.

Women as victimizers

In terms of women as offenders and perpetrators and therefore as victim-izers, official and most other measures indicate a gender patterning of crime (Davies, 2005). First, women commit far fewer crimes than men. Second, while women do engage in the full range of notifiable offences and therefore inflict damage upon property and do harms to the person, women tend to specialize in crime differently to men. Women's offending is largely characterized by the commission of theft-related offences, in par-ticular, shoplifting and therefore, for the most part we do harm (but not as much as men) to the retail sector by undermining their profit margins. Moreover, criminological theorizing of women's property-related crime and offending patterns dwells heavily upon reasons and explanations for their doing of crime that tend to downplay the significance of their offending and raise awareness of their multiple disadvantages and marginal economic position. This shows the influence of socialist feminism and its struggle for social justice which has tended to divert feminist atten-tion away from explaining female law-breaking. There has been a reluc-tance to admit that women might mean to do property crime and that some of their motivations are more akin to economic greed than need (Davies, 2003a, 2003b, 2005). This enhances the tendency to see women as vulner-able and socially and culturally victimized rather than as entrepreneurs and 'hot-shot wheeler-dealers' (Mellor, 2003) in crime similar to their male counterparts. Leaving property-related criminality aside, however, there are a number of significant and more serious aspects to women's offend-ing that tend to be masked by general patterns.

The subject of 'women who kill' is a constant fascination to undergrad-uate students (especially female students) judging by the numbers of dis-sertations they choose to do on this topic. Interest in women who kill is often rekindled by the media reminders of notorious female accomplices and child killers. In the UK, they include Myra Hyndley, Mary Bell, and more recently Rose West and we are sporadically reminded of the 'evil staring face' of Hyndley as her black and white photograph is reproduced in the media. More recently provocative headlines have not exactly shifted the fascination but have given it a different slant. Female-specific headlines are still rare but have more recently included: 'Mothers Who Kill: Not as Rare as We Think' (*Independent* 1999). Also, there appears to be concern once every ten years or so about girls' involvement in youthful violence. There has been TV *Public Eye* reports, for example, Robbins' report on the Ghetto Girls and the Peckham Rude Girls. Girl gangs were newsworthy again after the actress Elizabeth Hurley was robbed at knifepoint in Chelsea and threatened with a broken bottle allegedly by a gang of four teenage girls in 1994 (Knowsley, 1994). Almost a decade later, there was a surge of interest in young women's alcohol consumption leading to the female equivalent of men behaving badly, the 'Ladette' (Walklate, 2001).

Academic interest in women's apparently rising and occasionally extreme forms of violence has also more recently taken a different turn. In the US, there is a steady stream of studies on girl gangs and their use of violence. Attention is now upon women doing robbery and other forms of violent crime, often in connection to drugs (Sommers and Baskin, 1992; Sammers et al.,1993; Miller, 1998, 2001, 2002; Batchelor et al., 2001; Chesney-Lind and Pasko, 2004). In the UK and Canada, there would appear to be new areas for victimological inquiries and theorising connected to **feminal abuse** and killing including **femicide** (Jamieson, 1998), homicide, **infanticide** and other serious forms of violence (see, e.g., Brookman, 2004).

▶▶ **Feminal abuse**   *abuse pertaining to women.*

▶▶ **Femicide**   *the killing of a woman.*

▶▶ **Infanticide**   *the killing of an infant by or with the consent of the parents but usually by the mother.*

Traditionally, however, women both suffering from and perpetrating crime have been portrayed as the 'evil woman', the 'mad woman' and the 'bad whore' and it has been very slow progress for feminist criminological and victimological scholarship to overcome this legacy and be taken seriously. In the same way that we have been reluctant criminologically to contemplate that women might mean to do property crime, there is a reluctance criminologically, and a huge challenge to feminist criminological scholarship to take on the subject of women as perpetrators of child sexual abuse and infanticide (Davies, 2006). Yet, women are very often primary carers, and whether as babysitters, child-minders, nannies, teachers, friends, relatives or parents and mothers, they have ample opportunity to perpetrate abuse. As Williams points out: 'Child physical abuse is a prevalent occurrence; both sexes suffer it and both perpetrate it' (2004: 99). Even where women are suspected, they are in a more powerful position than their vulnerable victims and are shielded (Turton, 2000) and/or are seen as exceptions to the rule (Carrabine et al., 2004).

When there is literature on these subjects, it tends to be researched and authored by scholars belonging to the fields of psychiatry, behavioural sciences, mental and medical health, (see e.g. Finkelhor and Russell, 1984; Faller, 1987, Wilkins 1990; Elliot and Peterson, 1993), and their material is published in very specific journals such as *Child Abuse and Neglect* (e.g. Johnson 1989) and the *Journal of Sex Education and Therapy* (e.g. Laury 1992). The dissemination of this scholarship is from disciplines that are extremely marginal to criminology and is not easily accessed by criminologists. This suggests transgressive (Cain, 1990) approaches for understanding women as victimizers might be useful to victimology.

There are a number of 'syndromes' as studied in the health and medical fields including psychiatry and psychology. One example is Munchausen's Syndrome by Proxy (MSBP) or 'Munchausen's'- a name borrowed from Baron Munchausen and the hero of an extravagant and deceitful story of adventure. The nurse Beverley Allitt brought MSBP into the public spotlight. Allitt was jailed for the murder of four babies and injured nine others between 1991 and 1993 (BBC News, 1999). A Cardiff mother brought MSBP back to the Crown Courts where she admitted to two charges of child cruelty after subjecting her child to unnecessary surgical procedures causing risk and discomfort (BBC News, 2003). Another syndrome, Sudden Infant Death (SIDS) has also featured in topical news stories during the past decade as well as 'post-natal psychosis', an extreme form of post-natal depression, and a defence in England for infanticide until a child is the age of 2. Connected to interpersonal violence experienced by women, and of interest to socio-legal scholars, gendered pleas including the use of the 'plea of provocation' together with the notion of 'psychological self-defence' (Walklate, 2001) appear to be more widely reported in cases when women kill their male partners. In Australia, one report claims there is a history of domestic violence in more than 70 per cent of such cases (Bagshaw and Chung, 2000).

One recent headline has implicated a mother of infanticide: 'Cause of Death Unknown' (*Guardian*, 2003) and, taking up the challenge of exploring the facts and fiction of infanticide, criminologist Brookman (2004) cautions against confusing Sudden Infant Death Syndrome (SIDS) with infanticides. Recent statistics suggest that while homicide is predominantly a 'masculine' affair, female offending begins to parallel that of males in the instance of infanticide (Brookman, 2004). Also, woman-to-man and woman-to-woman inter-personal violence appear to be growth areas for criminological research (see, for example, Abel, 2001; Grady, 2002; Babcock et al., 2003; Bacon, 2004) and several surveys report significant levels of domestic violence perpetrated by women against men:

- A victimization survey of female-perpetrated assaults in the UK found that men reported being victimised by females more than women and experiencing the more severe forms of assault (George, 1999).
- The BCS (Home Office, 2004) estimates 9 per cent of men had been subject to domestic violence; sexual victimization or stalking in the 12 months prior to interview although not all of these will have been female-to-male violence.

QUESTIONS

What are the obstacles to exposing and explaining criminal victimization as perpetrated by women?

Are women still the 'Criminological Other' or can women now be 'real' offenders and criminal victimizers?

Summary

While this chapter has illustrated how the social relations of gender in the study of victims are being increasingly exposed, criminologically there is still an apparent reluctance to consider women as real criminals (Heidensohn, 1989; Davies, 2003a, 2003b,) and victimologically there is an apparently similar reluctance to acknowledge the full extent and range of the victimizations that women suffer and consequently to appreciate and understand more comprehensively what constitutes victimization and who counts as victims. Social stereotypes of femininity and motherhood enable women as victimizers to remain largely invisible, shielded from being suspected and accused by criminal justice and child protection agencies of the most serious forms of victimization. Thus criminologically and victimologically, women are not real criminals, they are not real victims and they are not real victimizers. Women fall within the blurred boundaries of what constitutes crime and victimization in society. Women largely remain invisible victims and invisible victimizers.

ANNOTATED BIBLIOGRAPHY

Davies, P. (2007) 'Lessons from the gender agenda' in S. Walklate (eds.) *Handbook of Victims and Victimology* Cullompton: Willan. This provides a thorough review and assessment of the salience of gender to understanding crime, social harm and victimization.

Hollway, W. and Jefferson, T. (2000a) 'The role of anxiety in fear of crime', **in T. Hope and R. Sparks (eds),** *Crime, Risk and Insecurity.* **London: Routledge; Hollway, W. and Jefferson, T. (2000b)** *Doing Qualitative Research Differently.* **London: Sage.** These two references collect together internet data from men and women and explore realistic and rational fears and whether they are mediated by social characteristics such as gender and age.

Pearce, J. and Stanko, E. (2000) 'Young women and community safety', *Youth and Policy,* **66: 1–18.** This is a good example of how recent feminist scholarship is beginning to recast women and girls outside of the traditional stereotypes about victimization, an article that focuses on young women and community safety.

Ristanovic, V. (1999) *Women, Violence and War.* **Budapest: Central European University Press.** This is an edited collection of articles on the theme of women, violence and war and as such conveniently brings together a number of case studies on the wartime victimization of refugees in the Balkans.

Szockyj, E. and Fox, J.G. (1996) *Corporate Victimization of Women.* **Boston: Northeastern University Press.** This collection includes theoretical perspectives on the subject as well as the ways in which women are physically exposed to hazards incurring miscarriages, respiratory ailments in the silicon chip industry (Simpson and Elis), the contribution of the pharmaceutical industry to compromising women's reproductive health (Finley), women's victimization in employment (Davis) and at work (Randall), in the marketplace where women can be harmed by products and services that aim to enhance their appearance (Claybrook) and before the law (Fox).

References

Abel, E.M. (2001) 'Comparing the Social Service Utilisation, exposure to violence, and trauma symtomology of domestic violence female "victims" and female "batterers"', *Journal of Family Violence*, 16(4): 401–20.

Askin, K.D. (1997) *War Crimes Against Women: Prosecution in International War Crimes Tribunals.* The Hague: Kluwer.

Babcock, J.C., Miller, S.A. and Siard, C. (2003) 'Toward a typology of abusive women: differences between partner-only and generally violent women in the use of violence', *Psychology of Women Quarterly*, 27: 153–61.

Bacon, B. (2004) 'Women's violence towards intimate partners: intergenerational explanations and policy considerations', paper presented to the British Criminology Conference, July, Portsmouth.

Bagshaw, D. and Chung, D. (2000) *Women, Men and Domestic Violence*. Commonwealth of Australia: University of South Australia.

Batchelor, S., Burman, M. and Brown, J. (2001) 'Discussing violence: let's hear it from the girls', *Probation Journal*, 48(2): 125–34.

BBC News (1999) 'Health experts to study controversial abuse syndrome', 19 August, available at: http://news.bbc.co.uk/1/hi/health/424772.stm

BBC News (2003) 'Mother faked son's illness for attention', 7 February, available at: http://news.bbc.co.uk/1/hi/wales/2737361.stm

Bennetto, J. and Judd, T. (2004) 'Murder cases under review to identify "honour killings"', available at: http://news.independent.co.uk/uk/crime/story.jsp?story=534253

Bishop, P. (2001) 'Bosnian Serbs jailed for rape and sexual slavery', *The Daily Telegraph*, 23 Feb.

Brookman, F. (2004) 'Infanticide: fact and fiction', paper presented to the British Criminology Conference, July, Portsmouth.

Brown, P. (1999) 'Companies to face naming and shaming for emission of cancer-causing chemicals', *The Guardian*, 8 Feb.

Budd, T. and Mattinson, J. (2000) *The Extent and Nature of Stalking: Findings from the 1998 British Crime Survey,* Home Office Research Study 210. London: Home Office.

Caiazza, A. (2001) 'Why gender matters in understanding September 11: women, militarism, and violence', Institute for Women's Policy Research Briefing paper No. 1908.

Cain, M. (1990) 'Realist philosophy and standpoint epistemologies or feminist criminology as a successor science?', in L. Gelsthorpe and A. Morris (eds), *Feminist Perspectives in Criminology*. Milton Keynes: Open University Press.

Campbell, B. (1993) *Goliath: Britain's Dangerous Places*. London: Virago.

Carlen, P. (1988) *Women, Crime and Poverty.* Buckingham: Open University Press.

Carlen, P. (ed.) (2002) *Women and Punishment: The Struggle for Justice.* Cullompton: Willan.

Carrabine, E., Iganski, P., Lee, M., Plummer, K. and South, N. (2004) 'Victims and victimization', in *Criminology: A Sociological Introduction*, London: Routledge.

Chan, W. and Rigakos, G.S. (2002) 'Risk, crime and gender', *British Journal of Criminology*, 42: 743–61.

Chesney-Lind, M. and Pasko, L. (2004) *The Female Offender: Girls, Women, and Crime*, 2nd edition. London: Sage.

Chigwada-Bailey, R. (2003) *Black Women's Experiences of Criminal Justice: Race, Gender and Class: A Discourse on Disadvantage*. Winchester: Waterside Press.

Christie, N. (1986) 'The ideal victim', in E. Fattah (ed.), *From Crime Policy to Victim Policy*. London: Macmillan.

Citylife (2004) 'Giving women a helping hand', *Citylife*, August 2004: 7.

Claybrook, J. (1996) 'Women in the marketplace', in E. Szockyj and J.G. Fox (eds), *Corporate Victimization of Women*. Boston: Northeastern University Press.

Cohen, S. (2002) *States of Denial: Knowing about Atrocities and Suffering*. Cambridge: Polity Press.

Connell, R.W. (1987) *Gender and Power*. Oxford: Polity.

Connell, R.W. (1995) *Masculinities*. Oxford: Polity.

Corporate Watch (2004a) 'Nestle SA'. Available at: http://www.corporatewatch.org.uk/profiles/food-supermarkets/nestle/nestle1.html

Corporate Watch (2004b) 'Monsanto Corporate Crimes'. Available at: http://www.corporatewatch.org.uk/profiles/biotech/Monsanto/monsanto5.html

Crawford, A., Jones, T., Woodhouse, T. and Young, J. (1990) *Second Islington Crime Survey*. London: Middlesex Polytechnic.

Cretney, A. and Davis, G. (1995) *Punishing Violence*. London: Routledge.

Croall, H. (1995) 'Target women: women's victimisation from white-collar crime', in R.P. Dobash, R.E. Dobash and J. Noaks (eds), *Gender and Crime*. Cardiff: Cardiff University Press.

Croall, H. (1998) *Crime and Society in Britain*. London: Longman.

Croall, H. (2001) *Understanding White Collar Crime*. Buckingham: Open University Press.

CWASU (2002) *Information on Trafficking in Women and Children for Sexual Exploitation*. Available at: http://www.cwasu.org/factsontrafficking1.htm

Davies, P. (2003a) 'Is economic crime a man's game?', *Feminist Theory*, 4(3): 283–303.

Davies, P. (2003b) 'Women and crime: doing it for the kids?', *Criminal Justice Matters,* 50: 28–9.

Davies, P. (2005) 'Women and crime for economic gain', unpublished PhD Northumbria University.

Davies, P. (2006) 'Victims, victimology and lessons from the gender agenda', paper presented at the British Society of Criminology Annual Conference, Glasgow, July.

Davis, P. (2007) 'Lessons from the gender agenda' in S. Walklate (ed) *Handbook of Victims and Victimology*. Cullompton: Willan.

Davies, P., Clark, A., Francis, P. and Thompson, J. (2001) *Domestic Violence in Rural Northumberland*. Newcastle: University of Northumbria.

Davies, P., Francis, P. and Jupp, V. (eds.) (1999) *Invisible Crimes: Their Victims and Their Regulation*. Basingstoke: Macmillan Press.

Davies, P., Francis, P. and Jupp, V. (eds) (2004) *Victimization: Theory, Research and Policy*. London: Palgrave.

Davies, P. and Jupp, V. (1999) 'Crime-work connections: exploring the invisibility of workplace crime', in P. Davies, P. Francis and V. Jupp (eds), *Invisible Crimes: Their Victims and Their Regulation*. Basingstoke: Macmillan Press, pp. 54–74.

Davis, S.M. (1996) 'Employment discrimination', in E. Szockyj and J.G. Fox (eds), *Corporate Victimization of Women*, Boston: Northeastern University Press.

Dignan, J. (2005) *Understanding Victims and Restorative Justice*. Buckingham: Open University Press.

Dobash, R.E. and Dobash, R.P. (1979) *Violence Against Wives: A Case Against Patriarchy*. Shepton Mallet: Open Books.

Dobash, R.P. and Dobash, R.E. (1998) *Rethinking Violence Against Women*. London: Sage.

Elliot, A.J. and Peterson, L.W. (1993) 'Maternal sexual abuse of male children: when to suspect and how to uncover it', *Postgraduate Medicine*, 94(1): 169–80.

Enarson, E. and Hearn Marrow, B. (eds) (1998) *The Gendered Terrain of Disaster*. Miami, FL: Florida Laboratory for Social and Behavioral Research: Florida International University.

Faller, K.C. (1987) 'Women who sexually abuse children', *Violence and Victims*, 2(4): 263–76.

The Feminist Majority Foundation (2001) 'Feminists against sweatshops'. Available at: http://www.feminist.org/other/sweatshops/sweatfaq.html

Finkelhor, D. and Russell, D. (1984) 'Women as perpetrators: review of the evidence', in D. Finkelhor (ed.), *Child Sexual Abuse: New Theory and Research*. New York: The Free Press, pp. 171–87.

Finley, L.M. (1996) 'The pharmaceutical industry and women's health', in E. Szockyj and J.G. Fox (eds), *Corporate Victimization of Women*. Boston: Northeastern University Press.

Fisher, B.S. and Gunnison, E. (2001) 'Violence in the workplace: gender similarities and differences', *Journal of Criminal Justice*, 29(2): 145–55.

Fox, J.G. (1996) 'Policy and social change', in E. Szockyj and J.G. Fox (eds), *Corporate Victimization of Women*. Boston: Northeastern University Press.

George, M.J. (1999) 'A victimization survey of female-perpetrated assaults in the United Kingdom', *Aggressive Behaviour*, 25(1): 67–79.

Gerber, J. and Weekes, S.L. (1992) 'Women as victims of corporate crime: a call for research on a neglected topic', *Deviant Behaviour*, 13: 325–47.

Gilchrist, E., Bannister, J., Ditton, J. and Farrall, S. (1998) 'Women and the fear of crime: challenging the accepted stereotype', *British Journal of Criminology*, 38(2): 283–98.

Gilchrist, E. and Blisset, J. (2002) 'Magistrates' attitudes towards domestic violence and sentencing', *Howard Journal of Criminal Justice*, 41: 4: 348–73.

Gilligan, C. (1982) *In a Different Voice: Psychological Theory and Women's Development*. Cambridge, MA: Harvard University Press.

Goodey, J. (2004) 'Sex trafficking in women from Central and East European countries: promoting a "victim-centred" and "woman-centred" approach to criminal justice intervention', *Feminist Review*, 76: 26–45.

Goodey, J. (2005) *Victims and Victimology: Research, Policy and Practice*. London: Longman.

Grady, A. (2002) 'Female-on-male domestic abuse: uncommon or ignored', in C. Hoyle and R. Young (eds), *New Visions of Crime Victims*. Oxford: Hart.

Hall, R. (1985) *Ask Any Woman*. Bristol: Falling Wall Press.

Hanmer, J. and Maynard, M. (eds) (1987) *Women, Violence and Social Control*. London: Macmillan.

Hanmer, J., Radford, J. and Stanko, E. A. (1989) *Women, Policing and Male Violence*. London: Routledge.

Hanmer, J. and Saunders, S. (1984) *Well Founded Fear: A Community Study of Violence to Women,* London: Hutchinson.

Harding, S. (ed.) (1987) *Feminism and Methodology*. Milton Keynes: Open University Press.

Heidensohn, F. (1989) *Crime and Society*. London: Macmillan.

Hester, M., Kelly, L. and Radford, J. (eds) (1996) *Women, Violence and Male Power*. Buckingham: Open University Press.

Hindelang, M.J., Gottfredson, M.R. and Garofalo, J. (1978) *Victims of Personal Crime: An Empirical Foundation for a Theory of Personal Victimisation*. Cambridge, MA: Ballinger.

Hollway, W. and Jefferson, T. (2000a) 'The role of anxiety in fear of crime', in T. Hope and R. Sparks (eds), *Crime, Risk and Insecurity*, London: Routledge.

Hollway, W. and Jefferson, T. (2000b) *Doing Qualitative Research Differently: Free Association, Narrative and the Interview Method*. London: Sage.

Home Office (2001) *The Criminal Injuries Compensation Scheme*. London: Home Office.

Home Office (2004) http://www.crimereduction.gov.uk/domesticviolence42.htm

Home Office (2005) *The Code of Practice for Victims of Crime. A Guide for Victims*. London: Office for Criminal Justice Reform.

Hough, M. and Mayhew, P. (1983) *The British Crime Survey*, Home Office Research Study, 76. London: HMSO.

Howarth, G. and Rock, P. (2000) 'Aftermath and the construction of victimization: The other victims of crime', *Howard Journal of Criminal Justice*, 39(1): 58.

Hudson, B. (1998) 'Restorative justice: the challenge of racial and sexual violence', *Journal of Law and Society*, 25: 237–56.

Hudson, B. (2000) 'Critical reflection as research methodology', in V. Jupp, P. Davies and P. Francis (eds), *Doing Criminological Research*. London: Sage.

Hughes, D.M. and Denisova, T. (2002) 'Trafficking in women from Ukraine', http://www.ncjrs.org/pdffiles1nij/grants/203275.pdf

Human Rights Watch (2004) *The Aftermath of Rape and Other Forms of Sexual Violence*. New York: Human Rights Watch.

Independent (1999) 'Mothers Who Kill: Not as Rare as We Think', 18 March.

Jamieson, R. (1998) 'Towards a criminology of war in Europe', in V. Ruggiero, N. South and I. Taylor (eds), *The New European Criminology: Crime and Social Order in Europe* London: Routledge.

Joe-Laidler, K. and Hunt, G. (2001) 'Accomplishing femininity among the girls in the gang'. *British Journal of Criminology*, 41: 656–78.

Johnson, T.C. (1989) 'Female child perpetrators: children who molest other children', *Child Abuse and Neglect*, 13: 571–85.

Jones, T., Maclean, B. and Young, J. (1986) *The Islington Crime Survey: Crime, Victimization and Policing in Inner-City London*. London: Gower.

Kahn, A.S., Jackson, J., Kully, C., Badger, K. and Halvorsen, J. (2003) 'Calling it rape: differences in experiences of women who do or do not label their sexual assault as rape', *Psychology of Women Quarterly*, 27(3): 233–42.

Kennedy, H. (1998) 'foreward', in M. Nuttall, *It Could Have Been You*. London: Virago.

King, R.D. and Wincup, E. (eds) (2000) *Doing Research on Crime and Justice*. Oxford: Oxford University Press.

Knowsley, J. (1994) 'Earrings, bracelets and baseball bats', *The Sunday Telegraph*, 27 November, p. 3.

Laury, G.V. (1992) 'When women sexually abuse male psychiatric patients under their care', *Journal of Sex Education and Therapy*, 18(1): 11–16.

Lees, S. (1997) *Ruling Passions*. London: Sage.

Lewis, R. (2004) 'Making justice work – effective legal interventions for domestic violence', *British Journal of Criminology*, 44(2): 2–4.

London Rape Crisis Centre (1984) *Sexual Violence: The Reality for Women*. London: LRCC.

Lynch, M.J. and Stretesky, P. (2001) 'Toxic crimes: examining corporate victimisation of the general public employing medical and epidemiological evidence', *Critical Criminology*, 10: 153–72.

Madge, N. (1997) *Abuse and Survival: A Fact File*. Cornwall: The Prince's Trust Action.

Marsh, I., with J. Cochrane and G. Melville (2004) *Criminal Justice: An Introduction to Philosophies, Theories and Practice*. London: Routledge.

Mawby, R.I. and Walklate, S. (1994) *Critical Victimology*. London: Sage.

Mayhew, P. (2000) 'Researching the state of crime: local, national, and international victim surveys', in R.D. King and E. Wincup (eds), *Doing Research on Crime and Justice*. Oxford: Oxford University Press.

Mayhew, P., Elliott, D. and Dowds, L. (1989) *The 1988 British Crime Survey*. London: HMSO.

Mellor, M. (2003) 'Money is not wealth', *Resurgence,* 217: 14–15.

Messerschmidt, J.W. (1993) *Masculinities and Crime*. Lanham, MD: Rowman and Littlefield.

Miers, D. (1989) 'Positivist victimology', *International Review of Victimology*, 1(1): 3–22.

Miller, J. (1998) 'Up it up: gender and the accomplishment of street robbery', *Criminology*, 36(1): 37–66.

Miller, J. (2001) *One of the Guys: Girls, Gangs and Gender*. New York: Oxford University Press.

Miller, J. (2002) 'The strengths and limits of "doing-gender" for understanding street crime', *Theoretical Criminology*, 6(4): 433–60.

Mintz, M. (1985) *At Any Cost: Corporate Greed, Women, and the Dalkon Shield*. New York: Pantheon Books.

Mirrlees-Black, C. and Byron, C. (1999) *Domestic Violence: Findings from the BCS Self-Completion Questionnaire,* Research Findings No. 83. London: Home Office.

Mooney, J. (2000) *Gender, Violence and the Social Order*. London: Palgrave.

Morley, R. and Mullender, A. (1994) *Preventing Domestic Violence to Women*, Crime Prevention Unit, Paper 48. London: Home Office Police Department.

Nelson, J.A. (1996) *Feminism, Objectivity and Economics*. London: Routledge.

Nuttall, M. (1998) *It Could Have Been You*. London: Virago.

Pain, R. (2001) 'Gender, race, age and fear in the city', *Urban Studies*, 38(5–6): 899–913.

Pearce, J. and Stanko, E. (2000) 'Young women and community safety', *Youth and Policy*, 66: 1–18.

Pearce, F. and Tombs, S. (1997) 'Hazards, law and class: contextualising the regulation of corporate crime', *Social and Legal Studies*, 6(1): 79–107.

Pearce, F. and Tombs, S. (1998) *Toxic Capitalism: Corporate Crime and the Chemical Industry*. Aldershot: Ashgate.

Peppin, J. (1995) 'Feminism, law and the pharmaceutical industry', in F. Pearce and L. Snider (eds), *Corporate Crime: Contemporary Debates*. Toronto: University of Toronto Press.

Perry, S. and Dawson, J. (1985) *Nightmare: Women and the Dalkon Shield*. New York: Macmillan.

Raj, A. and Silverman, J. (2002) 'Violence against immigrant women', *Violence Against Women*, 8(3): 367.

Randall, D.M. (1996) 'Exclusionary policies in the workplace', in E. Szockyj and J.G. Fox (eds) *Corporate Victimization of Women*. Boston: Northeastern University Press.

Ristanovic, V. (ed.) (1999) *Women, Violence and War: Wartime Victimization of Refugees in the Balkans*. Budapest: Central European University Press.

Ristanovic, V. (2004) 'War victimization of women'. Available at: http://www.penelopes.org Anglais/xarticle.php3?id-article=302

Rock, P. (1990) *Helping Victims of Crime: The Home Office and the Rise of Victim Support in England and Wales*. Oxford: Oxford University Press.

Rock, P. (ed.) (1993) *Victimology*. Aldershot: Dartmouth.

Ruggiero, V., South, N. and Taylor, I. (1998) *The New European Criminology*. London: Routledge.

Sheley, J.F. (1995) *Criminology: A Contemporary Handbook*, 2nd edition. London: Wadsworth.

Simmons, J. and Dodd, T. (2003) *Crime in England and Wales 2002/2003*. London: Home Office.

Simpson, S.S. and Elis, L. (1996) 'Theoretical perspectives on the corporate victimization of Women', in E. Szockyj and J. G. Fox (eds), *Corporate Victimization of Women*. Boston: Northeastern University Press.

Slapper, G. and Tombs, S. (1999) *Corporate Crime*. London: Addison-Wesley Longman.

Smith, C. and Wincup, E. (2000) 'Breaking in: researching criminal justice institutions for women', in R.D. King and E. Wincup (eds), *Doing Research on Crime and Justice*. Oxford: Oxford University Press.

Smith, D.K. (2001) 'Superannuating the second sex: law, privatisation and retirement income', *Modern Law Review*, 64(4): 519–43.

Sommers, I. and Baskin, D. (1992) 'Sex, age, race and violent offending', *Violence and Victims*, 7(3): 191–201.

Sommers, I., Deborah, R. and Baskin, R. (1993) 'The situational context of violent female offending', *Journal of Research in Crime and Delinquency*, 30: 136–62.

South Tyneside Women's Aid (2003) *South Tyneside Women's Aid Report 2002/03*. STWA.

Stanko, E. (1987) 'Typical violence, normal precaution: men, women and interpersonal violence in England, Wales and Scotland and the 'USA', in J. Hanmer and M. Maynard (eds), *Women, Violence and Social Control*. London: Macmillan.

Stanko, E. (1988) 'Hidden violence against women', in M. Maguire and J. Pointing (eds), *Victims of Crime: A New Deal?* Milton Keynes: Open University Press.

Stanko, E. (1990a) *Everyday Violence: How Women and Men Experience Sexual and Physical Danger*. London: Pandora.

Stanko, E. (1990b) 'When precaution is normal: a feminist critique of crime prevention', in L. Gelsthorpe and A. Morris (eds), *Feminist Perspectives in Criminology*. Milton Keynes: Open University Press.

Stewart, L. (2004) 'I am more angry at the system than at my rapist', *The Daily Telegraph*, Thursday, 15 April 2004: 21.

Swasy, A. (1996) 'Rely Tampons and toxic shock syndrome: Procter and Gamble's responses', in M.D. Ermann and R.J. Lundman (eds), *Corporate and Governmental Deviance: Problems of Organisational Behaviour in Contemporary Society*, Oxford: Oxford University Press.

Szockyj, E. and Fox, J.G. (1996) *Corporate Victimization of Women.* Boston: Northeastern University Press.

Turton, J. (2000) 'Maternal sexual abuse and its victims', *Childright*, 165: 17–18.

Tzvetkoya, M. (2002) 'NGO responses to trafficking in women', *Gender and Development*, 10(1): 60–8.

Upson, A. (2004) *Violence at Work: Findings from the 2002/2003 British Crime Survey.* London: Home Office.

US Department of State (2003) *Trafficking in Persons Report.* Available at: http://www.state.gov/g/tip/rls/tiprpt/2003/21262.htm

Venis, S. and Horton, R. (2002) 'Violence against women: a global burden', *The Lancet*, 359(9313): 1172–235.

Walby, S. and Allen, J. (2004) *Domestic Violence, Sexual Assault and Stalking: Findings from the British Crime Survey.* London: Home Office.

Walklate, S. (1995) *Gender and Crime.* London: Harvester Wheatsheaf.

Walklate, S. (1997) 'Risk and criminal victimization: a modernist dilemma?', *British Journal of Criminology*, 37(1): 35–45.

Walklate, S. (2000) 'Researching victims', in R.D. King and E. Wincup (eds), *Doing Research on Crime and Justice.* Oxford: Oxford University Press.

Walklate, S. (2001) 'The victim's lobby', in M. Ryan, S. Savage, and D. Wall (eds), *Policy Networks in Criminal Justice.* Basingstoke: Palgrave.

Walklate, S. (2002) *Understanding Criminology: Current Theoretical Debates*, 2nd edition. Buckingham: Open University Press.

Walklate, S. (2004a) 'Can there be a feminist victimology?', in P. Davies, P. Francis and V. Jupp (eds), *Victimization: Theory, Research and Policy.* London: Palgrave.

Walklate, S. (2004b) *Gender, Crime and Criminal Justice*, 2nd edition. Cullompton: Willan.

Watts, C. and Zimmerman, C. (2002) 'Violence against women: Global scope and magnitude', *Lancet*, 359(9313): 1232–7.

Wilkins, R. (1990) 'Women who sexually abuse children: doctors need to become sensitised to the possibility', *British Medical Journal*, 300(3000): 1153–4.

Williams, B. (1999) *Working with Victims of Crime.* London: Jessica Kingsley.

Williams, K. (2004) *Textbook of Criminology*, 5th edition. Oxford: Oxford University Press.

Women's Aid (2003) *Women's Aid Federation of England.* Available at: http://www.women-said.org.uk/about-wafe.htm.

Women's Aid Federation of England and Wales (2004) *Women's Aid Briefing Paper Domestic Violence, Crime and Victims Bill January 2004.* London: Women's Aid.

Worrall, A. (1990) *Offending Women: Female Lawbreakers and the Criminal Justice System.* New York: Routledge.

Wright, S. and Hill, P. (2004) 'Victims, crime and criminal justice', in J. Muncie and D. Wilson (eds), *Student Handbook of Criminal Justice and Criminology.* London: Cavendish Publishing Limited.

Zedner, L. (2003) 'Victims', in M. Maguire, R. Morgan and R. Reiner (eds), *The Oxford Handbook of Criminology*, 3rd edition. Oxford: Oxford University Press.

Young People, Victims and Crime

Peter Francis

Chapter aims

- To introduce discourses on youth, crime and victimization.
- To describe the incidence and prevalence of victimization among young people and acknowledge the relationship between offenders and victims.
- To discuss the importance of understanding youth crime victimization within socio-economic, cultural and political contexts.
- To examine the voices of young people within research and policy making around crime and victimization.

Introduction

When the words 'crime' and **'youth'** are paired together, the ensuing picture in most people's minds is that of the young person as offender. Given the frequency of offending by **young people**, this is perhaps not surprising. The peak age of offending for both boys and girls is 18 years; offenders under the age of 18 commit a quarter of all crime, and research informs us that offending decreases with age (Graham and Bowling, 1995). The 'problem of crime' is often equated with the 'problem of youth' (Muncie, 2004; Goldson and Muncie, 2006). The 'problem of youth crime' is reinforced by the media's stories of undisciplined youth, and of prolific, persistent and violent young offenders. In political and policy discourses, young people are presented as a perennial source of fear, anxiety and danger and in need of control. An ever-increasing battery of criminal justice powers and civil legislation reflects this, the aim of which is the formal regulation and pervasive monitoring and surveillance of young people and their education, work, leisure and recreational activities.

▸▸ **Youth**   *a number of criminologists have attempted to define the term youth, but Muncie (2004: 314) sums it up well: 'An ill-defined and variable period of the life-span between infancy and adulthood'.*

▸▸ **Young people**   *there is no definitive definition of young people. However, for the purposes of this book, and acknowledging that transition to adulthood is delayed and prolonged, the term young people is used to denote those children and young people under the age of 25.*

In contrast, the words 'youth' and 'victimization' are rarely co-joined. The focus upon young people as offenders has left us blind to the extent to which young people are victims of crime and fearful of the activities of other young people as well as adults. This is as much a criticism that can be directed towards criminology and victimology as it can the media and the state. For example, criminology has conventionally focused upon offending youth, exploring (and often appreciating) the activities and causes of their criminal and anti-social behaviour (Brown, 1998; Muncie, 2004). Beyond those studies on child abuse and domestic violence, victimology has paid scant attention to young people's experiences, perceptions and fears of crime, criminal justice and community safety. It is little wonder then that, as Sheila Brown (1998) has acknowledged, while young people have continuously been *ascribed* their status as offenders, it appears as if they have to *earn* their status as victims.

In the past 20 years there has emerged an embryonic if unfocused 'youth victimology' (Muncie, 2003). This has been informed by critical sociologies and criminologies of youth (see, for example, Furlong and Cartmel, 1997; MacDonald, 1997; Muncie, 2004) and by political and policy developments intent on reversing the democratic deficit in local decision-making (Pain and Francis, 2004). It is interested in the range of social harms experienced by young people. Research and scholarly activity have produced evidence that young people are victims of home circumstance and familial violence (Goodey, 1997); that they experience victimization and fear in the context of education, care and control systems; and that they undergo regular victimization as a result of the implementation of public policy and the activities of the state and its agencies and representatives (Muncie, 2003). It has identified that perpetrators are often other young people; that they are family members including parents; and that they are also representatives of agencies and organizations principally tasked with upholding young people's needs and rights. The paradox is, as Muncie (2003) has argued, that young people are routinely over-controlled and under-protected.

The aim of this chapter is to develop an understanding of the connections between young people, crime and victimization. The structure of the chapter is as follows. First, the chapter introduces the paradoxical positioning of young people, crime and victimization. Second, the chapter describes evidence of youth victimization drawn from a number of survey-based research studies of mostly school aged young people. Third, the chapter explores the connections between young people, victimization and social, political, cultural and economic contexts. Finally, the chapter examines attempts to give voice to young people in social research and policy-making.

Framing youth, crime and victimization

Throughout modernity young people have been 'framed' predominantly as offenders engaged in violent, criminal and anti-social behaviours in cities and towns across urban and rural England and Wales (Brown, 1998). As John Muncie (2003: 46–47) states:

> In political discourse young people tend to be a perennial source of anxiety and fear. Law and order enthusiasts, for example, continually warn of a delinquent syndrome in which youth delights in crudity, cruelty, violence and unruliness. ...
>
> Young people are also routinely portrayed not so much as depraved but as deprived. However, this deprivation is not viewed as one of material wealth and power (though this is usually the case), but of moral standards, parental guidance, training and self responsibility. Young people are typically viewed as being vulnerable: capable of being corrupted by all manner of 'evil' influences, unless their behaviour is tightly regulated and controlled. It is a control that is often justified in terms of giving young people 'protection' (from others and themselves).

Figure 8.1 is an extract from the front page of *The Independent* newspaper which highlights how the 'problem of youth' is often framed within political discourse and presented in the printed media.

Such constructions of youth have been supported by criminology's preoccupation throughout much of the twentieth century with understanding and appreciating young people (usually young boys) as offenders (Brown, 1998).

When young people are 'framed' as victims, it is often done so in a way that locates their experiences and the political and policy responses in the domain of health and social care. They are constucted as innocent victims not of crime, but of 'injury', 'harm' and 'abuse' experienced in familial and institutional settings (Brown, 1998; Walklate, 1989). Rather than being of central concern to criminologists, the victimization of young people is often constructed as the concern of social work, health and medicine and psychology and psychiatry. Box 8.1 offers illustration of the framing of the innocence of youth.

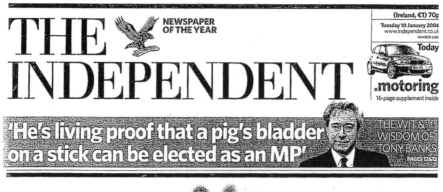

THE INDEPENDENT

.motoring
16-page supplement inside

'He's living proof that a pig's bladder on a stick can be elected as an MP'

THE WIT & WISDOM OF TONY BANKS
PAGES 12 & 13

BLAIR VS YOBS

Today, the Prime Minister announces his latest initiative to tackle youth hooliganism. But are his policies genuine or a gimmick?

Antisocial behaviour orders

In 1999 police and councils gained powers to tackle low-level vandalism and thuggery by issuing antisocial behaviour orders (Asbos). The scheme has been much revised and extended since then.

Ministers originally intended that 5,000 Asbos would be issued every year. The take-up has been lower, but has increased after a slow start. About 7,000 have been imposed since 1999. Nearly half are breached, which critics say threatens to criminalise children who break them.

However, ministers can point to research showing a drop from 21 per cent to 17 per cent in numbers of people who are worried about antisocial behaviour.

Fixed penalty notices

On-the-spot penalties are viewed by the Government as a key weapon against petty crime. Offenders are fined between £30 and £80, with the amount increasing by 50 per cent if they fail to pay within three weeks. The system went nationwide in April 2004.

More than 50,000 were issued in 2004, most for "disorderly behaviour while drunk" or "causing harassment, alarm or distress".

The Government says it nips yobbery in the bud. Opponents say it enables the better-off to pay their way out of trouble, with the poorer have to take their chance in court.

Child curfews

Local authorities, in conjunction with police, were given the power in 1998 to ban under-10s – later extended to under-16s – being out alone at night. Tony Blair said these curfews would stop young children "growing into a life of criminality", but the Police Federation complained about their "highly bureaucratic" nature. Three years later, not one curfew was in place.

Dispersal orders

Under the Anti-Social Behaviour Act of 2003, police can disperse groups of two or more under-16s in areas designated as centres of disorder. They have been enthusiastically adopted by local authorities and more than 400 are in place in England and Wales. There is also evidence that they have helped to lower levels of street crime.

However, the Home Office lost a test case in the High Court last summer brought by a 15-year-old from Richmond, south-west London, who argued the legislation breached his human rights.

Truancy

Since 2001, parents of persistent truants can be fined £2,500 or jailed for up to three months. The Government also suggested these mothers and fathers go on courses to improve their parenting skills.

There have been increasing numbers of truancy sweeps. Past government targets for reducing truancy have been abandoned and levels remain about the same as in 1997. About 50,000 children are missing from school in England at any one time.

Night courts

The idea of allowing courts in England and Wales to sit at nights and weekends was first aired by Jack Straw in 2001 when he was Home Secretary. The scheme was seen as a way of speeding up the criminal justice system, but was soon dropped. A £5m pilot project threw up a host of problems, such as finding cells for offenders.

Instant cash fines

Tony Blair sparked howls of derision six years ago when he proposed giving police powers to march delinquents to cash dispensers and impose instant fines for loutish behaviour. He said "a thug might think twice about kicking in your gate, throwing traffic cones around your street or hurling abuse into the night sky" if he thought he could be forced to pay £100 on the spot.

The Prime Minister backed down after the scheme was condemned by police and lawyers as unworkable and a threat to civil liberties.

Banning alcohol on public transport

A proposal that was put forward by the Prime Minister's respect unit as a way of to cut binge drinking and stop inebriated passengers causing havoc. The proposal – which would have stopped long-distance travellers having wine with a meal – fell apart within in hours as ministers distanced themselves from the move and opponents ridiculed it as "nanny statism".

REPORTS, PAGE 2

Figure 8.1   *The Independent* front page, 10 January 2006

Box 8.1   Framing the innocence of youth

A simple but useful illustration here is a child's victimization at the hands of their parents, such as physical and/or sexual abuse. Where the location of the victimization is the family, the child is often constructed as the 'ideal' victim (as structurally and physically powerless) of adult neglect, disorder and/or violence (caused by a disease – the disordered personality – and/or by the dangerous family environment – heavy drinking, teenage mother, etc.), and that the best response is the removal of the victim to a non-dangerous and safer place, be it another family or a residential care setting. In terms of political and media discourses, they often focus upon the 'innocence' of the victim and the 'demonic' nature of the offender, and the need to improve practice (Walklate, 1989). In terms of academic research, it can usually be found situated in early years, childhood, social work and youth and community studies.

Box 8.1 is meant to serve as illustration only. The reality is more complex and diffuse. All too often **childhood** (as distinct from adulthood) is constructed around conflicting and competing notions of innocence, truth and danger. Often the 'innocence' of childhood is called into question (Scraton, 1997). The experiences of the young victim may be questioned; and the young person is presented as 'dysfunctional' and 'dangerous'. For example, Morris (1987) presents a fourfold typology of the ways in which child sexual abuse has been explained:

- Often such abuse is explained as a 'fantasy' of the child.
- Often such abuse is explained as the child playing the role of 'seducer'.
- Often such abuse is explained as the fault of 'parenthood', or more accurately motherhood.
- Often such abuse is explained as 'harmless' because of the child's inability to understand and comprehend their experiences.

▶▶ *Childhood   often defined by notions of regulation and dependency, childhood, like youth, is an ill-defined and variable period of the life-span whose construction must be historically and theoretically conceptualized in specific socio-economic, cultural and political contexts.*

The construction of childhood changes over time, place and space. Certainly its construction is responsive to critical moments. Furlong and Cartmel (1997), for example, have suggested that the move from modern to late modern society has seen younger and younger people constructed as being a risk to rather than as being at risk from society.

As a consequence, the connections between youth and victimization have continued to remain at the margins of much criminological, media, political and policy discourse. As Brown (1998: 116–17) succinctly notes:

> Except in conjunction with the ideology of childhood 'innocence' – itself increasingly shaken by the demonization of ever younger age groups – the predominant categorizations of youth do not sit easily within a 'victim' discourse … in popular and policy discourse such issues are often treated with cynicism, disdain or vehement denial.

In the past two decades critical criminologists (see Brown, 1998; Muncie, 2003) have argued for a reframing of ways of understanding youth, crime and victimization. One such way has been by giving voice to young people and their experiences, and this has included young people's experiences of crime and victimization. A number of criminological studies have identified that young people suffer a high incidence of crime and are disproportionately likely to be victims, and that fear of crime has damaging effects on their lives. Indeed, for some criminologists, young people are more sinned against than sinners (see Hartless et al., 1995). Critical criminologists have also demonstrated that there is not always a clear-cut distinction between those most likely to offend and those most likely to be victims (Walklate, 1989; Mawby and Walklate, 1994). Much, though by no means all, of the criminal victimization that occurs in society takes place between young people.

Box 8.2 outlines some of the problematic ways in which the connections between youth, crime and victimization are commonly constructed.

Box 8.2   The paradoxical positioning of young people and crime

- Young people are often seen as a threat to social order, and widely imagined as committing crime, creating disorder or discomfort.
- Paradoxically, young people are sometimes viewed as particularly vulnerable, for example, to sexual abuse.
- Criminal justice and social policies have had a profound effect on young people, tending to regulate and control rather than protect them.

- Young people are very rarely consulted or have their views represented. When they are consulted, this is not necessarily done through formal mechanisms that effect change.
- Young people's experiences of crime and victimization appear to be very different to the ways in which they are labelled. They suffer far higher rates of victimization of a wide range of crimes than adults report in comparable surveys.

Source Pain et al. (2001)

Surveying young people as victims

Although Rob Mawby (1979) carried out a small-scale study of the victimization of 11–15-year-olds in two Sheffield schools during the 1970s and reported that two-thirds had been a victim of crime, the study of youth victimization did not emerge until the 1990s. The impetus for surveying young people about their experiences of crime, harm and policing emerged during the 1980s as a consequence of **left realist criminology**'s critique of the romanticism of much radical criminology and the pragmatism of much administrative criminology at the time (see, for example, Matthews and Young, 1992; Young, 1999).

▶▶ **Left realist criminology**   *emerged in the early 1980s, especially in the UK, as a critique of existing radical and traditional criminologies and conservative political administrations in power at the time. It was as though some radical criminologists found their older, rather aprioristic position untenable. Left realism's central critique is that existing and previous criminology has been partial, focusing only on one part of the process of crime, either on the offender, or the victim, or the societal reaction to crime or on the criminal behaviour itself. For Matthews and Young (1992), realism concerns synthesis rather than opposition in attempting to unite all aspects of the crime process.*

Left realism called for a social democratic response to crime and victimization that acknowledged the lived experiences of local communities. This involved researching the experiences of young people as offenders and as victims of crime through the use of the local victimization survey.

Three studies carried out in Scotland and two carried out in the north east of England provide some insight into youth victimization and fear of crime. Anderson et al. (1994) carried out questionnaire research with 1142 young people aged between 11–15 years in four schools across Edinburgh. The key findings from the study are presented here:

- Half of the sample reported being a victim of an offence against the person (17 per cent had something stolen from them, 37 per cent had been assaulted and 31 per cent had been threatened) during the previous nine months with boys more likely to report being a victim of crime than girls.
- The study found that perpetrators were often likely to be other young people, but the study also reports high levels of harassment directed at young people from adults. Some 10 per cent of offences against boys and 17 per cent of offences against girls were committed by people over the age of 21, with two-thirds of the girls reporting being harassed by adults on foot or in cars.
- Some, 83 per cent of the young people sampled had not reported their victimization to the police.
- Four in ten young men and six in ten young women reported being worried about the possibility of being attacked.
- Young people indicated heightened fears and anxieties about being a victim when the offender was older, a stranger and when they were alone.

Hartless et al. (1995) surveyed 208 12–14-year-olds in schools across Glasgow and 80 per cent of the sample reported being victimized in the previous year. Over two-thirds of the girls reported experiencing sexual harassment, while nearly two-thirds of the boys reported being a victim of assault and theft. In a survey conducted by Mori in a number of schools in Glasgow in 2003, 55 per cent of young people reported having experienced a negative incident over the previous year; 39 per cent reported being threatened and one in five reported having been physically attacked.

Brown (1995) carried out research with 1000 young people in Teesside, alongside a study of adult victimization and found considerable differences in incidence and prevalence of victimization. Young people reported experiencing more crime than the adult population. Finally, Goodey (1997) carried out research on 663 children in a school in the north of England and found that more girls (72 per cent) than boys (46 per cent) were worried when outside in public places. When age was taken into consideration, boys aged 11 reported greater levels of fear but this was outstripped by girls' fear as age increased.

The British Crime Survey (BCS) has only once surveyed young people under the age of 16, and that was in 1992. Unlike the Scottish studies discussed above that were conducted in schools, the BCS drew upon a sample of 1350 12–15-year-olds living in households across England and Wales. Nevertheless, analysis of the 1992 BCS as reported by Aye Maung (1995) offers evidence of youth victimization across England and Wales not dissimilar to the broad findings reported above. First, while much victimization was reported as occurring within the vicinity of the school environment with the perpetrator often known to the victim and of a similar age and sex, harassment, including sexual harassment and especially that carried out by adults often took place in public places away from the school environment. Second, vulnerability and risk differed by age and gender, as did fear. Some 56 per cent of young women aged 12–15 years said they worried about sexual pestering, while 48 per cent reported being worried about assault by a stranger. Young men in the same sample were less worried about sexual pestering (31 per cent); assault by a stranger (28 per cent); mugging (24 per cent) and burglary (15 per cent). Third, many of the young people who reported experiencing assaults and incidents of harassment often did not regard them as crime, whereas more traditional acts of theft and sexual harassment were more likely to be deemed as criminal by the young people. Aye Maung found that:

- Nearly a fifth of the sample of young people reported being a victim of something they regarded as being a crime ('since the summer holidays' – a period reported as approximately in the previous six to eight months).
- About one in ten young people reported experiencing a theft of property.
- Fewer that one in twenty young people reported a theft from the person, assault or adult sexual harassment that they deemed to be criminal.
- Young people experienced high levels of repeat and multiple victimization and that the majority of incidents went unreported.

Publication of the Aye Maung study did not lead to an avalanche of survey research into the experiences of young people. Nevertheless, four surveys carried out since 2000 provide contemporary insight into the nature and dynamics of youth, crime and victimization. These are discussed here:

- In 2003, the Crime and Justice Survey (Wood, 2005) provided the opportunity to ask young people aged 10–15 about their experiences of personal crime. Wood reports that over a third of the sample had experienced at least one personal crime over the previous 12 months – a figure well above the figure for those aged 26–65 (14 per cent). Second, Wood details that the type of crime experienced by young people changed with age (e.g. robbery being experienced by older age groups). Third, he notes that repeat victimization was particularly high among the sample with approximately 19 per cent of young people reporting experiencing five or more incidents in the previous year. Fourth, Wood argues that offending behaviour by young people was most strongly associated with being a victim of crime and that ethnicity did not appear to have a major impact on victimization rates for personal crime (Wood, 2005).

- As part of the national evaluation of the On Track multiple intervention programme, youth lifestyle surveys were carried out in 2003 with 30,000 young people in 29 secondary, 6 middle and 95 primary schools in England and Wales (Armstrong et al., 2005). Age ranges differed by school type (10–16 years of age in secondary schools; 7–11 years of age in primary schools) and survey questions asked young people about their experience of being a victim of crime and bullying over the past 12 months. Armstrong et al. found that:

  - 13 per cent of secondary school pupils reported being bullied in the last week; that bullying decreased with age and was experienced by boys more than girls. Risk of bullying was influenced by a range of factors including race, ethnicity, self-reported 'problem behaviour', status (e.g. excluded) and educational learning.
  - The risk of being a victim of crime also decreased with age. Some 64 per cent of Year 7 pupils reported experiencing crime, while 56 per cent of Year 10/11 reported being a victim of crime. Experience of crime differed by race and ethnicity.

- Since 2000, Mori have carried out research on young people for the Youth Justice Board (YJB) (see www.yjb.co.uk, accessed 24/09/2006). In 2004, the Mori youth survey of 5000 school children reported that 49 per cent of mainstream pupils had been a victim of crime in the last year. The study also reported that 13 per cent of the sample had been physically attacked, 23 per cent had been bullied and 26 per cent had been physically threatened. The Mori study is important in that it found that excluded young people reported higher prevalence rates apart from in relation to being bullied and having their property damaged or destroyed. The report suggests that excluded young people are more likely than young people attending mainstream school to be a victim of an offence of bullying. In the majority of cases, the perpetrators were also a young person although the report does suggest that offending differed by age and by type of offence.

- The final survey, based on survey data of 2420 children aged 9–16 years and reported by Deakin (2006) suggests that: first, the young people experienced diverse forms of victimization; second that the victimization was gendered; third, that harassment was the most common form of victimization and was perpetrated by other young people; and, finally, that 'asymmetry exists between the level of victimization experienced by children (denoting the likelihood of victimization occurring) and the number of children expressing fear' (Deakin, 2006: 387).

Each study described in this subsection offers insight into the experiences and perceptions of young people growing up across England, Wales and Scotland. They report that young people suffer a high incidence of crime and are disproportionately likely to be victims; that much victimization is not reported; and that fear of crime has damaging effects on their lives. In addition, many of the studies report that offending and victimization are unevenly distributed between young people, with certain groups experiencing higher levels of both, and that there is not always a clear-cut distinction between those most likely to offend and those most likely to be victims (Walklate, 1989). Some, though by no means all, of this victimization takes place between young people. While the complexities are apparent – the role of social networks, situations, places and relations – there is growing evidence of the dynamic interplay between young people's victimization and offending that requires further research and enquiry (see Deadman and Macdonald, 2004, for an interesting discussion on offenders as victims of crime).

Wood (2005: 6) reports that the strongest predictor of victimization amongst young people is criminal offending by the victim. He goes on to suggest that while any association would only develop over time – something the survey method is unable to secure – strong associations in the short term are likely to reflect lifestyle that constitute risks for both offending and victimization. In a similar vein, David Smith (2002) has suggested that crime victimization is the strongest predictor of self-reported offending. Smith also found that harassment by adults is reported as strongly related to rates of delinquency.

In reviewing the various surveys carried out into youth victimization it is important to note that comparisons between survey findings are difficult to make (Wood, 2005). Research design; the questions asked (and how the questions were asked – self-report; computer-aided; one-to-one; focus group); the wording of questions; the age group of the participants; the location of the research (for example, home or school; local area or national, etc.); the focus of the study (victimization in school, in public spaces, etc.); whether adults (teachers/parents) were present when the questions were asked, all make comparison difficult.

A further issue relates to the nature of the victimization reported by the young people. While many of the studies suggest high rates of under-reporting, it is conceivable that much that is experienced and reported by young people would not be recorded as crime by the police. For example, Aye Maung (1995) asks the difficult question of how many incidents perceived and reported by young people would be recorded as criminal by a police officer. Some experiences could be regarded as part and parcel of growing up rather than incidents that the police and court would process if they knew about them. This raises the question of how much youth victimization remains hidden.

A final issue relates to the ways in which young people growing up understand concepts such as 'crime', 'victim', and 'victimization'. For example, young people may not fully understand what it is to be a victim or offender.

Survey questions are likely to be written by adult researchers and may not be able to unpick and unpack young people's understandings and experiences. Of particular importance here is how young people conceptualize, understand and report the range of behaviours that they experience and engage in. Criminology remains limited in its understanding of the process of victimization among young people, and this has not been helped by the discipline's reliance on the victimization survey. After all, victimization surveys are limited in what they can achieve (see Box 8.3).

Box 8.3   Limitations of surveying young victims of crime

- Victimization surveys can assume a level of literacy and understanding among the sample population of young people that may not be available.
- Victimization surveys are premised on the idea that the young person is able to understand and recognize their victimization.
- Questions can reflect the agenda and priorities of those carrying out the research rather than the young people involved.
- Victimization surveys can be extractive. Young people are asked about their experiences of crime and victimization but do not necessarily receive anything in return (except, perhaps financial or material reward for being involved). Their hurt and distress may be enhanced as a result of answering survey questions.
- Victimization surveys count incidence and prevalence rather than researching the dynamic processes associated with growing up with crime and victimization (Maclean, 1991). They are unable to situate young people's experiences of crime and victimization within socio-economic, cultural and political contexts, nor do they take account of the changing nature of youth in transition.
- The surveys do not readily provide depth and detail of secondary victimization. Secondary victimization, according to Williams (forthcoming) occurs at the hands of criminal justice system staff or anyone else responding to an offence. It results from the insensitive treatment of victims of crime – often inadvertently – by the criminal justice system or by friends and acquaintances.
- Finally, victimization surveys are usually directed at those young people, who, by their very nature are 'easy to reach' – those children and young people attending school or resident in a household. But what of those young people deemed 'hard to reach' who may be excluded from school or home and/or who do not frequent places and locations accessible to the surveyor? They remain under-researched. Moreover, what about those young people above school age? These are the focus of the following section.

The study by Goodey (1997) is interesting in that it combined question-naire survey research with single sex discussions amoungst young boys. Acknowledging the danger of taking questionnaire findings at face value, Goodey utilizes group discussions with young boys to piece together the multiple and complex influences that affect how they experience fear. In the group discussions young boys articulated their fears differently than they did in the questionnaire.

QUESTIONS

What are the advantages and disadvantages of the victimization survey as a method of researching youth victimization?

How are risk and fear of crime connected to the vulnerability of young people?

How are youth victimization and offending related?

What factors can you identify that might make young people more or less likely to report their victimization?

Researching youth and victimization

In the past 20 years Sandra Walklate (1989, 2003, 2007) and Rob Mawby (Mawby and Walklate, 1994) have developed a critical victimology. In steering a path between positivist and radical victimologies, their 'brand' of critical victimology aims to get behind 'the mere appearance of things' to an understanding of the mechanisms which underplay and generate their appearance. For Walklate (2003: 41), exploration of the complexity of human interaction through time, place and space demands a research agenda which goes beyond the victimization survey and which can take account of and document these processes. The kind of framework supported by Walklate is one that locates victimization within a socio-economic, cultural and political context and which examines the processes that go on behind people's backs which contribute to the victims (and the crimes) we see as opposed to those we do not see. It is here that, for Walklate, not only may the processes of victimization best be understood, but also of how policy responses might best be located. For Walklate (2003: 42):

> Endeavours to research the real must take into account a number of processes which contribute to the construction of everyday reality: people's conscious

activity; their 'unconscious' activity (that is the routine activity which people engage in which can serve both to sustain and change the conditions under which that routine activity is constructed); the unobserved and unobservable generative mechanisms which underpin daily life; and the intended and unintended consequences of people's actions which inform both future action and knowledge.

For Walklate (2003), research may involve comparison, triangulation of method and longitudinal studies.

In order to develop an understanding of youth, crime and victimization further, this chapter will take a closer look at three research studies whose focus is about being young and growing up in late modernity. These studies are those by Carlen (1996); Macdonald and Marsh (2005) and Winlow and Hall (2006). Each study acknowledges the importance of carrying out research in the settings within which young people find themselves. Although they are not concerned exclusively with school aged young people nor solely with youth victimization, what they provide is insight into the dynamic, often complex and certainly fluid nature of young people's lived experiences of growing up, including their experiences of crime and victimization. More generally, each study demonstrates young people's experiences of social harm (Hillyard and Tombs, 2005), and highlights the need to understand youth victimization in a wider form than 'crime victimization' allows. Each study utilizes **qualitative methodologies** to get behind the 'mere appearance of things' (Walklate, 2003) and each develops a real understanding of the daily lives of young people living in a neoliberal society (Reiner, 2006).

▶▶ **Qualitative methodologies** *the qualitative approach is about people's attitudes, meanings, motives and behaviours and may involve a range of methods including observation, interviews and focus groups.*

The first two studies – by Carlen (1996) (Box 8.4) and Macdonald and Marsh (2005) – draw upon extensive research into the lives of homeless young people and young people growing up in poor neighbourhoods respectively.

Box 8.4 Pat Carlen (1996) *Jigsaw: A Political Criminology of Youth Homelessness*

In the following pages it will be shown that during the 1980s the British state failed to meet the minimum needs of increasing numbers of young citizens at the same time as targeting them for receipt of tighter disciplinary controls and, in the 1990s, even harsher punishment. During the same period it was revealed that while young persons suffer criminal victimization on a large scale, the crimes committed against them are seldom redressed. Young people themselves do not believe that police protection is extended to them in the same way that it is to older adults (especially older adults who are also householders) and they also feel excluded from debates about the forms, functions and possibilities of democratic policing. (Carlen, 1996: 2)

Thus starts Pat Carlen's political criminology of youth homelessness. Drawing upon in-depth interviews with 150 homeless young people in central England during 1992–95, Carlen pieces together a socio-economic, political and cultural debate about crime, politics and homelessness within a 'jigsaw' of analytical description, argument and counter-argument to present a range of competing and conflicting narratives and stories.

The first two chapters of the book offer an historical and contemporary discussion of the construction and governance of youth homelessness which argue that during the 1980s and 1990s homeless young people were recast as the 'socially expendable' outcome of dependency culture spawned by inept welfarism. However, it is Chapters 3 and 4 that offer the most insight into homeless young people's experiences of being a victim and survivor. Weaving together the political, policy, economic and academic literature, Carlen demonstrates the direct and indirect victimization of young homeless people within the home environment, on the street, in institutions and at the hands of care and regulatory professionals. Over two chapters, she argues:

- That the lives of young homeless people are fractured and shattered by the multiple, repeat and interconnected effects of affordable housing scarcity, unemployment, and cuts in welfare provision and that survival for them involves a reordering of political, moral and economic possibilities which can produce new modalities of living that can involve the mundane, the exotic and the criminogenic.
- That young homeless people do not constitute an underclass of different moral values. They constitute a threat to society because they are symbolic of the widening gulf between 'the moral pretensions of liberal democratic societies and the shabby life-chances on offer to the children of the already poor' (1998: 124); and that their crimes should be understood in the context of the factors that have led to their exclusion.

A reading of Carlen's study serves as a reminder of the limitations of the survey method. Most of the victimization of young homeless people is never counted in crime surveys, not reported to the police, and indeed rarely noticed at all, because of the 'invisibility' of homeless young people and their problems (Carlen, 1996; Wardhaugh, 2000) and the nature of the harms experienced. Yet homeless young people are more at risk from victimization before and while they are homeless, and from multiple and repeat victimization. Carlen's study provides the opportunity to examine the narratives and stories of homeless young, people in a way that opens to criticism simple definitions of youth, crime and victimization that deny context and meaning. It supports calls to examine social harms as experienced by young people. Carlen's study supports Walklate's (2003) claim that a more triangulated methodology and contextualized research brief can go beyond the mere presentation of things to an understanding of the complexity of human interaction through time, place and space. Furthermore, it highlights the continuum between experiencing victimization and acting as an offender; offers insight into the interplay between macro economic and social policy and micro analysis of the lived experiences of young people; and demonstrates the dynamic and fluid interconnections between being young, vulnerability and neo-liberal social and economic policies of the 1980s and 1990s in England and Wales (Reiner, 2006).

Carlen's study explores the experiences, the lives and the thoughts of young people living on the margins of respectability, engagement and participation. Research by Macdonald and Marsh (2005) further presents young people's victimization within a wider context of conflict and change in late modern society. Macdonald and Marsh (2005), in an attempt to develop a distinct perspective on **youth transitions**, provide a discussion of disconnected youth growing up in Britain's poor neighbourhoods characterized by high unemployment, high crime, high victimization and complex social networks (see also Johnston et al., 2000; Webster et al., 2004).

▶▶ **Youth transitions**   *it has already been noted that there is uncertainty about the term youth, and this is also the case for the term youth transitions. Taken literally, it presents a linear picture of young people moving through the life course and is a period in which life choices are made. However, in acknowledging the ways in which youth and their transition are historically, socially and politically constructed, and that youth transitions do not dovetail easily with other life-phases, youth transitions are best understood as referring to the general stages in life in which young people find themselves growing up and in which life chances are established. As Macdonald and Marsh (2005: 36) suggest, it 'is useful as a general, overarching concept; a metaphor that does not presume a particular sort of content, direction or length at the level of individual experience'.*

Box 8.5   Robert Macdonald and Jane Marsh (2005) Disconnected Youth Growing up in Britain's Poor Neighbourhoods

Based upon a study of young people growing up in the north-east of England, Macdonald and Marsh suggest that:

- There is not one uniform way that young people grow up in poor neighbourhoods; young people's lived experiences does really mean experien*ces*, and therefore individual transitions are complex, fluid and unpredictable. Critical moments, influenced by cumulative pressures and hardships all affect the lives that young people lead.

- Although individual narratives present individual stories, all the young people in the study demonstrated an enduring experience of economic marginality.

- Conservative theories of the underclass are simple and plainly wrong. For Macdonald and Marsh (2005: 199):

Conservative underclass theory fails to appreciate that individuals can react quite differently to apparently similar events and that this reaction is not fixed, clear or predictable (across cases or within individual biographies). A static view of 'underclass culture' ignores the complex and changing life experiences of young people who find themselves in difficult circumstances.

- Social exclusion theory which sees young people as members of a possible underclass because of structural exclusion from employment, is much more dynamic and complex. 'Social exclusion is best understood as a process or longer term experience, not a fixed, stable category reducible to, and measured by current joblessness' (2005: 202).

- Social exclusion does not connect in a straightforward way with the subjective experiences of young people from localities which, by all subjective definitions, were socially excluded.

They argue that any theory of youth transitions must take account of the historical, spatial and socio-economic contexts in which they are made.

Macdonald and Marsh's study provides a rich account of how the dynamics of the local interplay with the complexities of the macro socio-economic, cultural, political and the global to affect the lived experiences of young people growing up; and of the active role young people play within poor neighbourhoods. They demonstrate the impact deindustrialization can have on the young, the vulnerable and the marginalized. In particular, they report that experiences of direct and indirect victimization are widespread. Personal victimization in Britain's poor neighbourhoods is seen as affecting many of those interviewed – victimization to the home, to cars and to the individual were widespread as were incidents of harassment and violence. Moreover, Macdonald and Marsh suggest that risk and vulnerability to victimization may be related to an individual's (and their family's) position and embeddedness within the local community. Those with deep-rooted social networks alongside those with many interconnections were less likely to be victimized; 'incomers' and 'new arrivals' appeared to be more likely to experience victimization. Moreover, degrees of embeddedness impacted differently on the way victimization was experienced and the ways in which avoidance measures and mechanism for redress could be initiated. As they state, 'those who were better connected were not immune to criminal victimisation but could sometimes draw upon these connections to help reduce the risks, of, for instance, being burgled and to deal with the consequences if it did happen' (2005: 162).

The final illustration in this sub-section draws from Winlow and Hall (2006). Operating broadly within the ethnographic tradition, Winlow and Hall claim that their study attempts to craft a route between neoliberalist and left-liberalist perspectives on crime in order to offer a tale of insecurity, competitive individualism and violence. Their aim is to provide what they view as a more informed theoretical understanding of the relationship between violence, the economy and culture.

Box 8.6   Simon Winlow and Steve Hall (2006) Violent Night: Urban Leisure and Contemporary Culture

In an enticing, exotic and at times frightening narrative of the night-time economy's dynamic mixture of pain and pleasure and hedonism and violence, Winlow and Hall articulate how new trends in consumption alongside changes to the global and local capitalist economies have contributed to the construction of urban centres as simultaneously seductive and dangerous, particularly in the evening. Drawing upon interviews with young people, the police and others in the North-East of England, the book provides a sociological account of the fragmentation of the working class as they attempt to cope with the shifting demands of the advanced capitalist economy, particularly the shift from industrial capitalism to consumer capitalism. They highlight the:

- growing rift between the socially excluded and the rest of society;
- ways in which social bonds of industrial modernity have been eroded and replaced by instrumentalism and self-interest;
- shift from the world of work to that of leisure within a changing capitalist economy where the leisure services are replacing industrial capitalism as the main generator of profit;
- changing relations between young people from those that were robust and deep to those characterized by fluidity and superficiality;
- under-reported nature of alcohol-related violence;
- power of the consumer economy to shape 'everyday life to the extent that it creates the form of dissent that it prefers' (2006: 10).

Of specific relevance for the current discussion is Chapter 6 of their book, in which sample interview data with young victims of violence provides evidence of a capitalist consumer economy that places profit over safety; that highlights the dynamic inter-connectedness between victim and offender; and which raises fundamental questions as to the most appropriate way to survey and regulate the night time economy. Two-thirds of males and one-fifth of the females in the sample had experienced violence in the night-time economy. For Winlow and Hall, violence and its probability exist 'as the perpetual outcome of circular networks of inevitability, fear and revenge' (2006: 139). The ability to 'survive', to get through it, with a modicum of 'competence and dignity, perhaps even with panache' (2006: 139) is ingrained in their sense of self and the wider cultures from which they hail, providing the building blocks of masculine self-identity.

The three studies discussed above:

- Provide evidence of the paradoxical position of young people, crime and victimization in late modernity.
- Help 'contextualize' youth victimization in socio-economic, cultural and political contexts and offer insight into the impact neoliberalism has on being young and growing up.
- Support calls for a social harm perspective that allows for a better understanding of the experiences of people from the cradle to the grave.
- Offer insight into the very real yet fluid connections between youth victimization and offending.

- Direct attention towards the inadequacies of strategic and policy responses to young people, and situates understanding of them within the broader social, political and cultural landscape.

QUESTIONS

List the major qualitative methods of social research. Review your list and answer the following question: What are the advantages and disadvantages of using qualitative methods to research the lived experiences of young people as victims of crime?

How and in what ways do macro-economic and social policies and micro-lived realities interplay and impact on the experiences of young people growing up in England and Wales?

In what ways might a 'social harm' perspective contribute to an understanding of youth victimization?

Think about the way in which youth crime is 'framed'. To what extent is it possible to reframe the problem of youth and develop political and policy responses which are inclusive of them and their experiences?

Listening to youth?

Published in the late 1990s, Sheila Brown wrote on the cover of her book *Understanding Youth and Crime* (Brown, 1998) the words 'listening to youth?' Brown's book is a must read for all students of youth criminology. Her central argument is that while young people should be actively involved in politics and policy-making, they are constructed as 'Others' involved in crime, anti-social behaviour and harassment. While the idea of listening to young people is an established principle within English Law and public policy, enshrined within the Children's Act 1989 and the United Nations Convention on the Rights of the Child ratified by the UK government in 1991 (Willow et al., 2004), in just shy of 140 pages Brown demonstrates how modern narratives on youth, crime and victimization have been constructed around notions of innocence, danger and wickedness. Crudely put, for Brown, young people are under-involved, over-controlled and without voice:

> Since the young are a marginal category (or a constellation of marginal categories, if preferred, refracted through other social positionings and hierarchies of power), they are non-persons. Since they are non-persons, they are outside of claims of citizenship. Since they are not enfranchised, they stand outside of formal polity. Their 'powers' are inarticulated and thereby accorded qualities of danger *without reference to the voice of young people themselves*. (Brown, 1998: 118, *emphasis added*)

In the past 20 years there have been calls within critical criminology to listen to young people with the purpose of actively engaging them in the process of research and policy formulation (see, for example, Scraton, 1997; Brown, 1998; Muncie, 2003, 2004). 'Listening to young people' appears to be an orthodox mantra in critical criminology (Lyon et al., 2000; Pain and Francis, 2004). Not only is it a perspective which questions the orthodoxy of much administrative and mainstream criminological research on young people, it is a perspective that, as Pain and Francis (2003) argue, acknowledges the very real powerlessness of young people at every conceivable political, economic and social level, and argues strongly for the 'reframing' of ways of understanding youth and crime through a process of 'critical excavation' (Brown, 1998: 119). One such way is by representing the voices of young people within research and policy formulation.

Since the mid-1990s there has also emerged a political and policy agenda aimed at reversing the democratic deficit in decision-making by involving young people in local policy-making processes (Edwards and Hatch, 2003; DFES, 2004; Pain and Francis, 2004; Willow et al., 2004). It has been underpinned by a 'modernizing' agenda across local government; enabled by new public sector managerialism; and required under specific pieces of legislation (Crime and Disorder Act 1998 as amended by the Police Reform Act 2002; Local Government Act 2000; Every Child Matters 2004; Crime and Disorder Act Review 2006). It has supported calls for listening to youth and placing youth at the centre of local polity. For example, the Crime and Disorder Act 1998 widened the responsibility for crime beyond the police, and made it a requirement that each local area should bring together relevant local agencies and organizations in the management of crime reduction. The Act also directed these partnerships to regularly audit their local population's experiences of crime, fear and control and to develop a local strategy for the reduction of crime and disorder. The original guidance associated with the Crime and Disorder Act 1998 suggested that public consultation must include young people, and that young people must be viewed as *victims* of crime as well as offenders (Home Office, 1998; Pain et al., 2001).[1]

A review of the impact of the Crime and Disorder Act 1998 on the consultation carried out with young victims during the first round of audits and strategies suggested that there remains some way to go (Phillips et al., 2000; see Box 8.7).

Box 8.7   Young people as victims in crime and disorder strategies

In examining the extent to which the first round of crime and disorder strategies addressed children and young people as victims of crime, Mason found that young people were poorly represented as victims, and that 'many of the strategies combined (or equated) issues relating to the safety of young people with the problem of reducing juvenile crime' (Mason, 2000: 6). Mason also found that consultation with young people was not widespread, nor did it often lead to changes in practice where it had been carried out, so that 'strategies often cite the partnership's ideological commitment to the empowerment of young people, but only rarely do they demonstrate specific measures that work towards this goal' (Mason 2000: 28).

Source Pain et al. (2001)

Similarly, Edwards and Hatch (2003: 7) in a report on the nature and relationship between young people and communities state: 'There is some way to go to develop policies and services that add up to a serious commitment to young people not just in their early years but well into their teens.'

Despite the convergence of the criminological and political in terms of listening to youth, young people remain recipients of, rather than active participants in policy-making. In a study carried out in the northeast of England into the experiences of victimization and fear of crime among homeless young people and school-excluded young people, Pain and Francis (2003, 2004) report the difficulties of developing evidence-based policies that reflect the experiences of young people as victims. In doing so, they shed some light onto the very real problems of making youth voices count. For Pain and Francis (2004: 97) homeless young people 'epitomise the problematic ways that crime and youth are commonly constructed'. There is a relative paucity of information about them, particularly in relation to their victimization (see Carlen, 1996; Wardhaugh 2000). They are hard to reach, they experience a range of social harms and are over-surveilled and controlled. In using the term 'hard-to-reach' Pain et al. (2001) place primary importance on the social exclusion and invisibility in the policy-making process which many young people experience (Loader, 1996; Brown, 1998), and the way this contributes to vulnerability to victimization and fear. For Pain and Francis (2004: 96):

> There are grounds on which to suspect that victimization and the impacts of crime for these young people [hard to reach] are significantly higher than average, although they tend to be subject to criminalization and associated with high rates of offending too. However, evidence about hard to reach young people's experiences of victimization is sparse, due to the failure of traditional methods of research and consultation, and the lack of political will to reach them.

Reaching and including these groups in the process of research and policy formulation requires a combination of political will and alternative methodological approaches (Pain and Francis, 2003). In order to explore homeless young people's experiences of crime and victimization, and to understand what they saw as 'solutions' to their lives, Pain and Francis adapted a range of methods that fall under the heading of **participatory appraisal** (Chambers, 1997, 1999; Cooke and Kathari, 2001; see Pain and Francis, 2003, for a full discussion of the methodology used in this study). Illustration from the research of two of the techniques of participatory diagramming can be found in Figures 8.2 and Figure 8.3. Figure 8.2 presents a time line drawn by a young homeless women when asked about growing up, while figure 8.3 presents the findings of a group 'brainstorm' on solutions to youth homelessness. Both figures offer visual illustration of the experiences homeless young people have in relation to crime and social harm and of the possible ways in which youth homelessness may be tackled.

▶▶ ***Participatory appraisal*** *participatory appraisal derives from Participatory Rural Appraisal, widely used in the 'developing' world to facilitate change and empowerment in poor communities. They involve the use of participatory visual techniques as research tools within an action research framework.*

Drawing upon the experiences of 118 homeless young people, accessed through hostels, services and street locations, and utilizing participative research methodologies, Pain and Francis highlight a number of specific issues that arise in relation to the experiences of victimization for homeless young people.

- They identify, as have researchers before them (Carlen, 1996; Wardhaugh, 2000), that homeless young people are especially at risk from victimization,

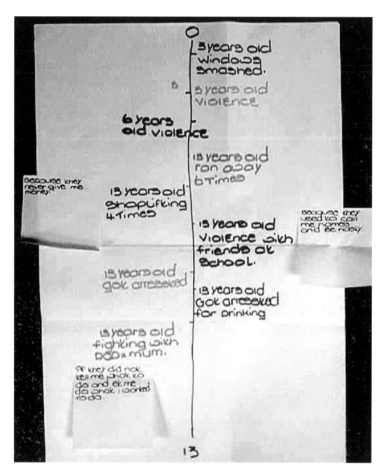

Figure 8.2 Timeline drawn by young woman

including repeat and multiple victimization. They report homelessness as a dimension of risk that sits alongside social variables of gender, race, age, class.

- They report that for many young homeless people the greatest risk is the home with many of their sample reporting experiencing sexual and physical abuse and/or witnessing violence in the home environment.
- They describe high levels of violence against young women.
- They record that there was a high risk of victimization on the street and in temporary accommodation for many of those involved.
- They detail evidence that many of those involved had experienced harassment, violence and procedural abuses directed at them by the police.

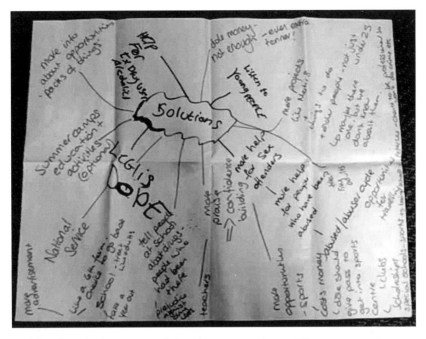

Figure 8.3 Group brainstorm on solutions to young people as victims

What is clear from a reading of their research is that homeless young people experience both victimization and offending at different times (or the same time), and that they are often related, both to each other and to the state of being homeless. All have experienced a range of social harms. Some offenders can also be viewed as victims, for example, having come out of care with little or no support, of police violence, or of poverty. While this observation fits with current understanding of youth and crime (in the general population, those young people who are most likely to offend are also most likely to be victims of crime), it contrasts greatly with popular images of young people and policy discourses. Yet, as Wardhaugh (2000: 99) argues, there is a need to 'conceptualize some individuals as being simultaneously victim and offender ... only then might they be understood, not as angels nor as devils, but as a complex and heterogeneous group of people'.

Despite considerable evidence of victimization among their sample, Pain and Francis (2004) go on to highlight a number of barriers to enhancing young people's engagement in local policy-making processes.

- They highlight the unequal power relations that place young people as recipients of rather than as stakeholders in local decision-making. This is exacerbated for those young people deemed hard to reach.
- They identify that young people – particularly those disconnected and victimized – often have more worrying and demanding issues to deal with than engaging in local democratic decision-making.
- They point out that taking seriously young people's experiences of crime and victimization invariably presents problems for the criminal and social justice response. This can maintain or even exacerbate local tensions, especially when one or more organizations (for example, the police or the local authority) are identified as victimizers by the young people involved.
- A final and crucial barrier to achieving action relates to ways in which the 'problem of crime' continues to be constructed as a problem of young people in much popular and political discourse and practice (Muncie, 2004; Goldson, 2000). Listening to young people sits uneasily within and alongside this culture of regulation, control and containment.

As Bren Neale (2004: 164) in a review funded by the Joseph Rowntree Foundation on the position and participation of young people as active citizens in local decision making concluded: 'Turning the principle of children's participation into practice is a complex task that involves changing the cultures of adulthood alongside those of childhood'.

Summary

To briefly summarize, four inter-related themes run through the chapter. The first relates to the problem of researching youth victimization. Significantly, there have been few studies conducted on young people as victims of crime and those that have engaged with young victims have predominantly done so through the use of the criminal victimization survey. While such studies have provided insight into the risks, fears and worries of young people, it must be acknowledged that victimization surveys are unable to situate and contextualize experiences.

Second, it has been suggested that there exists qualitative research on the lived experiences of young people. These studies have focused upon the lives and experiences of young people in transition, and as offenders and victims. They provide rich qualitative information about the connectedness between young people's lives, their experiences of social harms, the people they hang around with, and the neighbourhoods they live in.

Third, it has been uncovered that much victimization experienced by young people is carried out by other young people and that often young people are victims and offenders. The chapter also demonstrates the dynamic and fluid relationship between young offenders and victims, and highlights that in addition, young people also experience victimization at the hands of adults, often when they are in positions of care and control over them.

Fourth, it is acknowledged that over recent years there has been a movement towards promoting young people as citizens with an active contribution to make in political and policy arenas. However, beyond the rhetoric, it is argued that there are many individual, political, cultural and structural barriers to securing young people's engagement in the political and policy process.

To conclude, the problem of crime continues to be framed as the problem of youth. To develop knowledge and understanding about young people as victims, to promote young people as active citizens in politics and policy making, and to develop policies and practices that engage and respond to young people as victims of crime and social harm, there needs to be a re-framing of the youth crime paradox. This is the purpose of a critical criminology of youth (Muncie 2003).

ANNOTATED BIBLIOGRAPHY

Anderson, S., Kinsey, R., Loader, I. and Smith, C. (1994) *Cautionary Tales: Young People, Crime and Policing in Edinburgh.* **Aldershot: Avebury.** Although nearly 20 years old, this study into young people's experiences of crime and victimization remains an essential text. Not only does it provide an excellent discussion of the research carried out in Edinburgh, a critical reading of it highlights the problems of the victimization survey.

Brown, S. (1998) *Understanding Youth and Crime: Listening to Youth?* **Buckingham: Open University Press.** This book provides a critical introduction to the study of young people, crime and control and punishment. It explores political and policy developments on young people and reviews a range of literature on crime and young people.

Muncie, J. (2003) 'Youth, risk and victimization', in P., Davies, P. Francis and V. Jupp (eds), *Victimisations Theory, Research and Policy.* **Basingstoke: Palgrave.** This chapter is one of the few that have been written specifically from a critical perspective. The chapter demonstrates that young people are victims of home circumstance and familial violence; that they experience victimization and fear in the context of education, care and control systems; and that they undergo regular victimization as a result of the implementation of public policy and the activities of the state and its agencies and representatives.

Pain, R. and Francis, P. (2004) 'Living with crime: spaces of risk for homeless young people', *Children's Geographies,* **2(1): 95–110.** This article reviews research carried out by Pain and Francis into the victimization experiences of homeless young people in north-east England, using a range of participative research methods.

Note

1 Since the mid-2000s many CDRPs have co-joined with local Drug Action Teams (DATs) and operate as single partnerships. The Crime and Disorder Act Review 2006 makes it a requirement that CDRPs undertake six-monthly and annual strategic assessments of their local neighbourhoods.

References

Anderson, S., Kinsey, R., Loader, I. and Smith, C. (1994) *Cautionary Tales: Young People, Crime and Policing in Edinburgh.* Aldershot: Avebury.

Armstrong, D., Hire, J., Hacking, S., Armaos, R., Jones, R., Klessinger, N. and France, A. (2005) *Children, Risk and Crime: The On Track Youth Lifestyle Surveys,* Home Office Research Study 278. London: Home Office.

Aye Maung, N. (1995) *Young People, Victimisation and the Police: British Crime Survey Findings on Experiences and Attitudes of 12 to 15 Year Olds,* Home Office Research Study No 140. London: Home Office.

Brown, S. (1995) 'Crime and safety in whose "community"? Age, everyday life, and problems for youth policy', *Youth and Policy,* 48: 27–48.

Brown, S. (1998) *Understanding Youth and Crime: Listening to Youth?* Buckingham: Open University Press.

Carlen, P. (1996) *Jigsaw: A Political Criminology of Youth Homelessness.* Buckingham Open University Press.

Chambers, R. (1997) *Whose Reality Counts? Putting the First Last.* London: Intermediate Technology Publications.

Chambers, R. (1999) *Relaxed and Participatory Appraisal: Notes on Practical Approaches and Methods.* Brighton: Institute for Development Studies, University of Sussex.

Cooke, B. and Kothari, U. (2001) *Participation: The New Tyranny?* London: Zed Books.

Deadman, D. and Macdonald, Z. (2004) 'Offenders as victims of crime?: An investigation into the relationship between criminal behaviour and victimisation', *Journal of Royal Statistical Society Association.* 167: part 1: 53–67.

Deakin, J. (2006) 'Dangerous people, dangerous places: the native and location of young people's victimization and fear', *Children and Society*, 20: 376–90.

DFES (2004) *Every Child Matters: Change for Children.* London: DFES.

Edwards, L. and Hatch, B. (2004) *Passing Time: A Report About Young people and Communities.* London: Institute for Public Policy Research.

Furlong, A. and Cartmel, F. (1997) *Young People and Social Change: Individualisation and Risk in Late Modernity.* Buckingham: Open University Press.

Goldson, B. (ed.) (2000) *The New Youth Justice.* Lyme Regis: Russell House Publishing.

Goldson, B. and Muncie, J. (2006) *Youth Crime and Justice.* London: Sage.

Goodey, J. (1997) 'Boys don't cry', *British Journal of Criminology,* 37(3): 401–18.

Graham, J. and Bowling, B. (1995) *Young People and Crime.* London: Home Office.

Hartless, J.M., Ditton, J., Nair, G. and Phillips, P. (1995) 'More sinned against than sinning: a study of young teenagers' experiences of crime', *British Journal of Criminology,* 35(1): 114–33.

Hillyard, P. and Tombs, S. (2005) 'Beyond criminology', in *Criminal Obsessions.* London: Crime and Society foundation.

Home Office (1998) *The Crime and Disorder Act: Guidance on Statutory Crime and Disorder Partnerships.* London: Home Office Communications Directorate.

Home Office (2006) *The Crime and Disorder Act 1998 Review.* London: Home Office.

Hough, M. and Tilley, N. (1998) *Auditing Crime and Disorder: Guidance for Local Partnerships,* Crime Detection and Prevention Series Paper 91. London: Home Office.

James, A. and Raine, J. (1998) *The New Politics of Criminal Justice.* London: Longman.

Johnston, L., Macdonald, R., Mason, P., Ridley, R. and Webster, R. (2000) *Snakes and Ladders: Young People, Transitions and Social Exclusion.* York: Joseph Rowntree Foundation.

Jones, T. and Newburn, T. (2001) *Widening Access: Improving Police Relations with Hard to Reach Groups,* Home Office Police Research Series Paper 138. London: Home Office.

Loader, I. (1996) *Youth, Policing and Democracy.* London: Macmillan.

Lyon, J., Dennison, C. and Wilson, A. (2000) *'Tell Them So They Listen': Messages from Young People in Custody,* Home Office Research Study 201. London: Home Office.

Macdonald R. (1997) *Youth, the 'Underclass' and Social Exclusion.* London: Routledge.

Macdonald, R. and Marsh, J. (2005) *Disconnected Youth? Growing up in Britain's Poor Neighbourhoods.* Basingstoke: Palgrave.

Maclean, B. (1991) 'In partial defence of socialist realism: Some theoretical and methodological Concerns of the local crime survey', *Crime, Law and Social Change,* 15: 213–54.

Mason, D. (2000) *Building Safer Communities for Children: A Child-Focused Analysis of the First Crime and Disorder Strategies 1999–2002.* London: NSPCC.

Matthews, R. and Young, J. (eds) (1992) *Issues in Realist Criminology.* London: Sage.

Mawby, R. (1987) 'The victimisation of juveniles: a comparative study of publicly owned housing in Sheffield', *Journal of Crime and Delinquency,* 16: 98–114.

Mawby, R. and Walklate, S. (1994) *Critical Victimology.* London: Unwin Hyman.

Morgan, J. and Zedner, L. (1992) *Child Victims: Crime, Impact and Criminal Justice* Oxford: Clarendon Press.

Mori (2004) *Youth Survey 2004 for the Youth Justice Board.* London: Youth Justice Board.

Morris, P. (1987) *Women, Crime and Criminal Justice.* Oxford: Basil Blackwell.

Muncie, J. (2003) 'Youth, risk and victimisation', in P. Davies, P. Francis, and V. Jupp, (eds), *Victimisation Theory, Research and Policy* Basingstoke: Palgrave.

Muncie, J. (2004) *Youth and Crime,* 2nd edition. London: Sage.

National Crime Prevention (1999) *Living Rough: Preventing Crime and Victimisation Among Homeless Young People.* Canberra: National Crime Prevention.

Neale, B. (2004) 'Conclusion: ideas into practice', in C. Willow, R. Marchant, P. Kirby and B. Neale (2004) *Young Children's Citizenship Ideas into Practice.* York: Joseph Rowntree Foundation.

Newburn, T. and Jones, T. (2001) *Consultation by Crime and Disorder Partnerships* Draft report for the Home Office.

Pain, R. and Francis, P. (2003) 'Reflections on participatory research', *Area* 35(1): 46–54.

Pain, R. and Francis, P. (2004) 'Living with crime: spaces of risk for homeless young people', *Children's Geographies,* 2(1): 95–110.

Pain, R., Francis, P., Fuller, I., O'Brien, K. and Williams, S. (2001) *'Hard-to-Reach' Young People and Community Safety: A Model for Participatory Research and Consultation.* unpublished.

Phillips, C., Considine, M. and Lewis, R. (2000) *A Review of Audits and Strategies Produced by Crime and Disorder Partnerships in 1999,* PRCU Briefing Note 8/00, London: Home Office.

Reiner, R. (2006) 'Neo-liberalism, crime and criminal justice', *Renewal,* 14(3).

Scraton, P. (1997) *Whose Childhood?* London: UCL Press.

Smith, D. (2002) 'Crime and the life course', in M. Maguire, R. Morgan, and R. Reiner, (eds), *The Oxford Handbook of Criminology,* 3rd edition. Oxford: Clarendon Press.

Walklate, S. (1989) *Victimology.* London: Unwin Hyman.

Walklate, S. (2003) 'Can there be a feminist victimology?' in P. Davies, P. Francis and V. Jupp (eds), *Victimisation: Theory, Research and Policy.* Basingstoke: Palgrome.

Walklate, S. (2007) *Imagining the Victim of Crime.* Buckinghamshire: Open University Press.

Wardhaugh, J. (2000) *Sub City: Young People, Homelessness and Crime* Aldershot: Ashgate.

Webster, C., Simpson, D., Macdonald, R., Abbas, A., Cieslik, M., Shildrick, T., Simpson, M. (2004) *Poor Transitions: Social Exclusion and Young Adults.* London: Unwin Hyman.

Williams, B. (forthcoming) 'Victims in the criminal justice system' in P. Davies and P. Francis (eds), *Victims in the Criminal Justice System.* London: Polity.

Willow, C., Marchant, R., Kirby, P. and Neale, B. (2004) *Young Children's Citizenship Ideas into Practice.* York: Joseph Rowntree Foundation.

Winlow, S. and Hall, S. (2006) *Violent Night: Urban Leisure and Contemporary Culture.* Oxford: Berg.

Wood, M. (2005) *The Victimisation of Young People: Findings from the Crime and Justice Survey 2003,* Home Office RDS Findings 246. London: Home Office.

Young, J. (1999) *The Exclusive Society.* London: Sage.

Zedner, L. (2002) 'Victims', in M. Maguire, R. Morgan, and R. Reiner (eds), *The Oxford Handbook of Criminology,* 3rd edition. Oxford: Clarendon Press.

Old Age, Victims and Crime

Azrini Wahidin and Jason L. Powell

Chapter aims

Introduction

Age, science and social construction

Old age, crime and criminal victimization

Old age, vulnerability and the fear of crime

Reflections and future research directions

Summary

Annotated bibliography

References

Chapter aims

- To explore the relationship between old age, victims and crime.
- To outline the key debates in victimology in relation to ageing.
- To synergize gerontology and criminological theory.

Introduction

Crime is perceived to be an age war, with young offenders preying on innocent older victims ... Politicians have quickly, and quite unjustifiably, identified the elderly as particularly vulnerable to crime. (Mawby, 1988: 101)

Old age is shamefully seen like head lice in children and venereal disease in their older siblings. (Stott, 1981: 3)

In recent years, the experiences of individuals of the **life-course** have developed as an issue of concern in criminology (Powell, 2001). However, while there has been a wealth of research and scholarly activity relating to 'younger people' and crime (and more recently young people and victimization) (Davies et al. 2003; see Chapter 8 of this volume), research into the experiences and representations of 'older people', crime and victimization has been less well developed (Brogden and Nijar, 2000). Moreover, when comparing the criminological research on 'old age' to that of exploring race, class and gender, one might think that old age as a variable is of secondary importance. In this chapter it is our aim to demonstrate that researchers studying the relationship between older people, crime and victimization would benefit from a careful conceptualization of 'old age', which focuses on the ways in which it is socially constructed, represented and used by particular interest groups. It is only by deconstructing age in the study of criminology and victimology, we would argue, that we can begin to understand the place and significance of 'ageing' in disciplinary discourses on, and actual experiences of, criminal victimization.

This chapter explores old age as an important sociological dimension of analysis and dissects its relationship to victimization and contemporary crime. It is structured as follows. First, the chapter is concerned with examining how the notion of victim applies to older people within the life-course. Second, the chapter explores the relationship between old age and victimization, and highlights implications for the study of age and its relationship to victimization. The chapter concludes by suggesting that current political discourses position the concept of 'victim' along neo-liberal lines of 'responsibility' as opposed to the societal construction of the victim.

▶▶ **Life-course**   *The term life-course has replaced the term life stages to reflect the holistic understanding of the ageing process. The blurring of the life-course problematizes negative ageist stereotypes and practices and in turn produces more accurate and positive images that imply that later life is a time for vitality, creativity, empowerment and resourcefulness all attainable in old age.*

Age, science and social construction

There are two principal approaches to theorizing age – scientific and social constructionist. Scientific theories of ageing focus on the bio-psychological or pathological constituents of ageing. Social constructionist theories of ageing focus on how ageing is socially constructed. In western societies, age is usually presented numerically as the number of months and years from birth that an individual has lived. While this method of quantification is widely perceived as natural and 'the way things have always been', counting age is, in fact, a social construction which can be traced to the historical development of industrial capitalism and, in particular, the requirement to standardize conceptions of time across regional, national and global spaces (Phillipson, 1982).

The concepts of 'age' and 'ageing' have four main dimensions. First, age and ageing have a biological and physiological dimension – physical appearance changes over time (Moody, 1998). Second, age and ageing have a psychological dimension – mental functioning and emotional and cognitive capacities change over time. Third, age and ageing have a temporal-spatial dimension – the ageing of an individual takes place within a particular period of time and space. Fourth, age and ageing have a social dimension – socially defined expectations shape perceptions of how people of a certain age are supposed to behave, and influence how they are positioned in relation to gender, social class and ethnicity.

In short, 'old age' is a complex concept, and different uses and applications of the term can create complications when conducting research on the phenomenon of ageing. Indeed, different definitions of 'old age' are used today. For example, the term 'elderly' has been broadly applied by government departments to those aged 50 and over, while many researchers would favour retirement age (another contested term) as a marker for the onset of 'old age' (Chivite-Matthews and Maggs, 2002). The legal concept of 'pensionable age' has been defined as 'old age' (Biggs, 1993), yet those people requiring social and health care tend predominantly to be older people aged 70 and above.

Definitional and conceptual ambiguity cause difficulties for those interested in the relationship between old age and victimization. There are important implications here for how Western societies create and sanction crime control policies, and how the criminal victimization of older people is researched (Powell, 2001). For example, the recent analysis of sexual violence reported in the British Crime Survey (BCS) had a limited age range (see also Mirrlees-Black and Allen, 1998; Mirrlees et al. 1998). The authors explain this thus:

> Although the BCS includes respondents aged 16 and over, the questions on inter-personal violence were only asked of those aged between 16 and 59. This was for two main reasons. First older people have greater difficulty with or resistance to using a computer in this way ... Secondly, it was thought that issues of elder abuse (from family members other than intimates) might get confused with responses about violence from intimates and that these issues were more appropriately dealt with in a specialised survey. (Walby and Allen, 2004: 118).

Yet, whatever the issues, it is also clear that old age is an important variable for criminology. The United Nations estimated the global population of those over 60 years would double from 542 million in 1995 to around 1.2 billion people in 2025 (Krug, 2002: 125) (see Figure 9.1). Walker's more conservative estimate (1985) suggested that 'the population aged 65 and over is set to increase steadily (by one-fifth overall) between 1983 and 2021'. However, he continues, the largest rises are due to the numbers aged 75-and-over and 85-and-over: '30 per cent and 98 per cent respectively. By the end of this period women will outnumber men in the 85-and-over age group by around 2.5 to 1' (1985: 4). Whichever estimate is more accurate, **elders**, i.e. the elderly population merits more sustained sociological investigation because the general population is both ageing and growing in size. The elderly population also merits more sustained criminological investigation because of the widely acknowledged links – perceived and actual – between old age, criminal victimization, vulnerability and fear of crime.

▶▶ **Elders**   *the, blanket label of the 'elderly' can perpetuate a stereotype that the elderly population constitutes a homogeneous social group. The term elder will be used as a generic term to define those persons over the age of 50 in recognition of the positive aspects that old age can confer.*

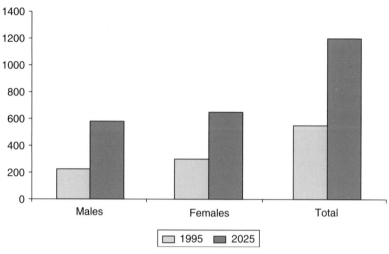

Figure 9.1 UN actual and projected global populations of men and women aged over 60 (in millions) 1995–2025

Source: See Krug (2002)

Old age, crime and criminal victimization

Despite the various conceptual and methodological issues detailed above, a number of criminologists have attempted to research the extent, nature and impact of criminal victimization of the elderly. Studies have utilized both quantitative and qualitative techniques, and despite questions concerning the reliability of some of the findings, a number of points can be drawn out as to the nature and extent of the criminal victimization of the elderly. These are detailed below in Box 9.1.

Box 9.1 Victimization of the elderly

- Older victims are more likely to be victimized in their homes (Jones, 2006).
- Older people who suffer material deprivation are most likely to be victims of crime (Pantazis, 2000).
- Older victims are less likely than crime victims in general to know their offender (Fattah, 1993; Fattah and Sacco 1989; Mawby 1988). Those older people who have been victimized once tend to fear repeated offences rather more than younger victims do.
- Younger people are more likely to be at risk of victimization than older people (Chivite-Matthews and Maggs 2002).

It can be seen from Box 9.1 that older people are no more at risk from most forms of criminal victimization than the wider population and, in fact, if anything, older people tend to experience less criminal victimization than their younger counterparts. Yet older people tend to express fear of crime much more. It is important to recognize that those individuals who are most concerned with the problem of crime and who express greatest fear of crime are not necessarily most likely to experience criminal victimization (Thomas and Hyman 1977). Indeed, there is no necessary connection between objective risk of criminal victimization and fear of crime. Rather, fear of crime is linked to a range of variables, key among which is vulnerability, which in turn is closely associated with old age. It is the connections between old age, vulnerability and fear of crime that are considered next.

QUESTIONS

Why and how, in popular imagery, is crime perceived to be an age war?

How are victimization and offending related to age?

Old age, vulnerability and the fear of crime

Fear of crime and fear of victimization have become part of the discourse of late modern risk society.

▶▶ **Fear of crime**   *is generally taken to refer to concern, worry or anxiety about crime, but there is research evidence to suggest that it encapsulates broader concerns about change and uncertainty.*

We are all haunted by the possibility that we could be the latest victim of a crime. However, individuals across the life-course may feel vulnerable for a number of reasons. Some may feel unable to protect themselves physically or economically (Pantazis, 2000). Some may be incapable of making a fast retreat. Others may feel unable to cope with the physical and emotional consequences of being victimized (Toseland, 1982). Also, it must be noted that fear and the notion of vulnerability are gendered (Dobash and Dobash, 1992, 2004).

Indeed, the fear of crime operates on a myriad of emotional and practical levels, from feeling vulnerable and isolated, to affecting personal well-being. As Moore and Tranjanowicz argue: 'Fear motivates people to invest and tie money in defensive measures to reduce their vulnerability. They stay indoors more than they would wish, avoid certain places, buy extra locks' (1988: 4).

Responses to the fear of crime can be found in the array of anti-theft devices; from CCTV cameras (Hughes, 1991; Coleman, 2004) to 'gated communities' (Hughes, 1991) and other forms of institutional segregation. And it is 'through such expert systems of power-knowledge that the lives of older people have been regulated, ordered, known, and disciplined' (Twigg, 2004: 65).

Research has identified four groups who particularly fall into this vulnerability category: women (Gordon et al., 1980; Warr, 1985), the poor (Taylor and Hale, 1986; Box et al., 1986, 1988), ethnic minorities (see Chapter 5 in this volume), and the old (Antunes et al., 1977; Baldassare, 1986; Braungart et al., 1980; Clarke and Lewis, 1982; Giles-Sims, 1984; Yin, 1985).

The 75-year-old-and-over group is the most vulnerable group within the elderly population. Walker (1985: 6) indicates, for example, that 'there is a very rapid increase in severe incapacity beyond the age of 70', in addition to which the elderly person is more likely to be living alone and to be housebound. This person is, typically, a physically frail widow. For such a person, who may be in a socially isolated position with diminishing or limited financial resources, 'expressed feelings of crime or insecurity appear to have many sources, and to be strongly influenced by beliefs, attitudes and experiences which have nothing whatever to do with crime' (Sparks, Genn and Dodd, 1977: 209). A pamphlet published in the UK by the charity Age Concern (1980: 3), as part of its Action Against Crime Campaign, states: 'Too many elderly people are worried. They have heard so much about crime and violence that they have become fearful, and worry reduces the quality of their lives'.

While older people would certainly benefit from more accurate information about the risk of victimization than they commonly receive through the mass media, their fear is related to the seriousness of the consequences if they were to be victimized, as well to the degree of the risk they face (see Skogan, 1987). When victimization occurs, it often happens in the person's own home, which is perceived as a serious violation of privacy and feelings of safety and tends to highlight people's feelings of dependency and vulnerability (Elias, 1986; Jones 1987). With regard to financial victimization, it is widely acknowledged that the legal framework relating to handling other people's money is extremely complex, but lacks safeguards for vulnerable older people (Powell, 2001).

Since the 1960s, fear of crime has been one of the major growth areas for both academic research and policy development (Fattah, 1995). Perhaps inevitably, the major output on both fronts has been from criminologists and criminal justice system professionals in the USA, but there has also been a growing international academic, scholarly and practitioner literature concerned with fear of crime and with measures to combat it. During the same period over 400 articles, conference papers, monographs and books have been written on some aspect or other of the fear of crime (Hale, 1996).

From this discussion it is possible to identify a number of factors which appear to contribute to fear of crime. Hale (1996) classifies these factors under the following six headings:

1. Vulnerability.
2. Environmental clues and conditions.
3. Personal knowledge of crime and victimization.
4. Confidence in the police and criminal justice system.
5. Perceptions of personal risk.
6. Seriousness of various offences.

Research studies that offer insight into the relationship between old age and the fear of crime are listed in Box 9.2. The key findings of these studies are then reviewed.

Box 9.2   Key studies on fear of crime and old age

Berrington, E. and Jones, H. (2002) 'Reality vs myth: constructions of women's insecurity', *Feminist Media Studies*, 2 (3): 50–75.

Chivite-Mathews, N. and Maggs, P. (2002) *Crime, Policing and Justice: The Experiences of Older People*. London: Home Office.

Jones, G.M. (1987) 'Elderly people and domestic crime', *British Journal of Criminology*, 27: 191–201.

Pantazis, C. (2000) 'Fear of crime', vulnerability and poverty: evidence from the British Crime Survey', *British Journal of Criminology*, 40: 414–36.

Powell, J. and Wahidin, A. (2004) 'Corporate crime and ageing', *Journal of Societal and Social Policy*, 4 (1): 44–56.

Berrington and Jones (2002) suggest that comprehensive data is required in the case of fear of elder sexual abuse. Despite a developing awareness of sexual violence, the rape crisis movement has found that many older women have had sexual experiences that may legally be classified as rape, yet do not consider themselves as rape victims..

Pantazis (2000) claims in her research that when older people feel vulnerable and fearful, their ability to withstand victimization may be substantially reduced. Pantazis (2000: 416) claims that the level of feeling unsafe among older people was conditional upon their level of deprivation and that multiple deprivations increase fear levels. The combined determinants of gender, poverty and age result in potentially higher rates of fear and vulnerability among elderly women than in other social groups.

Powell and Wahidin (2004) have explored the relationship between old age and corporate crime and the insecurity older people have towards pension provision by bonafide pension providers. They found that legal banking corporations took up to £11 billion from older people's pensions which contributed to the biggest financial scandal of the twentieth century. They also cite the embezzlement by Maxwell's pension of over £400 million which created a real fear of material deprivation among older people who saved pensions for over 20 years only to find their savings had been extracted by a head of a corporation.

Jones (1987) in his research suggests that when victimization occurs against older people, it often happens in the person's own home, which is perceived as a serious violation of privacy and feelings of safety and tends to highlight people's feelings of dependency and vulnerability. This can take the form of domestic violence against older women which in turn creates the problem of fear of crime against themselves by their partners and family members.

Chivite-Mathews and Maggs (2002) claim that survey analysis demonstrates that although victimization surveys indicate that young men have the highest risk of victimization, older women's fear of crime is three times higher than that of older men. They further suggest that in order to analyse the holistic nature of old age and fear of crime then we must recognize that it is a gendered phenomenon inter-related to age.

As this chapter demonstrates, what has been constructed as a 'problem' for elders – being potential victims of crime – may not be perceived as such by all older people. The analysis of the relationship between older people, victimization and the criminal justice system (see Brogden and Nijar, 2000) certainly challenges the stereotype that the elderly are a homogeneous, vulnerable social group. Where the elderly are identified as the most vulnerable in our communities is in respect of abuse of people who are dependent upon their assailant for essential daily care and vulnerable to fraud (Bennett et al., 1997). Older victims tend to report that crime has a high and long-lasting impact upon them compared to younger victims (Skogan, 1987). Pain succinctly argues:

> The structures of class, gender, race and ability are the key determinants of how older people experience old age. It is these which underpin where older people live, their socio-economic status and their risk of victimization, whether

from property crime, harassment in the community or abuse by carers within domestic spheres. (2003: 62)

One of the main reasons for low victimization rates among the elderly are that women and older people avoid going out at night because they do not feel safe doing so. Fattah and Sacco (1989) conclude in their study of crime against older people in North America that:

> While it may be fashionable to view fear of crime as an irrational response on the part of the elderly to a world that does not truly threaten them, such a conceptualisation is probably not appropriate. Rather than irrationality, elderly fear of crime may represent the exercise of caution by a group in society that frequently lacks the control necessary to manage the risk of criminal harm or to marshal the resources necessary to offset its consequences (1989: 226).

While they may be relatively unlikely to become victims of crime, their fears are understandable: if they are poor, in poor health, isolated, housebound and if they feel vulnerable, their ability to withstand victimization may be substantially reduced. As Powell (2001) explains, the level of feeling unsafe among older people is conditional upon their level of deprivation and multiple deprivations increase fear levels. The combined determinants of gender, poverty and age result in potentially higher rates of fear and vulnerability among elderly women than in other social groups. Older people are more fearful of crime than other groups within society. More research is required to identify the interrelationships between age, neighbourhood, poverty and fear of crime and its contribution to the social exclusion of older people.

QUESTIONS

What are the key issues in responding to the needs of elderly crime victims?

How are risk and fear of crime connected to the vulnerability of the elderly?

Reflections and future research directions

Having explored the relationship between the sociological study of old age and victimization and highlighted a number of implications for the study of age and its relationship to 'vulnerability', in this section we suggest that the marginalization of older people adds to hegemonic criminal justice practices leading to injustice and oppression in contemporary society. In order to prevent marginalization and multiple victimization, it is crucial to examine the role of victimological 'dominant assumptions' (Pain, 1997), criminal justice policy and social practices. A fusion of theoretical enquiry and active participation of older people and victims in victim policy process and victimological research would address pervasive cultural values central to the empowerment-marginalisation nexus based on 'age' and 'victimization'.

So how can the relationship between later life, crime and victimology be addressed? In our discussion we have examined how and why age and ageist discourses are deployed in the study of crime and later life. As the reader, you may ask why the older victim is presented by media reports, government policy and in some research as the archetypal victim. Second, you may ask why criminologists, victimologists and government policy advisers have produced a wealth of literature on young persons and offenders but have neglected problematizing age. One possible reason for the neglect of later life issues is that youth, as with the study of offenders, unleashes the voyeur and allows us to reminisce about our own youth styles. In contrast, the study of old age and crime as Pollak (1941), astutely observed approximately 60 years ago, evokes a different reaction:

> Old criminals offer an ugly picture and it seems as if even scientists do not like to look at it for any considerable amount of time ... On the other hand, if the thesis of the interrelationship between age and crime is to hold, an investigation of all its implications has to yield results, and with the tendency of our population to increase in the higher age brackets, a special study of criminality of the aged is required. (1941: 212)

If Pollak's view was accurate in 1941, it is even more so today. With the elder prison population representing the fastest growing age group in our prison system, we have reached an important juncture in the disciplines of **gerontology** and criminology.

▶▶ **Gerontology**   *interest in the study of human ageing has grown steadily throughout the twenty-first century. Gerontology is a broad discipline, which encompasses psychological, biological and social analyses of ageing. It is also the study of social welfare and social policy as it relates to ageing. The various strands within gerontology seek to problematize the construction of ageing and to identify the conditions experienced by elders in society. Gerontology raises questions about the role of the state in the management of old age to issues about the purpose of growing old within the context of a post-modern life course.*

Women and men in later life need improved health services, different types of housing, age-sensitive regimes, and a variety of aids when they become disabled. We have to recognize that the elderly inmate, due to the effects of ageing, has far different needs and places far different demands on a system that is designed for the younger inmate. But they also need a reason for using these things. 'In our society the purpose of life in old age is often unclear ... Old age is seen as a "problem" with the elderly viewed as dependants; worse still, they are often described as a non-productive burden upon the economy' (Phillipson, 1982: 166). Hence, it is not surprising that elders experience isolation and alienation when they are denied access to the sources of meaning valued by the society in which they live (Phillipson and Walker, 1986; Turner, 1988).

Summary

The limited knowledge about old age and crime and the absence of relevant policies and planning in this area, suggest that the criminal justice system should be turning its attention to

- an examination of existing formal and informal practices regarding elders, as the first step in developing an explicit and integrated set of policies and programmes to address the special needs of this group;
- developing a comprehensive and gender-sensitive programme for elders, which fosters personal growth and accountability and value-based actions that lead to successful reintegration into society;
- preparing all personnel of the criminal justice system to understand and appropriately address elder-specific topics and issues.

In terms of being able to address the needs of older people in the criminal justice system, the Prison Policy Unit for England and Wales should be able to institute the following

- adopt the age of 50 as the definition of an older victim;
- compile comprehensive data on the over-50s in the criminal justice system about processes of victimization;
- introduce specific programmes geared towards the needs of older people.

For many years, both gerontologists and criminologists have concentrated their attention exclusively in their respective fields (Malinchak, 1980). In this chapter, we have synergized criminological and gerontological theory to understand and problematise the complexity of ageing, victimization and crime and, in turn, place the needs of elders firmly on the research and policy agenda.

The evidence presented here demonstrates that although older people are portrayed as victims of crime, statistically they are least likely to be and the actuality of being a victim of crime in this respect is inversely dispropor-tionate to the fear of crime. However, one must stress that the experience of *fear* is very real to the individual and thus makes measuring degrees of fear impossible (Box et al., 1988). Sparks (1992) rhetorically asks, 'What is a rational level of fear? In other words, we argue, that if *fear* is *experienced* then ultimately; it is *real*.'

The consequences of Sparks' (1992) question are immense: there is the creation of what Estes et al. (2004) describe as 'No Care Zones', where vic-tim supports may disintegrate in the face of inadequate services and ben-efits for older people. On the other side, there may equally be the emergence of 'No Identity Zones', these reflecting the absence of spaces in which to construct a viable identity for later life compared to other age groups.

Traditionally, questions concerning discrimination in criminal processing have focussed on the effects of factors such as gender, ethnicity, disability, sexuality, socio-economic status and age (for those aged between 10–18), but have neglected later-life issues. Their experiences have remained marginalized in the debates around policy, and how the criminal justice system responds to these changes remains yet to be seen. By theorizing age, victimization and crime we hope to dispel and challenge some of the myths surrounding later life, crime and the older victim (see also Chapter 2 in this volume).

ANNOTATED BIBLIOGRAPHY

Bond, J., Coleman, P. and Peace, S. (eds) (1993) *Ageing in Society: An Introduction to Social Gerontology*. London: Sage. This book provides a compre-hensive coverage of gerontological issues while capturing the complexity inher-ent in the processes of ageing. The book emphasizes diversity in the experience of ageing as a function of cultural, social, racial/ethnic, and individual variability.

Brogden, M. and Nijar, P. (2000) *Crime, Abuse and the Elderly*. Cullompton: Willan. This book highlights how and why the criminal justice system as a whole has largely ignored older men and women. Brogden and Nijar in this volume bring together a comprehensive range of literature on the subject of elder abuse and victimization drawing upon key ideas from social gerontology.

Davies, P., Francis, P., and Jupp, V. (eds) (2003) *Victimisation: Theory, Research and Policy.* **London, Macmillan Press.** This book provides an accessible yet critical understanding of crime victimization in relation to theory, research and policy. The book provides an overview of the core areas relating to the study of victims and victimization including: victimological perspectives; researching victims of crime; crime and victimization and public policy and practice.

Mawby R. and Walklate S. (1994) *Critical Victimology: The Victim in International Perspective.* **London: Sage.** In this comprehensive text, the authors combine their experience of the emerging victims' movement to provide an accessible, theoretical and practical critique of victimology. Drawing on local, national and international sources (including Europe and USA). The areas covered are as follows: the risks of crime and how they vary from country to country; the impact of crime on the victim; the treatment of victims by the police, welfare agencies and courts; why governments have recently become interested in victim issues; policies and practices in other nations and what we can learn from them; what services are developing in the rest of the world; and how we can best ensure justice for victims while preserving the right of the defendant.

Pain, R. (1995) 'Elderly women and fear of violent crime: the least likely victims? A reconsideration of the extent and nature of risk', *British Journal of Criminology,* **35(4): 60–80.** This article assesses the relationship between the risk, space and fear of crime among elderly women and provides a good introduction surrounding old age, and the fear of crime. Her study demonstrates how age ought not to be abandoned as a frame of reference, in light of the relationship that the risk of violence is structured by age relationships.

References

Age Concern (1980) *Crime Prevention: Action Against Crime.* London: Age Concern.

Antunes, G.E., Cook, F.L., Cook, T.D. and Skogan, W.G. (1977) 'Patterns of personal crime against the elderly: findings from a national survey' *Gerontologist,* 17: 321–27.

Baldassare, M. (1986) 'The elderly and fear of crime', *Sociology and Social Research,* 70: 218–21.

Bennett, G., Kingston, P., and Penhale, B. (1997) *The Dimensions of Elder Abuse.* Basingstoke: Palgrave Macmillan.

Bernington, E. and Jones, H. (2002) 'Reality vs Myth: constructions of women's in security', *Feminist Media Studies*, 2(3): 50–75.

Biggs, S. (1993) *Understanding Ageing: Images, Attitudes and Professional Practice*. Buckingham: Open University Press.

Box, S., Hale, C., and Andrews, G. (1986) *Fear of Crime: Causes, Consequences and Control*, University of Kent Applied Statistics Research Unit Report to the Home Office.

Box, S., Hale, C., and Andrews, G. (1988), 'Explaining fear of crime', *British Journal of Criminology*. 28(3): 340–56.

Braungart, M.M., Braugart, R.G., and Hoyer, W.J. (1980)', *Age, sex and social factors in fear of crime'*, *Sociological Focus*, 13: 55–66.

Brogden, M and Nijar, P. (2000) *Crime, Abuse and the Elderly*. Cullumpton: Willan.

Chivite-Matthews, N. and Maggs, P. (2002) *Crime, Policing and Justice: The Experience of Older People*. London: Home Office.

Clarke, A.H. and Lewis, M. (1982) 'Fear of crime among the elderly', *British Journal of Criminology*, 22, 49–69.

Coleman, R. (2004) *Reclaiming the Streets: Surveillance, Social Control and the City*. Cullompton: Willan.

Davies, P., Francis, P. and Jupp, V. (eds) (2003) 'Victimology, victimisation and public policy', in P. Davies et al. (eds), *Victimisation: Theory, Research and Policy*, London: Macmillan Press.

Dobash, R. and Dobash, R. (1992) *Women, Violence and Social Change*. London: Routledge.

Dobash, R.P. and Dobash R.E. (2004) 'Women's violence to men in intimate relationships: working on a puzzle', *British Journal of Criminology*, 44: 324–49.

Elias, R. (1986) *The Politics of Victimisation*. Oxford: Oxford University Press.

Estes, C., Biggs, S. and Phillipson, C. (2004) *Social Theory, Ageing and Social Policy*. Milton Keynes: Open University Press.

Fattah, E. (1993) *Victimisation and Fear of Crime among the Elderly: A Possible Link?* Canberra: Australian Institute of Criminology.

Fattah, S. (1995) *Crime and Older People – Victimisation and Fear of Crime among the Elderly: A Possible Link?* Canberra: Australian Institute of Criminology.

Fattah, E.A. and Sacco, V.F. (1989) *Crime and Victimisation of the Elderly*. New York: Springer.

Giles-Sims, A. (1984) '*A* Multivariate analysis of perceived likelihood of victimisation and degree of worry about crime among older people', *Victimology*, 9: 222–33.

Gordon, M.T., Rigers, S., LeBailey, R. K. and Heath, L. (1980) 'Crime, women and the quality of urban life', *signs*, 5: 144–60.

Hale, C. (1996) 'Fear of crime: a review of the literature', *International Review of Victimology*, 4: 79–150.

Hughes G. (1991) *Understanding Crime Prevention*. Oxford: Oxford University Press.

Jones, G.M. (1987) 'Elderly people and domestic crime', *British Journal of Criminology*, 27: 191–201.

Jones, H. (2006) 'Elderly people and sexual violence', in: J.L. Powell and A. Wahidin (eds), *Foucault and Ageing*. New York: Nova Science.

Krug, E.G. (2002) *World Report on Violence and Health.* Geneva: WHO.

Malinchak, A.A. (1980) *Crime and Gerontology.* Englewood Cliffs, NJ: Prentice Hall.

Mawby, R. (1988) 'Age, vulnerability and the impact of crime', in M. Maguire and J. Pointing (eds), *Victims of Crime: A New Deal?* Milton Keynes: Open University Press, pp. 101–11.

Mawby, R. and Walklate, S. (1994) *Critical Victimology: The Victim in International Perspective.* London: Sage.

Mirrlees-Black, C. and Allen, J. (1998) *Concern about Crime: Findings from the 1998 British Crime Survey Research Findings No. 83*, Research Development and Statistics Directorate. London: Home Office.

Mirrlees-Black, C., Budd, T., Partridge, S. and Mayhew P. (1998) *The 1998 British Crime Survey,* Home Office Statistical Bulletin, 21/98. London: Home Office.

Moody, H. (1998) Ageing: Concepts and Controversies. Thousand Oaks, CA: Sage.

Moore, M.H. and Tranjanowicz, R.C. (1988) *Policing and the Fear of Crime Perspectives, Policing 3.* U.S Dept. of Justice Washington, DC.

Pain, R. (1997) '"Old age'" and ageism in urban research: the case of fear of crime', *International Journal of Urban and Regional Research*, 21 (1): 117–28.

Pain, R. (2003) 'Old age and victimisation', in P. Davies et al. (eds) *Victimisation: Theory, Research and Policy*, London: Macmillan Press.

Pantazis, C. (2000) '"Fear of Crime", vulnerability and poverty: evidence from the British Crime Survey', *British Journal of Criminology* 40: 414–436.

Phillipson, C. (1982) *Capitalism and the Construction of Old Age.* London: Macmillan.

Phillipson, C. and Walker, A. (eds) (1986) *Ageing and Social Policy: A Critical Assessment.* Aldershot: Gower.

Pollak, O. (1941) 'The Criminality of Old Age', *Journal of Criminal Psychotherapy*, 3: 213–35.

Powell, J. (2001) 'Theorizing gerontology: the case of social policy, old age and professional power in UK', *Journal of Ageing and Identity,* 6(3): 117–35.

Skogan, W.G. (1987) 'The impact of victimization on fear', *Crime and Delinquency,* 33: 135–54.

Sparks, R., Genn, H. and Dodd, D. (1977) *Surveying Victims.* Chichester: Wiley.

Sparks, R. (1992) *Television and the Drama of Crime: Moral Tales and the Place of Crime in Moral Life.* Buckingham: Open University Press.

Stott, M. (1981) *Ageing for Beginners.* Oxford: Blackwell.

Taylor, R.B. and Hale, C. (1986) 'Testing alternative models of fear of crime', *Journal of Criminal Law and Criminology,* 77: 151–89.

Thomas, C.W. and Hyman, J.M. (1977) 'Perceptions of crime, fear of victimisation, and public perceptions of police performance', *Journal of Police Science and Administration*, 5: 305–17.

Toseland, R. (1982) 'Fear of crime: Who is the most vulnerable', *Journal of Criminal Justice,* 10: 199–209.

Turner, B. (1988) 'Ageing, status politics and sociological theory', *British Journal of Sociology,* 40(4): 589–605.

Twigg, J. (2004) 'The body, gender and age: feminist insights in social gerontology', *Journal of Ageing Studies*, 18: 59–73.

Walby, S. and Allen, J. (2004) *Domestic Violence, Sexual Assault and Stalking: Findings from the British Crime Survey*', Home Office Research Study 276. London: Home Office.

Walker, A. (1985) *The Care Gap: How Can Local Authorities Meet the Needs of the Elderly?* London: Local Government Information Unit.

Warr, M. (1985) 'Fear of rape among urban women', *Social Problems,* 32: 238–50.

Yin, P.P. (1985) 'Fear of crime as a problem for the elderly', *Social Problems* 30: 240–45.

Criminal (In)Justice for Victims?

Pamela Davies

Chapter aims

- To provide an overview of the major landmarks in connection with victim assistance.
- To offer a critique of the victim's role and victim's participation in criminal justice policy-making and the practical administration of justice.
- To draw attention to some of the social inequalities and criminal (in)justices that some victims experience.
- To illustrate conflicts of interests, difficulties and tensions in accommodating victims needs.

Introduction

Over the past 40 years we have witnessed a changing and increasingly complex relationship between crime victims and the criminal justice system. While a small minority of the total number of crime victims are pulled into the criminal justice system to seek or help 'do justice', and while for many this experience is relatively unproblematic, for others it has unintended consequences which may incur further harm. Victims are now represented in the formal criminal justice system and as the various institutions and mechanisms for doing criminal justice expand and diversify, both formally and informally across the public and private spheres, the number of personnel that have the potential to impact upon the lives of those who have been criminally victimized is also changing.

This chapter offers a critical appraisal of the victim's role and victim's participation in criminal justice policy-making and the practical administration of justice. First, the role of the victim in criminal justice is briefly discussed. Second, some key landmarks that have occurred in connection with victim assistance over the past 40 years are considered. Third, some problems in the administration of justice for victims are considered. Fourth, some probation–victim relationships are considered and finally the state of victim-related support and activities is considered as we become firmly established in the third millennium. Some salient themes related to the notion of criminal justice 'balance' are explored in particular the notions of doing justice/achieving victimization, of promoting harmony/incurring harm, of duties and responsibilities, rights and needs.

The role of the victim in criminal justice

While the victim's role in the criminal justice process is important as a subject for victimological research and inquiry, the remainder of this text is testament to victimization being much more widespread. Indeed, the greatest amount of victimization that people experience in society takes place outside of the scope or view of the criminal justice system and some of the most vulnerable and neglected victims and forms of victimization in society remain invisible to the agencies of the criminal justice system (Davies et al., 2004; Goodey, 2005; Spalek, 2006). Mawby and Walklate have illustrated (1994: 33) the **attrition process** in criminal justice as follows: Only a minority of crimes are reported to the police with an even smaller minority of these cleared up and prosecuted. They explain that in the 1990s, out of a hypothetical population of 100, the BCS suggests 20–30 per cent a year or 25 people will be victimized. Of these, 30–40 per cent will report to the police and in less than 40 per cent of these cases will a suspect be identified resulting in perhaps two cases being prosecuted and possibly only one of the original 25 victims will experience being called as a witness in court. With fewer than half of all crimes reported to the police in 2002/03 and approximately only 3 cases in a 100 ever resulting in an offender being prosecuted or cautioned (CCJS, 2004; Victim Support, 2001), it is clear that victims experiencing any lengthy or sustained contact with any part of the criminal justice system in connection with a single experience of victimization remains as unique in the latter years of the twenty-first century as it did in the early 1990s.

▶▶ **Attrition process** *this refers to how incidents are processed and classified. In the criminal justice process the number of crimes dwindles. The true crime rate relates to when an offence is committed, official offenders are those who are convicted and have survived the process of attrition.*

The Criminal Justice System (CJS) includes three government departments: the Home Office, the Department of Constitutional Affairs and the Attorney General's Office and several separate agencies: the Crown Prosecution Service (CPS), the Court Service, Magistrates' Courts, and Crown Courts, the National Probation Service, the Police, the Prison Service and the Victim Support and Witness Service (Home Office, 2004a). As a whole, the criminal justice system is responsible for maintaining law, order and the administration of justice and it aims to reduce crime and to deliver justice on behalf of victims, defendants and communities. For those victims who engage directly with the criminal justice system and one or more of its agencies, theirs is an important role in helping to secure prosecution and achieve justice. To help victims in this role, there are several forms of support and assistance available. However, some encounters that victims have with the CJS may increase their suffering. This can arise from the way in which criminal justice personnel respond to victims, a phenomenon known as secondary victimization. Secondary victimization can be incurred by institutions or individuals during the police reporting and investigation stage or throughout the court, trial, and sentencing process. Secondary victimization is best known in rape cases and in particular a rape trial where the **adversarial system** is supposed to prove guilt, but where the reality of the rape victim's experience in court is that she has often been forced to relive her ordeal in the witness box almost as if to prove her innocence in the crime.

▶▶ **Adversarial system** *the Anglo-Saxon prosecution and judicial system where victims are defined as alleged victims and are pressured to adopt the role of witness.*

Traditionally, the victim has always had a role to play in reporting offences and providing evidence and information on crime and victimization in society to the police and other institutions of the criminal justice system such as the courts. Indeed, victims are crucial to most aspects of the criminal justice process and important to its smooth functioning. Beyond reporting offences to the police and identifying offenders, their role involves answering questions and giving evidence in court and, more recently, contributing to restorative justice and mediation schemes. The victim's formal role to each criminal justice agency is noted in Table 10.1. With the advent of restorative justice and other administrative initiatives in the last decade of the twentieth century, some victims have found their role in criminal justice matters extended. However, such victim centredness must be considered in the broader context of the police having taken over the prosecuting function in the middle of the last century. Since 1984, it has been the CPS that carries out the prosecuting function and that brings criminals to justice (Williams, 2004). Overall, the victim's role has been reduced by the existence of the intermediary of the CPS and victims have lost direct contact with prosecutors. This change also appears to have coincided with research that finds victims feeling ignored, used and uncomfortable at having little input into decision-making and with victims seemingly having limited knowledge or understanding of what is happening in their case. A substantial body of research has confirmed that some victims have found their treatment by the officials in the criminal justice system and their role according to the institutions of the criminal justice

Table 10.1 Victim's formal role with key criminal justice agencies

Criminal justice agency	Victim's formal role
police	Report crime to the police as soon as possible after the incident
	Help the police investigate the case, for example, make a statement, go to an identity parade
	Be prepared to go to court as a witness and give evidence if the offender goes to trial
	Tell the police (or CPS) if you prefer your name not to be read out in court. Ask the police (or CPS) if you wish to give evidence from behind a screen
Witness Care Units (Joint Police/Crown Prosecution Service Units)	Engage in a full needs assessment
	Victims have the chance to explain how the crime has affected them
	Victims have the option to complete a VPS and to give this to the police
Crown Prosecution Service	Be prepared to go to court as a prosecution witness
	Give evidence in court if the offender goes to trial
	Tell the CPS (or police) if you prefer your name not to be read out in court. Ask the CPS (or police) if you wish to give evidence from behind a screen
Magistrate's Court's	Be prepared to go to court as a prosecution witness. Give evidence in Magistrate's Court
Crown Court's	Be prepared to go to court as a prosecution witness. Give evidence in Crown Court
National Probation Service/Prison	If victims have any concerns about the release of a life sentence or serious sexual or violent offender from prison, these can be communicated to the probation service

system – police, prosecution and defence teams, courts and the compensation boards criminal injuries scheme – 'stressful, demeaning, unfair, disregarding of their feelings, rights, needs and interests' and furthermore 'Sometimes they see the system as a second victimisation which can be more unpleasant than the original crime' (Williams, 2004: 88).

According to Hoyle et al. (1999) the problems outlined above are common to all Western legal systems. In response, the Council of Europe and the United Nations (UN), through, for example, the 1983 Council of Europe *Convention on State Compens*ation for victims of violent crime and the 1985 United Nations charter for victim's rights: *Declaration of the Basic Principles of Justice for Victims of Crime and Abuse of Power* and the 1999 United Nations Handbook on Justice for Victims, have created obligations to keep victims involved in or informed about their cases. Essentially, however, as Maguire (1985) has explained, in order to improve communications between victims and criminal justice agencies, there is a need to address victims' needs for information, practical help and advice and emotional support. Victim Support confirm from their direct experiences of working with victims of crime since the early 1970s that victims can have a variety and mix of significant emotional, practical and financial needs. They argue that these needs ought to be officially recognized and further, that the activities of social and criminal justice agencies should ensure that nothing is done to increase victim's distress or add to their problems. Victim Support maintain that victims needs can be met and the effects of crime reduced by providing respect, recognition and support, information, protection and compensation (Victim Support, 2001). According to Mawby (2004), these needs are potentially and variously addressed by different agencies, support services and provisions and at different times. First, there is help at or shortly after the offence, which may be given by the police, a generalist victim assistance programme, or a specialist agency. Second, there is help at the court stage and finally there is help in the form of financial or other forms of compensation.

Some of these agencies and organizations are more **victim-oriented** than others. In crude terms, some forms of support are less victim-oriented than **system-oriented** and are designed to enable victims and witnesses, particularly vulnerable and intimidated witnesses to provide their best evidence in the prosecution and court process', other provisions are intended to limit prosecutional zeal and the worst excesses of the adversarial system that might lead to greater harm and secondary victimization (see, for example, the 1976 Sexual Offences Act, the 1988 and 1991 Criminal Justice Acts, the 1999 Youth Justice and Criminal Evidence Act and the 2003 Criminal Justice Act and Courts Act and Table 10.2). Such forms of support were introduced at least in part due to concern about the collapse of the criminal justice system should victims refuse or be prevented from cooperating whereas other provisions have materialized from concern about victims of specific types of serious violent and sexual forms of victimization and the impact these forms of victimization have on individual women and children (see, for example, Women's Aid and Refuge provisions, RCC's and Childline and Table 10.2). The question of whether or not initiatives can be considered victim-centred is increasingly debated and while this has been helpful in driving for the opinions of victims to be sought in project evaluations (Daly, 2002), it has also sparked controversy about victims' versus offenders' rights and about the politicization of the victim which alludes to victim's issues having become increasingly used for politicians' own ends.

▶▶ **Victim-oriented** *victim-oriented policies refer to support and assistance designed first and foremost to help the victim of crime.*

▶▶ **System-oriented** *system-oriented policies are mechanisms that are designed to help the criminal justice process run more smoothly and efficiently (for its own purposes), some of which involve measures intended to help the victim-witness provide better evidence. These are sometimes 'dressed up' as victim-oriented policies.*

In many respects, the legitimate role of the victim in criminal justice in the twenty-first century remains the same as it always has been, that is they represent a key holder and provider of information and evidence and adversarial and traditionally retributive legal systems as in England and Wales have in the past, militated against victims legitimate role in the legal process being extended beyond this. Legalistic mechanisms and retributive paradigms of justice have also prevented some victims of serious crime from receiving immediate help that could have aided their recovery and improved their ability to give cogent evidence (Williams, 2002). In other respects, however, the role of the victim in criminal justice appears to have become more prominent and we can point to a rash of government administrations, Home Office documentation, circular instructions, leaflet and booklet advice as well as legislative landmarks that support the general climate of opinion within victimology that compensatory and restorative justice measures as well as the feminist and voluntary movements, have changed and continue to change, the nature of the relationship between the victim and criminal justice over the past 40 years or so to one that is more participatory.

Landmarks in victim assistance

In the last decades of the twentieth century it is possible to point to several significant milestones or landmarks that have impacted upon and are connected to the support and assistance of victims. In Table 10.2 some key dates are highlighted from 1964–2006 together with the activity that date signifies. Such activity may be the creation of initiatives; the passing of legislation; the development of victim related schemes, significant achievements or events. Taken together, these 40 or so years of landmarks seemingly indicate the increasing importance of victims and victim centred justice that continues in to the twenty-first century. Table 10.2 is followed by commentary upon the impact of some of the key landmarks. Also discussed are examples of secondary victimization. During this period, England and Wales has witnessed the increasing importance of victims and recognition of their needs and these victim centred developments have been pushed forward by a combination of progressive victimological research, activist-led victim assistance and policy initiatives. The 'Landmarks' result from a complex interplay between these pressures for change spearheaded in particular in the 1970s by the role of the victims movement, and since influenced by the electorate, pragmatism and political expediency and, since the 1990s Victim Support has been particularly vocal in pushing for victims' rights, taking advantage of its unparalleled record in influencing and shaping government policy.

1950s and 1960s

Before the 1950s a victim of crime would have had very little to do with the criminal justice system. In this decade Margery Fry and a small group of reformers campaigned for compensation for victims which resulted in the Criminal Injuries Compensation Authority (CICA) being set up in the UK to administer the Criminal Injuries Compensation Scheme (CICS) for victims of violent crime. Today, the Authority is a non-Departmental Public Body comprised of approximately 550 staff whose job it is to administer the CICS throughout England, Scotland and Wales (CICA, 2004). There are various publications that can be accessed on-line via the Home Office and the Criminal Injuries Compensation Scheme web sites (CICA, 2001; Home Office, 2001) which describe the scheme and give guidance on who should apply and eligibility, things that affect claims (matters concerning helping the police, circumstances before, during and after an incident, criminal record) (CICA, 2005), how to apply for compensation and types of compensation (Personal Injury Award, Fatal Injury Award). It is a three stage process to apply for compensation:

Stage 1 – involves gathering the information you need
Stage 2 – check the guidelines on how awards are made
Stage 3 – complete an application form (This can be done on-line or in writing)

Table 10.2 Landmarks connected to the support and assistance of victims of crime in the UK (1964–2006)

Date	Support and assistance
1964	Criminal Injuries Compensation Authority set up in the UK to administer the Criminal Injuries Compensation Scheme (CICS) for blameless victims of violent crime
1972	Criminal Justice Act; ancillary order for compensation from the court without any application being made by the victim in addition to the main penalty; Community Service Orders introduced experimentally First Victim Support project set up in Bristol by NACRO, Police and Probation First UK Women's Aid refuge opened in Chiswick, London
1974	First Victim Support project set up in Bristol Women's Aid Federation established
1975	Community Service Orders (now Community Punishment Orders) introduced permanently
1976	Domestic Violence and Matrimonial Proceedings Act; provided protection from violence, through injunctions and police arrest, to married women Sexual Offences Act; limited protection of identity of raped women provided First Rape Crisis Centre opened in London
1978	Domestic Proceedings and Magistrates' Court Act; provided for an immediate hearing for the abused party in the magistrates' court
1979	National Association of Victim Support Schemes (NAVSS) formed (now known as Victim Support) as a registered charity
1982	Roger Graef's film on Thames Valley Police treatment of women reporting rape first shown on TV Criminal Justice Act; compensation as a sole penalty introduced First British Crime Survey published
1983	South Yorkshire Probation Service victim/offender mediation experiment
1985	Experimental mediation and reparation projects set up to work with serious offenders
1986	Childline telephone advice service established The Islington Crime Survey published – the first local crime and victimisation survey
1987	First Home Office funding for Victim Support
1988	Criminal Justice Act; discretionary awards under the CICS formalised, courts required to give reasons for not ordering compensation; video links in child abuse cases introduced; Home Office Circular 20/1988; Chief Constables asked to keep victims informed and produce leaflets about compensation and pass information on losses to Crown Prosecution Service
1989	CHANGE programme established in Scotland; court-ordered re-education programme for men who are convicted of violence towards their partners Victim Support launched the first Victim/Witness in Court project The Guildford Four are released from prison by the Court of Appeal

Table 10.2 (Continued)

Date	Support and assistance
1990	First Victim's Charter published by the government Home Office Circular 59/1990 instructs police to take victims' views into account when considering the cautioning of offenders Lothian Domestic Violence Probation Project established in Edinburgh (see CHANGE above)
1991	Criminal Justice Act; encouraged an even greater role for compensation through for e.g. compensation to be collected and passed on before fines; videotaped evidence in child abuse cases Home Office Probation Circular 61/1991 instructs probation service to provide information to the victim about the custodial process, and to obtain information from the victim about any concerns he/she may wish to be taken into account when the conditions (but not the date) of release are being considered Royal Commission on Criminal Justice established The Home Office agreed to fund Victim Support's Crown Court Witness Service The Birmingham Six are freed
1992	'Zero Tolerance' publicity campaign against male violence, Edinburgh
1993	Royal Commission on Criminal Justice reports to Parliament Stephen Lawrence stabbed to death
1994	Home Office Probation Circular 77/1994 'Contact with victims' and families', implementing the provisions of the Victim's Charter Victim Support's Crown Court Witness Service launched
1995	New Probation National Standards for writing of Pre-Sentence Reports to now include requirement to take victims' views into account when probation officers advise courts; Victim Support UK publishes The Rights of Victims of Crime. The Criminal Appeal Act; allowing for the establishment of the Criminal Cases Review Commission Criminal Injuries Compensation Act; set out a statutory tariff of injuries
1996	Victim's Charter, revised edition. 'One Stop Shop's and 'Victim Statements' to be piloted and evaluated National network of Victim Support's Victim/Witness Support schemes in place in Crown Courts Sex Offenders Act; introduced a register of sex offenders Rape Crisis Federation established CICS moved onto a tariff basis and placed on a statutory footing
1997	Criminal Cases Review Commission established and starts handling casework The Bridgewater Four are released from prison Pilot Victim-Impact Statements introduced in three police areas
1998	Crime and Disorder Act; introduces reparation orders requiring young offenders to make reparation to victims (where they consent) and other reparative interventions Speaking up for Justice; report published on vulnerable and intimidated witnesses in the CJS Victim Support launches Victim Supportline
1999	Youth Justice and Criminal Evidence Act; strengthened reparative measures in youth justice, removed the right of an unrepresented defendant to

Table 10.2 (Continued)

Date	Support and assistance
	cross-examine an adult rape complainant at trail, Part II details special measures (including screening, evidence in camera and by live/recorded video-link) to assist vulnerable and intimidated witnesses to give their best evidence in court, *Macpherson Report* published acknowledging police institutionalized racism in London's Metropolitan Police in connection with the death of Stephen Lawrence Victim Support gained Home Office funding to establish the Witness Service in Magistrates' Courts
2000	Criminal and Court Services Act; the Probation Service has a duty to inform victims of serious and violent and sexual offences, where the offender received a minimum 12-month sentence, of the expected release date of their offender should the victims wish to be informed Probation Inspection report published Updating of Probation National Standards for writing of PSR's to indicate whether the offender has undertaken any reparation for the crime
2001	Victim Personal Statement (VPS) introduced
2002	Victim's Charter (revised third edition) *Justice for All: A New Deal*; government White Paper proposing a new Bill to establish a Code of Practice
2003	Criminal Justice Act; allows for evidence to be given by live TV link, disallows gratuitous attacks on a witness's character in court Courts Act; through improved security at court combats threats and intimidation of witnesses Victim Support provides a Witness Service in all criminal courts *A New Deal for Victims and Witnesses*; government paper proposing a National strategy for a co-ordinated approach to supporting victims and witnesses, a needs based rather than rights based victim policy Home Office Restorative Justice Strategy published
2004	Domestic Violence, Crime and Victims Act introducing a Code of Practice and a Commissioner for Victims Compensation and Support for Victims of Crime; a consultation paper on proposals to amend the CICS and provide wider range of support for victims of crime. Victim and Witness Delivery Plan published by the Office for Criminal Justice Reform Witness Care Units (joint police/CPS) introduced
2005	*Rebuilding Lives - Supporting Victims of Crime*; a consultation paper on whether resources are appropriately focused on the needs of victims of crime CPS ten-point pledge for victims Witness Charter launched Pilot for Victim Advocates announced 7th July terrorist bombings in London killed 52 people
2006	Code of Practice for Victims of Crime enforced Commissioner for Victims and Witnesses and Victims' Advisory Panel established

Source: Adapted from Williams, B. (1999: 139–143) 'Landmarks in Support for Victims of Crime' and developed from a range of sources, primarily: Goodey (2005), Home Office (2005a, b), Victim Support (2004), Williams, K. (2004).

The actual form is 16 pages long. The rudiments of how to apply in writing for a personal injury award are illustrated in Box 10.1 where the subheadings of the 14 sections that comprise the form are shown. The Authority receives over 76,000 applications for compensation each year. The Home Office claims the scheme is one of the most generous in Europe (Home Office, 2004b), and probably in the world, spending in excess of £200,000,000 per year in compensation payments (CICA, 2004), more compensation than all the other European schemes added together.

Box 10.1   How to apply in writing for a personal injury award

Claim for compensation after a personal injury

1. Details of the injured person
2. Details of the person filling in this form
3. Details of any representative helping with this claim
4. Details of the incident
5. Details of the report to the police
6. Details of the report to any other authority
7. Description of injuries
8. Details of treatment
9. Loss of earnings and special expenses
10. Payments and compensation from other sources
11. Previous applications
12. Your remarks
13. Authorisation
14. Signature

Ethnic monitoring form

As Mawby notes (1988), criminal injuries compensation policies have developed so they are discretionary. He commented that the system: 'excluded victims of minor injuries, ignored non-injury compensation entirely, avoided any requirement to inform victims of their rights, and denied full or any compensation to a wide range of victim considered "undeserving"' (1988: 129). These discretionary rules, and the statutory tariff of injuries as introduced in 1995 have triggered many instances of victim disquiet especially related to the government's concern to limit the costs of the scheme by setting minimum and maximum claim levels and by its rules governing awards including restricting and deducting from payments (see Chapter 7 in this volume).

Victims have also been frustrated by the delays in the processing of applications. One victim has recently been outspoken about the surreal procedures followed by the Criminal Injuries Compensation Authority which she claims have delayed her recovery (Stewart, 2004).

1970s and 1980s

As already noted above, the 1970s can be distinguished by the relative visibility of the victims' movement and its impact upon victims of crime and the criminal justice system. Victim Support emerged, as did Women's Aid. Legislative achievements were also pushed through by the campaigning efforts and direct action of these groups (for e.g. the Domestic Violence and Matrimonial Proceedings Act 1976 and the Sexual Offences Act 1976). It is widely accepted by academic commentators that the 1970s can be characterized by activist-led victim assistance trailed by government administrations. The past 20 years have witnessed awareness of women and children's experiences of criminal victimization (Newburn, 2003). Women's Aid now has over 30 years of experience in working against violence and abuse against women and children. This organization now co-ordinates and supports a national network of over 500 local domestic violence services. In 2001/02, 143,337 women and 114,489 children were supported, with over 40,000 staying in their refuges. The figures in Table 10.3 show similar estimates for the period 2003/4–2004/5 with over 40,00 women and children being accommodated and supported by refuge-based services each year:

A further 35,000 individuals called their Helpline in 2003/2004 (Women's Aid, 2004) indeed use of all services, including outreach, advocacy

Table 10.3   Women and children accommodated and supported by refuge-based Services

Year	Women supported	Children supported
2003/2004	18,569	23,084
2004/2005	19,836	24,347

Table 10.4   Women and children's use of all services

Year	Women supported	Children supported
2002/2003	122,570	187,796
2003/2004	142,526	106,118
2004/2005	196,205	129,193

and support services has increased 60 per cent for women and 47 per cent for children from 2002–2005 as shown in Table 10.4.

While the landmarks agenda clearly labels a variety of government administrations, the efforts of voluntary bodies in bringing about these changes are less visible, so too is the pressure for change arising from victimological research.

In the early 1970s Sparks, Genn and Dodds (1977) conducted the first major survey of criminal victimization in Britain, the forerunner of the first national British Crime Survey which was conducted in 1981. These ground-breaking surveys revealed much greater amounts of victimization than those recorded in the 'official' crime figures and since the early 1980s the British Crime Survey and other victims surveys (see Anderson et al., 1994; Aust and Simmons, 2002; Bottoms et al., 1987; Crawford et al., 1990; Hanmer and Saunders, 1984; Jones et al., 1986; Kinsey, 1984,1985; British Retail Consortium, 2001) have been useful supplementary measures of the extent and nature of crime and victimization nationally, locally, in rural areas, against businesses and across specific sections of society (see also Chapter 3 in this volume).

In 1988, Van Dijk suggested that the UK was one of the countries with the highest distribution of victimagogic activities in Western Europe and that the UK was in the midst of what he identified as the third wave of the victim's movement, where we witness the 'institutionalisation of victim support'. This refers to the ways in which most feminist and other victim assistance schemes formed National Associations or were otherwise co-opted often by linking into their funding, by central or local government (Van Dijk, 1988: 120–2). If we take Van Dijk's (1988) characterization of the period 1980–87 as a period of 'the institutionalisation of victims support and the call for justice' whereby there was increased professionalization of victim support services and increased acknowledgement that victims are consumers of the criminal justice system who place demands upon it, we might extend this period beyond 1987 to 1989. At the same time as van Dijk was writing of the institutionalization of victim support, Shapland was warning that independent 'fiefs' (including the police, CPS, courts, judiciary, prisons) – comprising the separate agencies of the criminal justice system – were in danger of abrogating any responsibility to victims. In so doing the criminal justice system's non-development of policy she warned, could contribute to the growing unrest of the 'peasants' – the victims – or those who represent their interests. Shapland suggested the danger was that another adversarial 'fiefdom' for victims would be created (Shapland, 1988: 193–4). Garland has since similarly characterized this era as dominated by the managerialist ethos where the state views crime victims as customers seeking better service delivery (Garland, 1996).

1990s and 2000s

From 1990–98, the landmarks indicate significant victimagogic activity, some of which is indicative of victims calls for justice being responded to by the criminal justice system. This is evident in the issuing of detailed guidelines in particular for police, the courts and probation through circular instructions, National Standards and the Victim's Charter (Home Office, 1990, 1996) which could be seen as an attempt to co-ordinate government policy on all matters affecting victims in the criminal justice system. It is also evident in the gradual bowing to pressure for a more humane system from the victim's perspective and for increased participatory rights to strengthen the victim's position within the criminal justice system. For many commentators on the changes in England and Wales however, the landmarks achieved by the mid to late 1980s were slow in arriving (Rock, 1986; Maguire and Pointing, 1988) and this criticism could also be extended to include the changes up to a decade later. In addition to the slow official recognition of the victim's role in the criminal justice system, since the 1990s, and in particular the introduction of the Victim's Charter in 1990, there has been further criticism of the half-hearted efforts on behalf of the Home Office to really take on board the notion of victim's rights (Mawby and Walklate, 1994; Spalek, 2006; Victim Support, 1995). It is also important to acknowledge that behind the official landmarks since the early 1980s, not only were Victim Support taking increased advantage of their political influence and their track record in successfully working as partners with the police, (on a typical day the police will refer 3,000 victims to Victim's Support (Wilson, 2004)), but also some victim advocates were sympathetic towards to the growing arguments for a less retributive and more humane and restorative approach to victims and criminal justice generally.

Such an approach involves putting right the harm caused by an offence, negotiating a balance between the offender's accountability to the harmed and on the victims entitlement to reparative redress and participation in the process of determining how an offence should be dealt with (Dignan, 2005). Ultimately a restorative paradigm sees the individual as the primary victim not the state (Karmen, 2001; Smith and Hillenbrand, 1997; Zehr, 1990).

While there was some ad hoc critical commentary upon various landmarks throughout the 1990s there has been mounting concern and comment upon that decade in respect of problems in the administration of justice. The impact of this in terms of the criminal justice 'fiefdoms' creating more harm rather than promoting greater harmony (Wright, 2004) are considered below.

In terms of victim-related activities in the 2000s, this period is dominated by the introduction of the Code of Practice for Victims of Crime (Home Office, 2005b) and its underpinning legislation. The Code governs services provided in England and Wales by no less than 11 organizations connected to the criminal justice process. These government measures have given impetus to a needs-based strategy for victims and witnesses whilst Victim Support has continued to expand its service so that it now provides a Witness Service in all criminal courts.

QUESTIONS

Review the landmarks connected to the support and assistance of victims of crime as detailed above.

Where do you think the pressure for change in policy and practice connected to victims of crime came from in (a) the 1960s? (b) the 1970s? (c) the 1980s? (d) the 1990s? and (e) in the early years of this century?

Outline some of the tensions that exist in the criminal justice system in England and Wales between meeting the needs of victims of crime and securing a criminal conviction.

Problems in the administration of justice for victims

The origins of the independent body the Criminal Cases Review Commission date back to 1991, with advances made in 1995 to establish the Commission before it began its work in 1997. Its primary purpose 'is to review possible miscarriages of justice in the criminal courts of England, Wales and Northern Ireland and refer appropriate cases to the appeal courts' (CCRC, 2006: 1). Its work involves reviewing the convictions of those who believe they have been wrongly found guilty of a criminal offence, or wrongly sentenced. Miscarriages of justice can occur when any of the suspects' rights as set out under the European Convention of Human Rights are breached. For example, where legal assistance or a public and independent hearing is denied or where a suspect is denied the right to remain silent. They can also occur when safeguarding legislative rules under the Police and Criminal Evidence Act (PACE) 1984 and Criminal Procedure and Investigations Act 1996 have been broken, for example, by non-disclosure of evidence, poor identification or unreliable confessions.

The Commission began work on an estimated backlog of 250 cases and in the first few years it received about 800 cases per annum. In 2001, the Commission referred 39 convictions to the Court of Appeal, in 2002, it made 31 referrals to the Court of Appeal and in 2003 it made another 32 referrals (http://www.ccrc.gov.uk/latestnews/latestnews.html). In 2004, BBC News

Table 10.5 Criminal Cases Review Commission 'Productivity'

Year	Applications received	Cases reviewed
2004/2005	955	825
2005/2006	938	1012

OnLine reported that the Commission had a backlog of 1,200 cases comprising about a third of all applications to date (BBC News Online, 2004). The most recent statistics on applications and completed reviews of cases show an increase in 'productivity' as shown by the figures in Table 10.5.

Additionally, in 2005/2006, there were 73 re-applications and the backlog fell from 368 in March 2005 to 247 in March 2006. As of 2006, the Commission had received 8,540 applications (CCRC, 2006).

There was popular dissent about the fairness of the British criminal justice system of law and its institutions and processes in the 1980s when a series of infamous cases including the Guildford Four and the Birmingham Six questioned the effectiveness of the system in securing the conviction of the guilty and the acquittal of the innocent. The Commission and the work it does is official recognition that the legal system can create new tragedies and that the innocent are victimized and ultimately the Commission can refer cases to the Home Secretary where it feels a Royal Pardon should be considered.

For most of the 1990s, British criminal justice continued to suffer damning criticism and problems in the administration of justice for victims. In 1993, Stephen Lawrence became a murder victim in London. The *MacPherson Report in* 1999 implicated the Metropolitan Police who were deemed guilty of institutionalized racism and as having contributed to further victimizing the Lawrence family in the inquiries following their son's murder. Brown (1999) has defined institutionalized racism in the following way – a sustained failure for the police service, for example, to respond to situations objectively. Rather, the police service as a whole exhibit entrenched assumptions and preconceptions that make them suspicious of black people as offenders and victims leading to treatment that falls far short of how they or any other person would expect to be treated. The death of Stephen Lawrence and other high profile crimes drew attention to rough justice for victims generally and for child victims in particular. Such crimes would appear to have stimulated and justified increased penal populism (Goodey, 2005) and greater expressive forms of punishment (Garland, 2001). As Edwards (2004) notes, such measures highlight the centrality of victims in the arguments used to promote and justify particular penal responses.

Probation–victim relationships

The probation service was pivotal to the inter-agency development of the first victim support initiative in the early 1970s (Goodey, 2005; Spalek, 2003; Table 10.1) and has had a tangential role in the growing impetus towards restorative justice originally though Community Service and Probation Orders and later also through other sentences of the court. During the 1980s, debates around the notion of solving conflict and repairing damage through 'reintegrative shaming' 'making good' and 'making amends' were aired (Braithwaite, 1989; Wright, 1982, 1996) and reparation pilot schemes as well as mediation and conferencing commenced (Tudor, 2002). Probation services were often key players in many of these schemes. During the 1990s the service underwent metamorphic changes resulting the National Probation Service with a new ethos and National Standards (Home Office, 1995). These events, together with the publication of the Victim's Charter in 1990, saw the advent of new responsibilities and duties being placed upon the service regarding victim-contact and victim-focused delivery, the provision of information to victims and risk management of offenders. For the Probation Service this series of changes culminated in 2000 (Home Office, 2000) with the confirmation of certain statutory duties towards victims of crime and firmly established probation's role with regard to victims of crime as restorative in nature.

Since the Victim's Charter 1990, where the Home Office suggested increased victim-contact work for the probation service, the service, having little direction and support on how to implement these changes, responded to these new requirements in a positive but piecemeal way (Home Office, 2000) with implementation continuing to be 'hesitant and variable' (Crawford and Enterkin, 2001). However, by the time of the publication of the second Victim's Charter in 1996, significant changes in the relationship between the probation service, offenders and victims had taken place in many areas (Williams, 1999b) and by the turn of the century local services had adopted different models for their victim-contact service delivery (Crawford and Enterkin, 2001; Spalek, 2003). Some had developed specialist victim units, while in other areas work with victims was increasingly incorporated as a mainstream concern of probation staff (Williams, N. 1999b). Research on the nature of these changes warned of potential clashes of interests, ambiguities and of tensions for the probation service (Crawford and Enterkin, 1999, 2001; Johnstone, 1995, 1996; Spalek, 2003), whose remit and role had traditionally been offender-centred. Issues over rationale, philosophy, coherence, consistency, clarity and resources have also been raised (Johnstone, 1995, 1996; Crawford and Enterkin, 1999, 2001; Spalek, 2003) as well as concerns about insensitive practice (Johnstone, 1995, 1996; Kosh and Williams, 1995; Williams B., 1999; Williams, N. 1999).

On a typical day, 900 probation reports are written (Wilson, 2004) and since revising arrangements for incorporating a victim perspective into pre-sentence reports (PSRs) in 1992, 1995, and 2000, all of these are now required to contain a section on victim impact and damage done as well as an assessment of the offender's attitude to the victim and awareness of the consequences. In practice, PSR authors will often have a single interview with an offender and authors are often entirely reliant upon the offender for information about the victim as CPS packs of information are not always available prior to the interview with the offender (Dominey, 2002). Information derived directly from the offender ought, however, to be supplemented by written information from the CPS and possibly a victim impact statement. One other key aspect of probation officers 'and trainees' work with many of the 218, 342 offenders under supervision each day (Wilson, 2004) is group work with offenders where incorporating a victim perspective ought to be now standard practice.

The development of a victim-oriented approach in the probation service has taken place over a relatively short period of time and specifically in terms of direct contact with victims, this work has had a pronounced effect on the practicalities of doing probation work, upon resources and upon the service as a whole that is making efforts to put a victim perspective at the core of its policy and practice. Nevertheless, concerns appear to have arisen from sympathetic commentators and critics from within the probation service as well as from those concerned with researching the changes as they affect victims. Spalek, for example, has argued that a consumerist notion of victimization has been adopted within the probation service which homogenizes victims and marginalizes their social and economic circumstances and perpetuates notions of an 'ideal victim' (Spalek, 2003, 2006). Crawford and Enterkin (1999, 2001) suggest there are some positive benefits for victims of serious crime in terms of their receiving of factual and contextual information and through victim-contact work and experiences of contributing to a report considering conditions of prisoner release, they found victims were positive and that some victims derived a greater sense of justice. However, these authors also note that victim-contact work can also remind victims of their anxieties and Dominey (2002) has also drawn attention to critics of the practice of direct contact between report writers and victims of domestic violence. Eadie and Knight (2002) have also commented on the difficult task of ensuring dialogue between agencies primarily working with perpetrators of victims of domestic violence in order to ensure that women's safety is not compromised. Crawford and Enterkin (2001) also note that victim-contact work can remind victims of their secondary status within the criminal justice system and that there is a need to clarify the appropriate use and impact of information derived from victim contact work. Dominey (2002) has concluded that the quality of assessments made in PSRs will depend upon the extent to which report writers have received training in the area of victimology and that victim issues are more important to some reports than others.

Victimagogic activities: The state of the art

The period from 1998 to date takes us into the third millennium. At the time of writing, this period has witnessed a series of important changes in penal law starting with the 1998 Crime and Disorder Act and culminating in the Domestic Violence, Crime and Victims Act 2004 and the Code of Practice for Victims of Crime. State compensation is under major review (Home Office, 2004b), the number of criminal justice agencies and institutions and victim-oriented parties are proliferating while academic comment continues to reflect on the role of the victim both within and without the criminal justice system.

We can note the continued expansion and development of principles and practices that fall within a restorative framework of justice especially in connection with youth justice policy. The concept of reparation featured strongly in the 1998 Crime and Disorder Act and Youth Justice and Criminal Evidence Act 1999 (Dignan, 2002, 2005) and some of the implications of this are explored by Hazel Croall in Chapter 3 of this volume (for a broader level of debate on restorative justice see the comprehensive collection of articles in the Special Issue of the *British Journal of Criminology* – Vol. 42 No. 3. The articles consider the 'Practice, Performance and Prospects for Restorative Justice' and the implications for specific types of victims, victimizations and communities.) Voluntary organizations including Victim Support and Women's Aid continue to campaign on behalf of victims generally and for women and children as victims of domestic violence and abuse specifically. Both groups have provided responses to the recent consultation papers from the Home Office and Law Commission. There have clearly also been significant changes over the last 40 or 50 years in respect of how the police relate to victims of crime. Many of the changes brought about since the mid-1970s including the campaigning and activist led efforts of the women's movement and Victim Support, as well as Roger Graef's film in 1982 have been individually researched and critically reviewed elsewhere (see Mawby and Walklate, 1994).

Into the third millennium, the Metropolitan Police have a duty to respond to hundreds of recommendations arising from the Macpherson Report

(Macpherson, 1999) and this has been central to the administration and implementation of victim statements. A Victim Statement or Victim Impact Statement (VIS) can be a pro-forma or free-form victim-information statement where victims are invited to formally state what physical, financial, psychological, social or emotional effects the offence had on them and the wider impact of the crime including upon their family. The VIS is sent to the CPS and in the event of a guilty plea or verdict the contents of the VIS are communicated to the court. The police, CPS and courts can take account of the contents of the VIS in making prosecution, bail and sentencing decisions (Hoyle et al., 1999). Another form of victim statement is the Victim Personal Statement (VPS) where the victim is offered the option of relating to the criminal justice agencies how a crime has affected them and to enable victims to give more information about the impact of crime. This is a two-stage process where the initial stage takes place when the victim's witness statement is taken and the second stage relates to any longer term effects of the crime (Walklate, 2002). The police should now ask victims if they wish to make a VPS when they have finished filling in their witness statement, the statement might be made on video or for vulnerable victims by an appropriate adult. More usually it will take the form of a written statement which can include information as noted in Box 10.2. VIS and VPS are collected by the police and they form part of the case papers. While both forms of victim statement are in the spirit of victim's procedural rights (Walklate, 2002), some see their introduction as part of the enhancement of the role of the victim in the criminal justice process, others see these changes as more pragmatic initiatives whereby victims are encouraged to contribute to the smooth functioning of the criminal justice system by complying with the needs of the individual 'fiefdoms' to ensure effective prosecutions.

Box 10.2   Victim Personal Statement – example of what might be included

Name of Victim: _____

Name of Offender: _____

Date of Offence(s): _____

- I would like to be told about the progress of my case
- I would like any extra help or support that is available when I appear as a witness at the trial and if the offender is given bail

(Continued)

- I feel extremely vulnerable and rather intimidated by the whole thing, the offender, the police, the courts, everything
- I am especially worried about the offender being given bail
- I would like you to know how the crime has affected me

    o physically – description of injuries, treatment, effects (including evidence if desired)
    o emotionally and psychologically – indicating if racial hostility was part of the crime or if victimization was because of faith, cultural background or disability (including evidence if desired)
    o finanically – including loss of wages or income, expenses incurred. Whether a claim from the offender for any injury, loss or damage suffered will be made

I would also like you to know about

    o property damage and loss – to clothing, glasses, tools, home (description and value, cost of repair)
    o There are also some other issues: – how life has changed as a result of the crime. How the crime has caused/made worse medical or social problems

Name: _____

Signature: _____

Date: _____

Similar opinions to those mentioned above are to be found surrounding the One Stop Shop – a service where information about case progress is offered to victims via police. The information includes core information from the police as well as the CPS and the courts and includes: the charges, date of hearings, plea and trial; outcome, verdict and sentence (if these are all applicable). The aim is to keep victims informed about progress in selected cases (Hoyle et al., 1999). In discussing the relationship between victims and the criminal justice system, as with any of the 'fiefdoms', but the police in particular, the notion of power remains important and tensions between individual police officers and personalities, between roles and functions can ultimately determine a victim's experience of the criminal justice system (Davies, 2004). Thus early research findings and more general critiques on victim statements drawn from findings across other nations suggest it is likely that underlying issues of justice, implementation and participation will determine outcome (Walklate, 2002).

QUESTIONS

Giving responsibility for keeping more serious victims of crime informed to the probation service is unique (Williams, 2005) and victimologically controversial. Consider the impact this has upon the nature of the service to victims.

Victim Statements are also victimologically controversial. What are the arguments for and against the introduction of victim statements?

Summary

While it has not been possible to comment in detail on each and every landmark connected to the support and assistance of victims of crime this chapter has focused upon some social inequalities that arise in respect of achieving criminal justice. It has shown how some victimagogic activities are victim driven while others are service driven. Government papers since 2002 have signified a more co-ordinated strategy for victims and as Goodey (2005: 127) has noted victim-centred justice forms one of the three goals of criminal justice reform in England and Wales. *Justice for All: A New Deal* proposed: (1) tough action on anti-social behaviour, hard drugs and violent crime; (2) rebalancing the criminal justice system in favour of the victim: and (3) giving the police and prosecution the tools to bring more criminals to justice. Under goal number two, the Domestic Violence, Crime Victims Act 2004 has introduced the Code of Practice for Victims of Crime (Home Office, 2005b). The consultation paper *Rebuilding Lives – Supporting Victims of Crime* (Home Office, 2005a) also signifies a continuing strategy to focus on the needs of victims of crime. This recent shift of balance towards the victim has had considerable European influence since the 1980s (see Goodey, 2005) but for most commentators this does not amount to any substantive rights-based constitution for victims in the UK. As Spalek has noted, in Britain, victims are depoliticized as 'consumers' and 'active citizens' and victim's rights are thus narrowly constituted (Spalek, 2006). Greater emphasis on victims' needs has recently conjured up distracting distinctions and comparisons between victims' and offenders' rights. Edwards argues there are more important focal points for debate and that the rhetoric of rights and the metaphor of 'balance' in particular within the criminal justice system preclude a comprehensive analysis of the issues raised by victim involvement and forms of victim participation within criminal justice (Edwards, 2004). Perhaps more modest aims for improving the role victims play and experience in the criminal justice system should be as van Dijk suggested in the mid-1980s (Maguire and Pointing,1988: 2.): 'The ideal victim package of victim services seems to be a mixture of community-based care provision and a less bureaucratic criminal justice system' (also quoted in Goodey, 2005: 4).

This chapter has drawn attention to some of the social inequalities and criminal (in) justices that some victims experience as part of their role in criminal justice matters. It has provided a critical appraisal of the victim's role and victims' participation in criminal justice policy making and the practical administration of justice. Social inequalities are evident in the role of the victim in criminal justice generally and in relation to some types of victims in particular, several problems in the administration of justice have shown unequal and unfair treatment of some who come into contact with various agencies of the criminal justice system and in exploring more recent victimagogic activities, relationships between the probation service and victims illustrate conflicts of interests and difficulties in accommodating victims needs similar to the tensions that have previously been explored (Davies, 2004) in respect of the police and victims of crime.

ANNOTATED BIBLIOGRAPHY

Davies, P. (2004) 'Crime victims and public policy', in P. Davies, P. Francis and V. Jupp (eds), *Victimisation: Theory, Research and Policy* Basingstoke: Palgrave/Macmillan. This chapter examines the victim's representation or traditional lack of representation in criminal justice policy and practice. It points towards several tensions between victims and the police and police and victims and explores some developments in the victim's role in the trial, sentencing and punishment process.

Edwards, I. (2004) 'An ambiguous participant': the crime victim and criminal justice decision-making', *British Journal of Criminology,* 44: 967–982. Having made the case for moving the focus of debate away from an analysis of the role of the victim in the criminal justice system that is rooted in the notion of balancing victim's and offender's rights, Edwards argues for a new framework where the concept of victim participation in criminal justice can be analysed. Edwards illustrates some of the ambiguities that can arise in a victim's participatory role through the Victim Personal Statement Scheme.

Domestic Violence, Crime and Victims Act 2004 and **Home Office (2005b) *The Code of Practice for Victims of Crime. A Guide for Victims.* London: Office For Criminal Justice Reform.** The Domestic Violence, Crime and Victims Act 2004 provides legislative backing to *The Code of Practice for Victims of Crime*. Essentially the Code contains service standards in connection with victims of crime. The Code demonstrates a continued focus upon service standards and services and responses that victims can expect to get as initiated under the Victim's Charter 1996.

References

Anderson, S., Kinsey, R., Loader, I. and Smith, C. (1994) *Cautionary Tales*. Aldershot: Avebury.

Aust, R. and Simmons, J. (2002) 'Rural crime: England & Wales', *Home Office Statistical Bulletin*, 1/02. London: HMSO.

Bottoms, A.E., Mawby, R.I. and Walker, M.A. (1987) 'A localised crime survey in contrasting areas of a city', *British Journal of Criminology*, 27: 125–54.

Braithwaite, J. (1989) *Crime, Shame and Reintegration*. Oxford: Oxford University Press.

British Retail Consortium (2001) *The 9th Annual Retail Crime Survey*. London.

Brown, H. (1999) 'The victims of racist violence', *Criminal Justice Matters: Victims* 35: 16–18.

CCJS (2004) *An Introduction to Criminal Justice*. London: Centre for Crime and Justice Studies.

CCRC (2006) *Annual Report and Accounts 2005/2006 Criminal Cases Review Commission*. London: CCRC.

CICA (2001) *The Criminal Injuries Compensation Authority: A Guide to the Criminal Injuries Compensation Scheme 2001*. Glasgow: CICA.

CICA (2004) Home Page https://www.cica.gov.uk/portal/page?-pageid=115,64686&-dad=portal&-schema=P

CICA (2005) *Compensation for Victims of Violent Crime: A Short Guide*. London: CICA.

Crawford, A. and Enterkin, J. (1999) *Victim Contact Work and the Probation Service: A Study of Service Delivery and Impact*. Leeds: Centre for Criminal Justice Studies, University of Leeds.

Crawford, A. and Enterkin, J. (2001) 'Victim contact work in the probation service: paradigm shift or Pandora's box?', *British Journal of Criminology*, 41: 707–25.

Crawford, A., Jones, T., Woodhouse, T. and Young, J. (1990) *Second Islington Crime Survey*. London: Centre for Criminology, Middlesex Polytechnic.

Daly, K. (2002) 'Restorative justice: the real story', *Punishment and Society*, 4(1): 55–79.

Davies, P. (2004) 'Crime victims and public policy', in P. Davies, P. Francis and V. Jupp (eds), *Victimisation: Theory, Research and Policy*. Basingstoke: Palgrave Macmillan.

Davies, P., Francis, P. and Jupp, V. (2004) *Victimisation: Theory, Research and Policy*. Basingstoke: Palgrave Macmillan .

Dignan, J. (2002) 'Reparation orders', in B. Williams (ed.), *Reparation and Victim-Focussed Social Work*. London: Jessica Kingsley.

Dignan, J. (2005) *Understanding Victims and Restorative Justice*. Maidenhead: Open University Press.

Dominey, J. (2002) 'Addressing victim issues in pre-sentence reports', in B. Williams (ed.), *Reparation and Victim-Focused Social Work*. London: Jessica Kingsley.

Eadie, T. and Knight, C. (2002) 'Domestic violence programmes: reflections on the shift from independent to statutory provision', *Howard Journal of Criminal Justice*, 41(2): 167–93.

Edwards, I. (2004) 'An ambiguous participant: the crime victim and criminal justice decision-making', *British Journal of Criminology*, 44: 967–82.

Garland, D. (1996) 'The limits of the sovereign state: strategies of crime control in contemporary society', *British Journal of Criminology*, 36(4): 445–71.

Garland, D. (2001) *The Culture of Control: Crime and Social Order in Contemporary Society*. Oxford: Oxford University Press.

Goodey, J. (2005) *Victims and Victimology: Research, Policy and Practice*. London: Pearson Longman.

Hanmer, J. and Saunders, S. (1984) *Well Founded Fear: A Community Study of Violence to Women*. London: Hutchinson.

Home Office (1990) *The Victim's Charter: A Statement of the Rights for Victims of Crime*, revised 2nd edition. London: Home Office.

Home Office (1995) *National Standards for the Supervision of Offenders in the Community*. London: Home Office.

Home Office (1996) *The Victim's Charter: A Statement of Service Standards for Victims of Crime*. London: Home Office.

Home Office (1998) *Speaking up for Justice*: Report of the Interdisciplinary Working Group on the Treatment of Vulnerable or Intimidated Witnesses in the Criminal Justice System. London: Home Office.

Home Office (2000) *National Standards for the Supervision of Offenders in the Community*. London: Home Office.

Home Office (2001) *The Criminal Injuries Compensation Scheme 2001*, London: Home Office.

Home Office (2004a) *Justice and Victims* London: Home Office http://www.homeoffice.gov.uk/justice/index.html

Home Office (2004b) *Compensation and Support for Victims of Crime*. London: Home Office.

Home Office (2005a) *Rebuilding Lives: Supporting Victims of Crime*. London: Home Office.

Home Office (2005b) *The Code of Practice for Victims of Crime: A Guide for Victims* London: Office for Criminal Justice Reform.

Hoyle, C., Morgan, R. and Sanders, A. (1999) *The Victim's Charter: An Evaluation of Pilot Projects*. Research Findings No 107. London: Home Office Research, Development and Statistics Directorate.

Johnstone, P. (1995) 'The Victim's Charter and the release of long-term prisoners', *Probation Journal*, 42(1): 8–12.

Johnstone, P. (1996) 'Probation contact with victims: challenging throughcare practice', *Probation Journal*, 43(1): 26–8.

Jones, T., MacLean, B. and Young, J. (1986) *The Islington Crime Survey* Aldershot: Gower.

Karmen, A. (2001) *Crime Victims,* 5th edition. London: Wadsworth.

Kinsey, R. (1984) *The Merseyside Crime Survey: First Report.* Liverpool: Merseyside Metropolitan Council.

Kinsey, R. (1985) *The Merseyside Crime and Police Surveys: Final Report.* Liverpool: Merseyside Metropolitan Council.

Kosh, M. and Williams, B. (1995) *The Probation Service and Victims of Crime: A Pilot Study.* Keele: Keele University Press.

Maguire, M. (1985) 'Victims' needs and victims' services', *Victimology*, 10: 539–59.

Maguire, M. and Pointing, J. (eds) (1988) *Victims of Crime: A New Deal?* Milton Keynes: Open University Press.

Mawby, R.I. (1988) 'Victims' needs or victims' rights: alternative approaches to policy-making', in M. Maguire and J. Pointing (eds), *Victims of Crime: A New Deal?* Milton Keynes: Open University Press.

Mawby, R.I. (2004) 'The provision of victim support and assistance programmes: a cross-national perspective', in P. Davies, P. Francis and V. Jupp (eds), *Victimisation: Theory, Research and Policy.* Basingstoke: Palgrave Macmillan.

Mawby, R.I. and Walklate, S. (1994) *Critical Victimology.* London: Sage.

Macpherson, W. (1999) *The Stephen Lawrence Inquiry*, report of an inquiry by Sir William Macpherson, London: The Stationery Office, Cm 4262–1.

Newburn, T. (2003) *Crime and Criminal Justice Policy,* 2nd edition. London: Longman.

Rock, P. (1986) *A View from the Shadows.* Oxford: Oxford University Press.

Shapland, J. (1988) 'Fiefs and peasants: accomplishing change for victims in the criminal justice system', in M. Maguire and J. Pointing (eds), *Victims of Crime: A New Deal?* Milton Keynes: Open University Press.

Smith, B.E. and Hillenbrand, S.W. (1997) 'Making victims whole again: restitution, victim-offender reconciliation programmes, and compensation', in R.C. Davis, A.J. Lurigio and W.G. Skogan (eds), *Victims of Crime*, 2nd edition. London: Sage.

Spalek, B. (2003) 'Victim work in the probation service: perpetuating notions of an "ideal victim"', in W.H. Chui and M. Nevis (eds), *Moving Probation Forward.* Harlow: Pearson.

Spalek, B. (2006) *Crime Victims: Theory, Policy and Practice.* Basingstoke: Palgrave Macmillan.

Sparks, R., Genn, H. and Dodd, D. (1977) *Surveying Victims: A Study of the Measurement of Criminal Victimization.* Chichester: John Wiley and Sons.

Stewart, L. (2004) 'I am more angry at the system than at my rapist', *The Daily Telegraph,* Thursday, 15th April 21.

Tudor, B. (2002) 'Probation work with victims of crime', in B. Williams (ed.), *Working with Victims of Crime: Policies and Practice.* London: Jessica Kingsley.

Van Dijk, J. (1988) 'Ideological tends within the victims movement: an international perspective', in M. Maguire and J. Pointing (eds), *Victims of Crime: A New Deal?* Milton Keynes: Open University Press.

Victim Support (1995) *The Rights of Victims of Crime.* London: Victim Support.

Victim Support (2001) *Manifesto 2001.* London: Victim Support.

Victim Support (2004) *30:30 Vision: Victim Support at 30 and the Challenges Ahead.* London: Victim Support.

Walklate, S. (2002) *Understanding Criminology: Current Theoretical Debates,* 2nd edition. Buckingham: Open University Press.

Williams, B. (1999) *Working with Victims of Crime: Policies, Politics and Practice.* London: Jessica Kingsley.

Williams, B. (ed.) (2002) *Reparation and Victim-Focused Social Work.* London: Jessica Kingsley.

Williams, B. (2005) *Victims of Crime and Community Justice.* London: Jessica Kingsley.

Williams, K. (2004) *Textbook of Criminology,* 5th edition. Oxford: Oxford University Press.

Williams, N. (1999b) 'Probation work with victims of crime', *Criminal Justice Matters: Victims,* 35: 20–1.

Wilson, D. (2004) 'The politics and processes of criminal justice', in J. Muncie and D. Wilson (eds), *Student Handbook of Criminal Justice and Criminology.* London: Cavendish.

Women's Aid (2004) http://www.womensaid.org.uk/about/about-wafe.htm

Women's Aid (2006) *Annual General Report 2006.* Women's Aid: Causeway.

Wright, M. (1982) *Making Good: Prisons, Punishment and Beyond.* London: Unwin Hyman.

Wright, M. (1996) *Justice for Victims and Offenders: A Restorative Response to Crime,* 2nd edition. Winchester: Waterside Press.

Wright, M. (2004) 'Preventing harm, promoting harmony', in P. Davies, P. Francis and V. Jupp (eds), *Victimisation: Theory, Research and Policy.* Basingstoke: Palgrave Macmillan.

Zehr, H. (1990) *Changing Lenses: A New Focus for Crime and Justice.* Scottsdale, PA: Herald.

Web addresses

www.victimology.nl

www.unodc.org

www.victimsupport.org

http://news.bbc.co.uk/hi/english/static/in-depth/uk/2001/life-of-crime/miscarriages.stm

http://www.ccrc.gov.uk/latestnews/latestnews.html

Index